KATHERINE DUNHAM

JOYCE ASCHENBRENNER

Katherine Dunham:
Dancing a Life

UNIVERSITY OF ILLINOIS PRESS

URBANA AND CHICAGO

Library of Congress Cataloging-in-Publication Data
Aschenbrenner, Joyce.
Katherine Dunham : dancing a life / Joyce Aschenbrenner.
    p.   cm.
Includes bibliographical references (p.) and index.
ISBN 0-252-02759-0 (cloth : alk. paper)
1. Dunham, Katherine.
2. Dancers—United States—Biography.
3. Choreographers—United States—Biography.
I. Title.
GV1785.D82A73   2002
792.8'028'092—dc21   2001007541

Contents

Introduction

IN AN AGE in which celebrity is brief, the name or accomplishments of Katherine Dunham may not be widely recognized. Although her impact on American culture was acknowledged by a Kennedy Center award in 1983, the lingering impression is that of a popular theatrical personality and dancer in the middle decades of the last century. Those more familiar with her achievements know Katherine Dunham's significance transcends that image. She founded and directed the first self-supporting African American dance company. The Katherine Dunham Dance Company achieved critical and popular acclaim, introducing African and Caribbean dance and culture to U.S. and international audiences. She created a dance technique that blended African-based movement with ballet and modern dance to liberate the knees and pelvis, fundamentally changing American dance. Her dance school in New York in the 1940s educated a generation of artists who helped shape the course of American theater.

Perhaps even more significant, throughout her career as an educator, Dunham has consistently championed a view of dance instruction that involves developing the total person. From the 1960s to the present, she has applied this philosophy in promoting cultural awareness and social skills among children and youth in the economically depressed city of East St. Louis, Illinois, as a basis for an active community life. She has remained committed to this project into her nineties, despite ill health and numerous invitations from friends and colleagues to move and establish programs in cities with greater economic and cultural resources.

It is her community enterprise that inspired me to write this biographical work. Like Dunham, I had changed my career emphasis during the social ferment of the sixties. Largely as a result of discussions with an African American colleague, I turned from a research focus on Muslim kinship and society in South Asia to look at my own society, concentrating on black family and social organization. In 1969–70, as a research associate in urban studies at the University of Chicago, I worked with Raymond Smith, a Caribbean studies specialist, and David Schneider, an authority on American kinship, on a large-scale project involving Latin American, Appalachian, and African American families.[1] After this project was completed, I took a position at Southern Illinois University at Edwardsville. I was attracted by the thriving black studies program based in the university's Experiment in Higher Education, one of the more creative programs funded during the War on Poverty era.

Katherine Dunham was director of the Performing Arts Training Center, part of the Experiment in Higher Education in East St. Louis. Along with Buckminster Fuller and others, she had been invited to join the Southern Illinois University system by Chancellor Delyte Morris, who was interested in developing the cultural life in southern Illinois.

When I went to southern Illinois, I knew very little about dance and nothing about Katherine Dunham, although I discovered later that a relative had attended a Dunham performance in Portland, Oregon, in the 1940s. In the drab cultural climate of World War II, the audience responded enthusiastically to Dunham Company performances.[2] She was synthesizing ballet, African, East Indian, and other movement into a dazzling, dynamic new choreography. The originality of her technique was partly an outgrowth of her training in anthropology, which she studied at the University of Chicago, and her fieldwork in the Caribbean. When, in the 1970s, I attended Dunham's course, "Dance Anthropology," I began to understand that she was espousing a revolutionary approach to both dance and anthropology by regarding dance as central to the study of anthropology.

Although I did not learn to perform Dunham dance technique, I did grow in my understanding of dance, and I expanded and modified my view of anthropology by observing and participating in her East St. Louis programs. I saw that Katherine Dunham, who had studied with some of the trailblazers in anthropology—Robert Redfield, Bronislaw Malinowski, and Melville Herskovits, among others—had retained much of the freshness of thought and humanism of those early anthropologists, qualities that had been dulled and diluted by professional and academic developments in the field. I felt it was important to look at her development as an anthropologist and where she fits in the history of the field, both as a writer and as a dancer and choreographer. Her continual encounters in world cultures and participation in them through dance expanded and honed her intercultural skills, which she translated into her stage presentations.

My comprehension of the significance of Dunham's gifts to her own and later generations deepened through further experiences. In 1976, I attended a National Endowment for the Humanities summer seminar at Brown University, for which I wrote a study of the influence of African American dance—especially Dunham dance technique—on American culture. I later expanded it into a monograph that was published by the Congress on Research in Dance.[3] In the meantime, I visited Dunham in Port-au-Prince, Haiti, several times, first residing in the hotel where she and Dunham Company members had stayed many times; then, on a later trip, I joined her at Residence Dunham. I was shocked at the progressive deterioration of the material and social environment in Port-au-Prince; by my third trip, the garbage was piling up in the streets so that cars could barely navigate, and because of the breakdown in civil authority and resulting violence, we were unable to travel in the city. During these visits, I was able to observe Dunham's complex integration into Haitian society, and I came to understand her commitment to Haitian people and its relation to her views on art and society. Her commitment was given expression in a 1992 fast protesting the treatment of Haitian refugees, supporters of President Jean-Bertrande Aristide who were fleeing political reprisals.

Through the years, I have been associated with Katherine Dunham in many capacities—as a student; as an instructor and observer at Dunham technique seminars; as a friend, acting curator, and education coordinator of the Dunham Museum; as a board member of the Katherine Dunham Centers for Arts and Humanities; and as a personal friend. My association with Katherine Dunham over the past twenty-six years and our shared anthropological backgrounds have led me to reflect on her study of relationships in dance, culture, and society. I have learned much from her and her colleagues through the years and have gained a deep respect for her and her achievements. She has been my mentor on many levels and in many capacities.

As a result of this participation in aspects of Katherine Dunham's mission, I began to envision an undertaking to elucidate her views on anthropology and dance and how they relate to her social activism. Although many biographies have been written dealing with Dunham as a dancer and choreographer, no one has treated in detail her innovative role in dance anthropology and her efforts to realize her views of the social responsibilities of artists and educators.[4] My approach in the present work is to interweave biographical details with some general observations about her life's work. This task includes identifying the elements in her earlier life that contributed to her views on dance and anthropology and documenting how these affected her exceptional legacy. Her record of achievements comprises a successful dance company, a unique dance technique, innovative educational institutes, pioneer work in dance anthropology, and community cultural programs. The present work does not purport to be a comprehensive biography. Katherine Dunham has published two memoirs and is in the process of writing another; these served as primary sources for the current work, as did interviews with Dunham and her friends and colleagues.

Attempting to do justice to the many facets of the life and career of Katherine Dunham, I have enlisted the help of many of her friends, students, and former company members. This treatment is thus not limited to Katherine Dunham but also includes the many people around her whom she has involved in her mission. From the beginning, Katherine Dunham's career has been a group enterprise. Her work has depended on her ability to lead and inspire, and to understand her, one has to have some acquaintance with her friends, colleagues, and followers.

In striving to portray a complex personality such as Katherine Dunham, the writer faces a daunting challenge. In the first place, her published memoirs, *A Touch of Innocence*, which she wrote in the third-person voice, and *Island Possessed* need to be addressed in detail,[5] since they reveal so much of what is central in her life.[6] In *A Touch of Innocence*, her poignant, soul-plumbing childhood account, she expressed her artistry in a different venue, surprising commentators not for the first or last time. It received widespread critical acclaim. Reviewers commented on its literary excellence, considered unusual for a celebrity, especially a dancer. In reviewing the book for the *New York Times Book Review*, Elizabeth Janeway remarked on Dunham's "ability to handle the English language with beautiful accuracy";[7] Langston Hughes stated that she danced and wrote equally well and admired her "gift for physical detail" that he felt was sometimes "too real for comfort."[8] Other reviewers noted the lack of self-pity and the objective treatment of the personal horrors and tragic family situations she described, as well as her vivid characterizations of family members and friends. In an article entitled "The Hard Way," a reviewer in the *Hartford Courant* commented on the force and power of the narrative, which she thought exemplified "all the compassion and brilliance that have distinguished [Dunham's] art."[9]

Such a powerful document offers a biographer both advantages and disadvantages; the benefits are obvious, but the author's deft self-characterization can impede the biographer's task of providing new insights. When

Katherine Dunham is questioned about her childhood, she repeats events she describes in *A Touch of Innocence,* undoubtedly because they clearly represent formative life experiences. While much of my treatment of Dunham's childhood in chapter 1 is based on this literary work, it is augmented by more recent comments by Dunham and others. My commentary, based on personal experiences and interviews, selects and expands on certain aspects of her recollections. This interpretation represents what I believe is the significance of these early events to her later achievements.

In contrast to *A Touch of Innocence, Island Possessed*—Dunham's account of her anthropological education and long-term field (read "life") experiences—received less favorable treatment, especially in the *American Anthropologist*, the "flagship" anthropological journal.[10] At the time, anthropology was caught up in specializing and becoming "scientific," and Dunham's holistic approach was not appreciated. This was her autobiographical work that really spoke to me as an anthropologist and ultimately led to the present undertaking. Many of the events I discuss in chapters 2, 4, and 6 are based on this second memoir.

Barbara Myerhoff referred to the "third person" created through the collaboration of an oral historian and a narrator.[11] In basing an account on a literary, constructed self as well as on a living person, the biographer performs a delicate balancing act in which an attempt is made to grant a voice to every side—the literary subject, the author, her family, friends, and colleagues, and the living person. Some parts of her life are known to me only through these written accounts, while others were clarified through interviews with those who knew her at various times and in different capacities. Finally, crucial perspectives were gained through a long-term friendship and conversations with Katherine Dunham herself. For me, there is a sense of dealing with not only a "third person" but also a multiple person constructed of all of these "selves"— the literary self, the memoirist's constructed self, the person through the eyes of others, the self-concept of the living woman, and the biographer's perceptions, each corresponding to distinct viewpoints and to different time periods and activities in the person's lifetime. The biographer's task—a monumental one—is to recognize and integrate these personae into a recognizable whole.

Many of those I have known and interviewed through the years have died or have become physically infirm. I am indebted to those who are no longer with us who shared their memories and delight in their roles in the Dunham mission: the late Tommy Gomez, Lucille Ellis, Talley Beatty, Pearl Reynolds, Ronald ("Ronnie") Marshall, and John Brooks. Others who have assisted me are named in the body of the narrative. I would like to express special appreciation to Katherine Dunham for her encouragement and inspiration in this undertaking. My friend and colleague Charlotte J. Frisbie read the manuscript during its final stages and provided valuable advice and commentary. Jeanelle Stovall and Donna Pollion assisted with dates and details of events. I also thank the University of Illinois Press editors who worked with me: Judy McCulloh, for having faith in my will to finish this work, and Jane Mohraz, for holding my feet to the fire in providing details and consistency.

Some who have published materials about Katherine Dunham through the years have not shared their writings with her or informed her of their work. She is understandably unhappy about this lack of courtesy. I therefore felt committed to making my manuscript available to her prior to publication, which I have done at various stages of the writing. However, I assume full responsibility for any errors or misinterpretations in the text.

I have grown in my understanding during this challenging task. It is my hope that those who read it will learn a fraction of what I have absorbed in researching and writing it.

1 More Than a Touch
of Innocence

> The anthropological method has been absorbed and as-
> similated into a way of looking at the world with a kind
> of exact, tolerant, but not uncritical justice.
> —Elizabeth Janeway

KATHERINE DUNHAM was born in Chicago, Illinois, in 1909.
Her family included her father, Albert Millard Dunham; her mother,
Fanny June (Guillaume); an older brother, Albert Jr.; and children from
her mother's first marriage. They resided in Glen Ellyn, a small suburb
of Chicago. According to Dunham's memoir, her mother possessed Indian, French Canadian, English, and probably African ancestry; her father
descended from a union of a Malagasy (Madagascan) man and a West African woman. Katherine's mother was considerably older than her father.
Dunham describes her as charming and beautiful, with great intellect and
considerable property. Her father, too, was an extraordinary man who ran
his own business and moved his family into white or nearly all-white
communities, where he protected them with aggressive intransigence.

Prejudices expressed by her mother's side of the family, which was
"nearly white," toward her father and his relatives left a deep mark on
the child. Katherine sensed malignities around her, personified in the
"Crandalls," a phantasmic and sinister family that her brother, who was
four years older, attempted to help her exorcise.

Their mother died when Katherine was only four, and their father left
the children with their aunt Lulu on Chicago's South Side. Again Katherine encountered prejudice as African Americans from the South began

to flood north to escape the increasing impoverishment in the South and the passage of Jim Crow laws. Older black Chicago residents found themselves losing privileges and benefits formerly attained through white paternalism. Her aunt lost her beautician patronage, as her former white customers retreated before the oncoming tide of black southerners.

Privations caused by Aunt Lulu's loss of business led to a court challenge to her custody of Katherine and her brother, brought by the children's maternal relatives. Since Katherine's testimony was used in the case against her aunt's custody, she felt responsible. Because of conflicting allegiances within the family, loyalty and betrayal became important issues in her life. Placing herself in the center of family conflict, she identified with her father's side, yet she felt a moral imperative to understand both points of view. When she was older, she felt disloyal to her stepmother when she and her father visited her mother's socially conscious family, who lived in a neighborhood that "passed" for white. Yet it was while listening to their conversations that she conceived the idea of producing a cabaret for a church fund-raiser.

These formative experiences, as recounted in her memoir, launched her impulse to act as go-between, as an intermediary between classes and races and, later, as a "culture broker" for her dancers, her students, and people of different cultures. Dunham came to understand that her obligations and her personal attachments did not stop at either side of the color line. As a woman and an artist, she maintained close bonds with white intellectuals and artists, as well as with African and African American intellectuals, artists, and politicians. Although most of her dancers have been African American, she also has had many white students, including some notable ones. She has employed both black and white secretary/assistants, and her property manager for twenty-five years in Port-au-Prince, the late Rosie Rubenstein, was Israeli.

When the children were taken from their aunt Lulu, ultimately to live with Albert Sr. and his new wife, they were at first unwilling to accept Annette Poindexter Dunham as their mother. The stepmother could not live up to Katherine's fantasies of her birth mother. Her mother was never discussed, and photographs of her were hidden away; this air of secrecy heightened the emotional impact on the girl when her father told her that watercolors on the wall were painted by her mother. That knowledge, along with memories of her mother and of her parents playing music together, created in the girl's mind an idealized picture of her mother as the center of a harmonious, cultured family life. Annette, a former schoolteacher, could not compete in her imagination with the beautiful Fanny June, artist, musician, and assistant school principal.

Annette Dunham proved to be a very caring parent and often took the children's side against their father. Katherine learned to value her stepmother's loyalty and concern and came to appreciate the increasing difficulty she had in trying to preserve a degree of normality for the children. Katherine even resented the fact that her father sometimes used qualities of his first wife as weapons against Annette when they quarreled. In this context, she felt that to think about Fanny June or her first family was a kind of betrayal, similar to that perpetrated against Aunt Lulu.

Annette Dunham finally won the girl's total loyalty by her increasing sympathy for Albert Jr. in his conflict with his father and her continuing support of the boy, even when it brought Albert Sr.'s wrath down on her. Although she sometimes seemed weak and ineffectual when dealing with her husband, his son noted somewhat ironically that she usually saw that things went her way in the end. In her eighties, with the advantage of hindsight, Katherine Dunham referred to her as the "iron lady," perhaps with her brother's comment in mind.

Katherine Dunham came to recognize early on that the oppressed may oppress others. Her mother's first family ridiculed and scorned her part-Indian grandmother and her retarded half-brother; and they cheated and generally showed disdain for her father and his family. The young child's compassion and empathy for these misused relatives matured into her later humanistic causes. But her father, who in the opening pages of *A Touch of Innocence* was characterized as a hunter, was also seen as an oppressor. Albert Sr., who brought home vicious guard dogs rather than playful puppies, seemingly out of a need to dominate and arouse fear, provided a baleful motif in the childhood account. He rejected his son when he did not share his life goals and sought to suppress his dreams. She saw her brother as a vulnerable and poorly matched opponent to her father; in her mind, these and later events cast him as the ultimate victim. In the bitter conflict between Albert Sr., the man of business, and Albert Jr., or "Al," the dreamer, Katherine's allegiance was squarely on the side of her brother. She suffered intensely along with him as their father censured his aspirations to become a scholar and opposed his plans to attend college.

In publications and conversations, Katherine Dunham has employed the metaphor of the Greek mythical Iphigenia in describing her problematic relationships with her father and brother. In 1944 or 1945, her friend and guide Erich Fromm cautioned, "Be careful that you don't become an Iphigenia."[1] Such an image appealed to her sense of the dramatic. In *A Touch of Innocence*, after describing her childhood fear for her brother's safety in the face of her father's anger and her felt need to protect him, she characterized her youthful self as a "blind seeker after an unattainable planet, Iphigenia already begun."[2]

The myth of Iphigenia evokes universal human experiences. According to the legend, she was sacrificed by her father, despite the pleas of her mother, to satisfy the divinities and save his people. When the gods relented, she was rescued and was helped to flee to another country, where she was forced as priestess to preside over sacrifices of her compatriots. Thus, she sustained a guilt that could only be assuaged by a courageous act: she saved her hostage brother's life at the risk of her own. Only then was she reunited with her people, now freed, serving them as priestess.

The text of the Iphigenia myth—entrapment in family conflict, victimization, guilt, self-sacrifice, and a drive to escape, as well as a search for social continuity and personal identity and fulfillment in service—represents the dynamics of family relationships shaping Katherine Dunham's moral development. Fromm, a Jungian, helped her interpret her experience in the light of such universals.

The evidence in Dunham's career for the themes relating to a search for identity and an impulse to serve is manifold. The motifs of family conflict and entrapment of both siblings, victimization and exile of the brother, and the drive to escape are central in her early life. The children's father was driven by the ambition to own and operate a successful dry-cleaning business, a nearly impossible goal for a black man in the early part of the century, particularly one who had experienced many financial and emotional setbacks. The son experienced the brunt of all the father's failures and shortcomings, and the stepmother was powerless to stem the brutal behavior of the father toward his son.

When a dust wheel to clean carpets, purchased by their father to expand the family business, broke down, he raged and ordered his son into the cavern housing it to make repairs. To young Katherine, who imagined monsters in the gaping abyss, it seemed a nemesis: "the silent, waiting Presence, formless and without definition . . . this Something, inescapable, deliberate, already set in motion to reach out blindly and without reason . . . to draw unto oneself one Albert Millard Dunham, Jr., before his full season—began its motion in these places and these years and under these conditions."[3] Her reaction to the wheel is reminiscent of her fears surrounding the diabolic Crandalls; both presage the "mind parasites" that, in her eighties, she felt were threatening everyone and everything she valued.[4]

Katherine empathized with her brother's fears but also with her father's feelings of defeat; she associated the gradual disintegration of the dust wheel with the deterioration of the family. In her father's scheme of things, his son was expected to carry on the business and succeed where he had not. The boy visualized a different future; he was an excellent student and read and studied at every opportunity, thus enraging his father.

The authority and strength of the man was matched by the youth and determination of the boy. As Albert Jr. grew older, the conflict between the two became more extreme. When he announced his intention to attend the University of Chicago, having received a tuition scholarship, his father disowned him, and he received little family support—merely what his mother and sister could spare from household expenses. Katherine later partly attributed his premature death to the hardships he suffered while attempting to support himself and keep up his studies. Their father also eventually drove away her mother and herself with his violent fits and his penury, especially by his refusal to help his son.

The guilt Katherine felt over her brother's plight and her anger toward her father formed the basis for the Iphigenia theme. In *A Touch of Innocence*, she wrote that before he left for the university, Albert Jr. had advised her, "Don't ever give up. You'll make it all right!" He seemed to imply that she would succeed even if he did not, although, in her mind, he was far superior to her, morally and intellectually.[5] This perception imposed a terrible onus on her; in a sense, his task was to show her the way, and she then had to fulfill his expectations and accomplish what he was unable to do. He knew that her way was different from his own, and throughout her early years he was a wise counselor; in later years, she was to look to other sagacious guides to fill that role.

The impulse to escape, to follow her brother into a better life, was the propelling force that sent her first to the University of Chicago and later around the world. Her brother had comforted her when things were unbearable by painting a picture of education at the university and then travel, even to Africa. Harboring "negative feelings" toward home and family when they were children, she and her brother felt that "they were not born into the families they were supposed to," a not uncommon view of rebellious offspring.[6] A Jungian psychologist has half-humorously explained such estrangement with a story of "The Mistaken Zygote," describing the relief felt when the alienated person discovers her "true family": "When an individual's particular kind of soulfulness, which is both an instinctual and a spiritual identity, is surrounded by psychic acknowledgement and acceptance, that person feels life and power as never before. Ascertaining one's own psychic family brings a person vitality and belongingness."[7]

As an adult, Katherine Dunham, in her first encounter with Haitian peasants, experienced a "wonderful feeling of belonging. . . . I felt I was finally at home."[8] Her lifelong crossing of geographic, cultural, and social boundaries and her occult explorations into the ancient past and the distant future appear to be an unending search for the justice, peace, and amity that she longed for and never found at home or, in later years, in Haiti or elsewhere. Despite her valued mentors and many friends and followers, ultimately, as a reviewer of *A Touch of Innocence* observed, she had learned to trust no one but herself and to live by her own standards.[9]

Diversity and Dramaturgy

From the outset, cultural values and differences were associated with dramatic events in Dunham's mind. In her memoirs, she described the origins in her early years of many of her later actions and interests: she imagined herself "alternately explorer, big game hunter, shipwrecked castaway, and physician to a tribe of powerful but friendly aborigines."[10] Curiosity about other people and their ways of life and a "yearning for adventure" led her to scale bluffs near her home to visit a woman who had formerly toured on a theatrical circuit; she came away with a feather boa, a beaded bag, and long leather gloves.[11] Theatrical influences appeared throughout her childhood; she later remarked, "Play games in grade school must have been my theater."[12] During her stay in Chicago with her father's relatives, she observed rehearsals of a never-to-be-produced musical directed by her uncle, Arthur Dunham, who was a vocal coach and choral director, and promoted by her aunt Clara; these memories "stayed with her and may have inspired in some small way her own eventual choice of a theatrical career."[13] While Aunt Lulu was at work, she secretly attended many vaudeville shows and "forerunners of the Broadway Revue" at the Grand and Monogram theaters, with a stage-struck relative who was taking care of her. This was her "first initiation into the cult whose preliminary rituals she had only glimpsed in the rehearsals . . . in Aunt Clara's flat."[14]

Other secrets and arts of the stage were gradually revealed to her. She spent happy times with Aunt Lulu as her aunt plied her trade as a beautician; later she would experiment with homemade cosmetics and remedies, and on a visit to Annette Poindexter Dunham's relatives at a resort in Wisconsin, she observed her uncle, a self-taught beautician, masseur, and chiropodist, with healing hands deftly regenerate wealthy patrons. The connection between magic, healing, and the cosmetic arts was firmly established in her mind: "The girl never tired of examining her uncle's hands during the sacred stagesetting seconds when, spread open, they were held motionless, near but not touching the recumbent votary. This, he explained to her, was the most important part of the treatment, because without the transference of life fluids from body to body, the magic contact could not be made, and any amount of skill or technique would be worthless."[15]

The powerful combination of drama, medicine, and magic—here stemming from her uncle's Indian and African heritage—impressed itself on the child, and she would later recognize kindred spirits in the Haitian *voudun* performances. Because of this preconditioning, the transformation of the ritual performance onto the Broadway stage did not involve a great leap in her mind, although to others it was a radical departure.

The steps leading from *observer* to *performer* are also patent in Dunham's narrative. Her birth mother had played the piano and her father the guitar, and as a young child, she heard them playing together in harmony—a memory of a more pleasant time in her father's life. Her father introduced her to piano lessons, but the piano was not for her; she enjoyed more active pursuits. While practicing the piano, she reported, "her mind would wander to dancing class, to basketball practice, and to the coming spring track events."[16] Although she was an excellent athlete and was elected president of the Athletic Club at school, she had to forgo sports and acrobatics because of arthritis in her knees; dance became her fundamental means of expression. She joined the Terpsichorean Club, a high school dance club. After watching a fellow student perform at a recital, she yearned to study ballet, but it was not offered as part of the curriculum. Increasing duties demanded by her father at home also kept her from participating in dance and sports as much as she wanted to.

Already Dunham was suffering from knee problems that were to plague her throughout her dancing career. A doctor advised her to stop dancing, but she refused to listen to what she perceived as soul-destroying advice. "If I hadn't danced I wouldn't have been able to walk," she declared years later.[17]

Her determination to continue dancing and her disappointment at not being able to perform the *hopak*, a Ukrainian dance, at a school recital led her to propose a cabaret to raise money for her parents' African Methodist Episcopal (AME) church—a bold undertaking in the face of a rather staid congregation. This action at the age of fifteen initiated a life pattern: if the conditions for a desired end were not present, she created them. At the cabaret, which she named the "Blue Moon Café," she performed the *hopak*; she was also impresario, producer, star, and director. As she later described it, the wife of a chiropodist, who was a former "Floradora soubrette," "joined forces wholeheartedly with the young producer and delved into her camphor-scented trunks to bring forth her version of the tightly corseted dresses of the Floradora girls, topped off with a mauve-colored velvet hat, rakishly tilted, from whose wide brim flowed a sweeping ostrich plume."[18] In her memoir, Dunham recalled her conversations with the "old woman at the top of the cliff" and the costume items she had brought home; she delved even further into the past: "The afternoons she had long ago spent at the Monogram Theatre moved out of an almost forgotten dream world into sharp reality; and she drew as generously on this folk material as on the school recital, the Terpsichorean Club rehearsals, and scenes from movies."[19]

The cabaret was not a total triumph, because she became ill and could not perform some of her functions. Still, it achieved modest success, and her performance was praised, which engendered a desire for even greater accomplishments in theater.

Katherine Dunham was a determined young girl, and her leadership qualities were already emerging. Earlier, when attending a school where she felt ostracized, she had restored her self-confidence by, as she put it, "a common device of the imaginative and self-willed"—establishing a secret society, "The Eagle Eye." She described it as "relentlessly exclusive" and totalitarian, whose members were sworn to secrecy and wore beaded headbands as an insignia.[20] In later life, she recalled a loyal friend among the group, a red-haired girl named Audrey who stuck with her in the face of social rebuffs.

In recruiting a group to fight against unfairness as a child, Dunham undoubtedly learned strategies of social control that years later were effective in maintaining discipline and morale in a troupe of dancers touring under conditions of social discrimination and physical discomfort. But the adult Dunham did not admire the tactics she employed as leader of "The Eagle Eye," using such terms as "fascistic" in describing them. Still, she recognized the psychological motivations and dynamics of a small, close-knit outcast group. When she directed a Federal Writers Project, she explored the role of cults among the underprivileged, and she maintained a lifelong friendship with one of those groups, the Nation of Islam, as well as with the controversial Louis Farrakhan.

Although loyalty is a positive trait to Dunham, exclusivity is not. In 1992, in the context of articulating her thoughts about the existence of a Dunham tradition, she remarked that she does not believe in establishing a "cult," although male dancers seem to desire such affiliation.[21] Personal observations, as well as comments by others, indicate Dunham is a highly charismatic leader whose strength is in teaching and spurring others on to their highest achievements rather than in establishing a closed cadre of followers.

Touching the Heritage

Katherine Dunham and her brother grew up in socially and racially integrated surroundings; their sojourn on Chicago's South Side was relatively brief. Many of their experiences—at least superficially—differed little from those of other lower-middle-class children in the United States at the time. There was more equality then as far as being poor was concerned. Other immigrant groups encountered similar types of discrimination; racial lines had not yet hardened into isolated enclaves. That came later, after the "Great Northern Drive" from the South (1917–20) and the race riots of 1919, when whites reacted violently to competition for jobs and housing.[22] Dunham discovered in her later travels that in the United States "race," or skin color, has historically carried a peculiarly American symbolism; the rigid dichotomy of black and white derives from economic and social benefits to white Americans, including immigrant groups.

Although Dunham and her family did not live in segregated neighborhoods, they encountered and resisted racism. Her father fought to live in primarily white neighborhoods, where he thought his business would prosper. At school, the girl stubbornly refused to sing a song with the line, "I jumped on a nigger and thought he was a horse," and, with her family's support, she persuaded the teacher to eliminate the song from the chorus repertoire. Her brother, who was very popular at school, was forced to relinquish a third term as class president because there were objections by a minority of students. But in a dramatic incident involving cruelty to horses, which was anathema to their father, a white neighbor came to his assistance in chastising a sadistic bigot—a white man—who had called him base names, forcing the man to leave.

In these instances, Katherine Dunham came to recognize that white people could be intolerant or decent, and she was able to distinguish between those who were prejudiced and those who were not. She also experienced in definitive ways the possibility of overcoming and circumventing racial biases. Decades later, she attributed her social activism partly to her father's example. Her later efforts to fight and overcome racism on behalf of others were based on her knowledge, gained in her early years, of the importance of the fight and the possibility of success in the struggle. But while she recognized the social and political reality of race, she was not trapped into looking at the world in terms of black and white. Although she has focused on African and African American cultures and is dedicated to increasing opportunities for black Americans, she has not identified herself as a black nationalist but has looked for human universals in her art and in human relationships.

It was her discovery and cultivation of African American traditions, however, as well as her determination to achieve recognition of their value, that enabled Katherine Dunham to realize her childhood ambitions. She had become familiar with African American cultural expressions early in her life. Her father had told the children African trickster tales while they were young, and, as mentioned earlier, she had learned herbal and cosmetic secrets, possibly traceable back to Cleopatra and beyond, from relatives and acquaintances.

When she and her mother traveled with a friend to Alton, Illinois, visiting St. Louis as well, they encountered many of the recent southern immigrants. At first, she recognized her kinship to these people only at a surface level, one that was imposed by a society that, as Martin Luther King Jr. maintained, judges people by the color of their skin rather than by the content of their character. After all, her aunt Lulu had lost her business because of whites' fears of new southern arrivals on the South Side. But on that trip, according to Dunham, she was aroused to a profound sense of kinship and an aesthetic and spiritual appreciation of the culture of the newly arrived southerners: "she had never before seen in people such abandon and naked joy and fullness of meaning, just in standing and listening and waiting for catfish and enjoying whatever soft creole humor they were passing back and forth." She described "diamond stickpins and pointed yellow shoes with mirrors in the toes and broad-striped suits and shirt" and women "carrying organdy parasols of all colors and wearing many finger rings and necklaces of big glass beads and pastel-shaded silk stockings and dresses cut low over high, cone-shaped bosoms."[23] Clearly the acute observer was at work, storing up details for future enterprises of which she had no knowledge.

Although she admitted she also saw these things on later visits, that night "she felt deeply stirred by the multiple raw potentialities . . . the music that drifted out from every doorway as they drove away . . . followed her and struck so far down into a substance that had never stirred or made itself known before that now, at this moment, began a possession by the blues, a total immersion of the baptismal font of the Race. *This music would sometime be her only tie to these people.* Deeper than prayer and closer to the meaning of life than anything else."[24] Her affirmation voiced feelings parallel to those later expressed about Haitian people and culture. With African traditions in mind, she wrote of the southerners: "they turned inward, way, way, inward, deep into something people are supposed to know about and don't look at, or knew a long time ago and lost touch with."[25] But she felt they were ready to give up their birthright and adopt "life destroying" middle-class values.

In these passages, Katherine Dunham the anthropologist, the artist and interpreter of African traditions, as well as the social philosopher was speaking. A great deal of experience had intervened, helping her interpret a profound childhood experience. Among Haitian peasants, she was to find a culture rich in African traditions, sure of its legitimacy, widely and deeply expressive. In both St. Louis and Haiti, she was initially an observer rather than an insider, a learner rather than a practitioner; she would later state that cultural attributes often associated with race were learned, not genetically inherited.[26]

Her reference to the "baptismal font of the Race" underlines the fact that Dunham was never baptized in a Christian church. Her father was not a faithful churchgoer, though her stepmother made her attend church services. She hated the AME church, although her cabaret was held under its auspices and for its benefit. The repressive, sober Methodist approach to spiritual life was not attractive to the vibrant young spiritual explorer, nor was the emotional exhibitionism of the visiting revivalist. Instead, she turned to her own sense of the supernatural, to the evening star that on most nights was framed in her tiny bedroom window. One night, she wrote, it woke her with "a gentle caress": "She opened her eyes in peace, filled with the certainty that she would never again feel the isolation or the fear of loneliness. . . . The choreography of her inner being stirred at this instant."[27] She sometimes addressed the star as "God" and always asked for strength, courage, and knowledge of the right thing to do. "When everything else seemed unreasoning and unheeding, the Star with its cold unwinking serenity somehow gave her confidence in the presence of some divinity, somewhere in that vast outer space, dispassionately guiding destinies according to a plan so blindingly obvious as to appear obscure."[28]

As a nonagenarian, Katherine Dunham is still a mystic, searching for cosmic direction and viewing human progress and morality from a perspective of timelessness. However, she is also a humanist, her attention directed to ongoing events and her mind and body firmly implanted in her surroundings. Perhaps it was just such disparate proclivities that gave rise to the creative tensions she reconciled and transformed into art.

In writing her memoir, she used the strategy to protect herself that is inherent in all art: the objectification of feelings and events to comprehend and gain some control over them. The account is written in the third person, and a note to the reader states, "This book is not an autobiography. It is the story of a world that has vanished."[29] Later queried about this, she explained that it was a protective strategy for herself and her family: "I didn't touch that book until after my mother died . . . it was too close to me, I was too tender, to be objective."[30] She distanced early painful experiences by referring to her childhood self as "the girl" or "Katherine" and by shaping her memories by means of metaphors or objective correlatives.[31] For example, "the closed room" signified the trauma associated with her birth mother's death, closing off hope for a normal, loving family. The gray sweater reminded her of childish disloyalty to her aunt who gave her the sweater, and the dust wheel symbolized the dissolution of the family as a result of her father's obsessive goals. The cello lessons represented her brother's cultural and intellectual aspirations and her father's opposition to them, and the "Star" symbolized her own private vision. The white canvas shoes belonging to her mother, which her father forced her to wear when her own wore out, embodied the social humiliation she felt at never having the "right" clothes or a "normal" family. Her father's guitar, deteriorating in the flat over the family business, recalled his youthful dreams when he had played it with a group of musicians in the Palmer House and courted a "glamorous divorcée," her first mother; its condition mirrored the deterioration of his aspirations.

In *A Touch of Innocence*, Katherine wrote about her father's sexual overtures to her at a time when such revelations took a great deal of courage. She depicted in dramatic terms her actions in resisting his advances and attaining a moral advantage over him. Later, with adult wisdom and the knowledge of "the complex nature of men," she forgave him;[32] but to break away from the domineering influence he represented in her life, she had to reject his authority.

Entering a junior college in Joliet, she became acquainted with great literature and grew more reflective about herself and more aware of her own potential. She had a vivid dream about a body of water, taking on different forms, that connected her with her distant past and would carry her into the future. The joining of a sense of fatalism with a clear sense of purpose and obligation was a contradiction enabling her to take on a perplexing, discordant world, whose irrationalities she felt she had encountered from birth. By the end of *A Touch of Innocence*, she had moved to Chicago, reunited with her brother, who was recovered from a bout with tuberculosis, and was prepared for anything as "the great wide world opened before her."[33]

2 At the University of Chicago

> [T]here in . . . that city so deadly dramatic and stimulating, we caught whispers of the meanings that life would have . . . there is an open and raw beauty about that city that seems either to kill or endow one with the spirit of life.
>
> —Richard Wright, Introduction to St. Clair Drake and Horace Cayton's *Black Metropolis*

WHEN KATHERINE DUNHAM LEFT Joliet in 1928 to matriculate at the University of Chicago, she began her higher education in the broadest sense of "education." In the liberating atmosphere of the city, she experienced freedom from parental restrictions and the independence of earning her own living; in its heady milieu, she enjoyed artistic inspiration, intellectual challenge, and social stimulation. She would later remark that she hated the hypocrisy and racism she found in Chicago, which would "take innocents by surprise and deeply wound the trusting."[1] But the hazards of an environment often described as "wide open" and "raw" were navigated with the guidance of wise and caring mentors: her brother, Albert Millard Dunham Jr.; her dance teacher, Ludmilla Speranzeva; her university instructors, especially Robert Redfield and Melville Herskovits; and her friend and guide Erich Fromm. They would be among the first of many counselors to whom, along with her "spirit guides," Katherine Dunham would turn for help in comprehending and responding to her personal calling.

At the time she arrived, the city was a whirlpool of social, intellectual, and economic forces. Chicago had an international reputation of radicalism because of its strong labor movements in the late nineteenth century and the 1930s. Eugene V. Debs, the Socialist party's candidate for president, came out of the Chicago labor movement.[2] In his memoir, Studs Terkel, regarded by some as a personification of Chicago, cited his own involvement with such groups as the Anti-Fascist Refugee Committee, befriending opposition survivors of Franco's regime; Friends of the Abraham Lincoln Brigade, which helped those who fought in the Spanish Civil War; and the Civil Rights Congress, a supporter of such political dissenters as the Rosenbergs.[3] He described "Bughouse Square" on the Near North Side, where the socialists Emma Goldman and Lucy Parsons, the widow of a "Haymarket martyr," and many others spoke and where "somebody [was] always invoking the name of Eugene V. Debs."[4]

Richard Wright contended that the "most incisive and radical Negro thought" came from Chicago.[5] Arna Bontemps compared the black literary scene in Chicago of the 1930s with the Harlem Renaissance: it was "without finger bowls but with increased power."[6] The novelists Richard Wright and Frank Yerby; the poet and novelist Langston Hughes; the writers Arna Bontemps, William Attaway, and Margaret Walker; the poet Gwendolyn Brooks; the philosopher Albert Dunham; the sociologists Charles Johnson and Horace Cayton; the anthropologists St. Clair Drake and Katherine Dunham; the artists Charles White and Charles Sebree; and the actors Canada Lee and Ruth Attaway were all indelibly marked by their sojourns in Chicago. Robert Abbott of the *Chicago Defender*; Ida B. Wells, a journalist and social reformer from Memphis; A. Philip Randolph, who organized the Brotherhood of Sleeping Car Porters in Chicago and nationally, and Elijah Muhammad, the head of the Nation of Islam, among others, set the standards for "race men and women" who championed civil and human rights.

In a study entitled "Richard Wright and the Chicago Renaissance," Robert Bone maintained that the great migration of black southerners to Chicago during and after World War I, along with other social and cultural forces, led to the development of Chicago as a black literary center in the 1930s.[7] Richard Wright, its most famous exemplar, emigrated from Mississippi with his parents in 1917 and wrote about adjustment to city life. The harsh realism of his writing reflects, as Dunham put it in *A Touch of Innocence,* the "bitter hatred" that grew out of the migration. Bone regarded Wright's work about black migration, *Twelve Million Black Voices,* as the central document of the Chicago Renaissance.[8]

By the late 1920s, when Katherine Dunham arrived, the South Side was heavily populated with black residents from the South. The center of the "Black Belt" was Forty-seventh and South Park streets, where, according to popular parlance, "If you're trying to find a certain Negro in Chicago, stand on the corner of 47th and South Park long enough and you're bound to see him."[9] In this area, known as Bronzeville, black theater, blues, and jazz flourished, and black-owned businesses, black churches, and other black institutions thrived. Her brother found an apartment for her in this area, in the artistic and intellectual community nurtured by the nearby University of Chicago. Here Katherine Dunham began her new life.

She was mentally prepared for living and working in this social environment. In rebellion against oppressive parental restrictions, she was open to all experience, responding like a newly unfettered creature faced with unlimited space and boundless possibilities. Her potential was still nascent; unlike her brother, she was not an outstanding student. She loved to dance but had little training. Subscribing to few orthodoxies and motivated by a desire to learn and an innate sense of destiny, she was drawn to people and situations that enriched her perspective, and she intuitively avoided those which would be destructive to her growth.

Katherine Dunham has at various times remarked that she was naive and that she did not know or realize something discrediting about someone or some occurrence; she has spoken of "the wisdom of innocence."[10] Undoubtedly, her childhood experiences of injustice contributed to feelings of malaise and a dark view of humankind, taking form in the childhood "Crandalls" and, much later, "mind parasites." Still, negative influences did not preoccupy her conscious mind, and she focused on the exhilarating things that were happening to her, the kindness and generosity of people she met who were creating and accomplishing in many media.

While Chicago was to her an exciting, exotic place, the years of the Great Depression were very difficult. She suffered many privations, including unheated quarters and studios, lack of sufficient warm clothing, and little money for food. She recalled that she and her girlfriend would get slices of bread from a cafeteria line in a popular local restaurant and then persuade the server to put gravy on them, until the proprietors finally caught on to what they were doing. She did not have much money for new clothes, and rather than wear her heavy coat, which was old and unfashionable, she wore a lightweight coat through the bitter cold of a Chicago winter. She has painful memories of this time, the pain that comes with poverty and the lack of entrée into social circles commensurate with her potential and ambitions.

Later on, when she had a little more income, she was expected to send money every month to her parents, who were also having serious financial problems. For a time, her friend Erich Fromm, whom she met through her work at the university, helped her with this obligation. Albert Jr. also gave her financial assistance when he could.

Albert felt responsible for Katherine's move to Chicago, and he took his fraternal duty toward her seriously. He had sent her the application for entrance to the university and the application that led to her employment at the Hamilton Park library, in a white middle-class neighborhood. When she threatened to quit because of her employers' racist attitudes and practices, her brother pointed out that she needed the income if she wanted to go to the university and continue dancing.

Albert had earned the respect of his teachers and fellow students and was established as an intellectual (he was awarded a Phi Beta Kappa key in his senior year). He realized that his younger sister was not oriented toward a purely academic career, nor was she yet accepted in the dance world. As she later recounted, "He saw me floundering around, not knowing exactly where to place myself socially, and I certainly was not intellectual. So he [started] the Cube Theatre for me to have a place to expand creatively and to meet the people that he thought I would meet."[11] To provide a social and cultural milieu that he could share with her and in which she would meet important people in the cultural life of Chicago, Albert, along with his friend Nicholas Matsoukas, founded the experimental Cube Theatre. She speculated about his motives years later: "somehow he must have sensed . . . I would have a much harder time surviving if I didn't express myself in some of the performing arts."[12]

At the Cube, located in a former art colony called Harper Neighborhood in Hyde Park, Katherine Dunham met people of the "Bohemian elite," which included those of diverse social backgrounds. Most were white, but many "Negroes" were included in the group. She later stated that group members felt themselves to be the "prime motivators of the New Negro rage."[13] At the time, the commonly used term for people with African ancestry was *colored; Negro* was favored by the young and was equivalent to *black* in the 1960s or *African American* in the 1990s.[14] According to Alain Locke, the "New Negro" represented "the development of a more positive self-respect and self-reliance; the repudiation of social dependence and . . . of the double standard of judgment with its special philanthropic allowances [as well as] the rise from social disillusionment to race pride [and] the belief in ultimate esteem and recognition."[15] The characteristics Locke enumerated echo principles exemplified by her parents as well as those promoted by the "Black Pride" movement in the 1960s; they have been embodied in Dunham's life work, and her espousal of these principles led her to identify with young people in the 1960s and 1970s.

She performed in some of the theater productions and met such writers as Locke, Bill Attaway, Arna Bontemps, Langston Hughes, James T. Farrell, Meyer Levin, Ben Hecht, the actors Ruth Attaway and Canada Lee, and the artists Charles White and Charles Sebree. Her closest friends at this time—besides Frances Taylor, her future sister-in-law—were the actress Ruth Attaway and her playwright brother, Bill, and the painter Charles Sebree. Members of the Cube group would attend performances by visiting artists and then invite them to a show in the little theater. Among the visitors were Louis Armstrong, W. C. Handy, and Paul Robeson. Robeson commented to her that he felt she needed to continue in theater.[16] In his memoirs, Handy recalled, "During my six-months stay in Chicago . . . University students and educators had me for their guest. I was associated with a little theatre movement . . . out of which came Katherine Dunham."[17]

Through performances and discussions, Dunham was introduced to patrons of the Cube, including the denizens of Chicago's affluent North Shore, where she attended parties. "It was a strange social life," she commented many years later.[18] Among those living on the "Gold Coast" was Inez Cunningham Stark, president of the University of Chicago's Renaissance Society from 1936 to 1940, who was a critic, lecturer, and art connoisseur.[19] As president of the Renaissance Society, she brought, among others, the architect Charles Le Corbusier and the composer Sergei Prokofiev to Chicago; Dunham met the latter at a party in Inez's home. Mark Turbyfill and Ruth Page, dancers and choreographers with the Chicago Opera, also became her friends and colleagues. Page came from a wealthy Indiana family and had toured with Anna Pavlova; she was, according to Dunham, an "inventive" dancer. In her memoirs, Page referred to Dunham as "a discovery of the poet Mark Turbyfill," remarking that he wanted Dunham to become the first black ballerina.[20] They both proved to be genuinely helpful to the young aspirant in the early part of her career.

As her social contacts widened, Dunham initiated her practice of creating "small gatherings" of people who she thought should meet one another other and who otherwise perhaps would not. In inviting them to her apartment, she was beginning to challenge social boundaries, inaugurating her role as a catalyst for social and cultural exchange. Throughout the Chicago years, professors, students, composers, musicians, painters, designers, writers, anthropologists, psychologists, as well as dancers and actors, took part in these affairs.

Dunham invited Etta Moten to dinner when she came to Chicago in 1931 from Kansas City, where she had studied music, to perform in a play that, as it happened, was set in Haiti. Moten, who later appeared on Broadway and toured extensively as Bess in *Porgy and Bess*, married the publisher Claude Barnett, who owned the *Chicago Defender*. She characterized the young Dunham as "quietly interested in you . . . it seemed as though she had always known you."[21] Even though by that time Dunham was something of a celebrity in Chicago, Moten found her to be very friendly and not in the least arrogant. Moten recalled that she was thrilled at meeting an actor in a popular radio program who was also present that evening. Dunham kept in touch with the singer through the years. In 1994, Moten, a widow in her eighties, still lived in Chicago in the same house on Martin Luther King Drive that, according to a former Dunham Company member, she lived in when they visited her while on tour in the 1940s.[22] She had a fine selection of African sculpture that her husband collected. Dunham visited with her in 1966 in Dakar, Senegal, where she was attending the First World Festival of Negro Arts.

Among other visitors to Dunham's apartment were the linguist Alfred Korzybski; the ethnomusicologist Alan Lomax; Benjamin Davis Jr., a future brigadier general; the writers Arna Bontemps and Meyer Levin; the novelist and anthropologist Zora Neale Hurston;[23] the anthropologists Robert Redfield, Bronislaw Malinowski, and A. R. Radcliffe-Brown; her fellow student Fred Eggan, who later taught at the University of Chicago; and artists in all media.

Dunham took part in literary and, to a lesser extent, political discussions at the Cube and at the Dill Pickle Club on Chicago's North Side. Among her acquaintances was Studs Terkel, who performed at the Chicago Repertory Group, a North Side theater in friendly competition with the Cube. The Repertory Group often played in union halls, taverns, and soup kitchens and on picket lines; it produced Clifford Odets's play *Waiting for Lefty*, focusing on the labor movement, in which Canada Lee also acted.[24] The play encouraged audience involvement, placing actors portraying union members throughout the theater; they shouted "Strike" during an emotional climax at the end. Terkel and others performed scenes from Odets's play at a union hall, where feelings were intense.

While on a visit to Dunham in 1993, Terkel recalled that during one performance the audience attacked the actor who played a union snitch.[25] In his memoirs, he reported that while on his way to a performance, he was stopped by members of the Chicago "Red Squad" and given a warning. He wrote, "The many of us were caught up in the radiance of commitment. . . . Some of the gods did subsequently fail; but those were not doubting times . . . they were fervent years."[26]

The Writers' Section of the National Negro Congress, in which many of the members were communist sympathizers, was led by Richard Wright, whom Dunham met at the Lincoln Center on Oakwood. Although he joined the Communist party, Wright reported that he had many differences with party members, both black and white, and was ostracized by the Chicago cell. He complained that they gave short shrift to the experiences of American Negroes because they attempted to downplay race in favor of class solidarity.[27]

Dunham was more involved in artistic and social activities than in politics. In her memoir, she noted that communism was "making inroads" at both the Cube Theatre and the Dill Pickle Club, and she described the "deception and hypocrisy" and "heavy-handed attempts" to mix the races.[28] Her relationship to the labor movement, however, would emerge at several points in her career, through her involvement in the New Deal Federal Theater Project and in contacts with such labor leaders as A. Philip Randolph and Harry Bridges of the International Longshoremen's and Warehousemen's Union.[29]

Like Terkel, Dunham supported the Abraham Lincoln Battalion; those idealists who volunteered to fight in the Spanish Civil War found support at the Cube Theatre. Langston Hughes, who visited the theater when he was in town, served for a time as correspondent in the war.[30] Dunham knew people in the Illinois contingent that fought in Spain. "I was angry about the war," she stated sixty years later. She choreographed "Scenes from the Spanish Earth" to perform at a benefit for Spanish Civil War victims and re-created this ballet in her 1939 performance at the Windsor Theater in New York.[31]

Dunham was not interested in ideology but espoused humanitarian ideals and practice; her concern has been about people rather than abstract causes. She remarked in her memoir that during this period the "injustice of man to man became a dominant theme in my life."[32] In later years, both Dunham and Terkel would be harassed by authoritarian and often bigoted officials as a result of the political implications of their humanistic views and actions.

The creation of "Scenes from the Spanish Earth" involved a merging of artistic and social concerns, revealing a growing perception of the relationship between dance and society. At the same time, Dunham was rapidly developing as a dancer. Her dance teacher, Ludmilla Speranzeva, had studied at the Chauve Souris Dance School, noted for mime and acting. The branch of ballet Speranzeva taught, in Dunham's words, "worked on the theory that dance had been too long treated as a precious, elite artform in Russia."[33] The combination of dance with a story line that she learned from Speranzeva significantly influenced Katherine Dunham's choreography. She also studied ballet with Adolph Bolm of the Civic Opera, who was Turbyfill's teacher. Through Speranzeva, she met the great Spanish dancer La Argentina and her partner, Escudero, as well as Vera Mirova, who specialized in Balinese, Javanese, and East Indian dance. She attended performances by the Isadora Duncan Dance Company and the Ballet Russe, and she met the choreographers Michel Fokine and Léonide Massine. Dunham would take three or four lessons from some of these artists when they were in town. They were charmed by the young dancer, and she was offered scholarships; but she remained true to her own private vision that led her to be independent.

With the encouragement of Speranzeva, her brother, and her friends Ruth Page and Mark Turbyfill, Dunham began to teach dance. This was for her a logical, if consequential, step; her destined role was not to be a member (a "polka dot," as she later called the practice of including a black dancer or two in a company) of a white dance company. Her leadership qualities, first apparent in the church cabaret in Joliet, reasserted themselves, this time in a more fertile cultural milieu.

There were serious problems that had to be overcome before she could organize a dance group. The most pressing need—that of finding a place to work—would plague her throughout her career. Her students were middle class but black, and most studios would not accommodate them. She could not work in Turbyfill's studio, so he offered to teach ballet to her students on street corners; she met with him on El (Chicago's elevated train) platforms, anywhere they could, to discuss plans. Of course, money, too, was a perennial problem. When she first began to teach, she would rent space here and there, with the assistance of teachers and friends. Her first studio was a converted barn; when the furnace burst, she tapped the city gas main for free gas. When this was discovered, she was charged with theft; after that, the gas company refused to provide utilities. She had bronchitis all winter, and the students, too, caught colds.

At one point, Ruth Page advanced her money to rent a studio; her brother also gave what he could from his fellowship. Speranzeva came to her assistance, allowing her to use her studio and, after she returned from the Caribbean, rented a studio for Dunham in her own name. The course of following what she felt was the right path, finding the means to accomplish her goals, and inspiring and accepting support from those who believed in what she was doing was evident in those early Chicago days.

As her class started to perform in recitals, she began to explore choreographic patterns and movements, and she and Turbyfill assembled the most promising students to establish a school. The technique was basically balletic, and she named the group Ballet Nègre, indicating a kinship with the Ballet Russe. Another difficulty had to be overcome, that of finding students who were willing to work hard to attain the high standards Dunham set from the beginning. Despite a successful debut at the annual Chicago Beaux Arts Ball, the group did not receive invitations to other events. When no long-term financial support was forthcoming, they were forced to disband.

Although Dunham studied ballet with Turbyfill and others, it was not her forte. Page noted that she had started training too late to develop a "real talent" for classical ballet.[34] Page also maintained that the "time was not yet ripe" for black ballet dancers, which raised an entirely different question. She was referring to the fact that the dance establishment, as well as the public, did not believe that ballet was appropriate to the physique and gifts of black dancers. John Martin, a dance critic for the *New York Times*, wrote as late as 1963 that an Afro-American should not be drawn into ballet, since it is "alien to him culturally, temperamentally and anatomically." He pointed out the differences between fluidity and "erectness" of the spine and contrasted the pelvic movement in Negro dancers to that of the European: "When the Negro takes on the style of the European, he succeeds only in being affected, just as the European dancer who attempts to dance like the Negro seems only gauche."[35] Arthur Mitchell, formerly of the New York City Ballet and founder of the Dance Theatre of Harlem, and Janet Collins, former leading ballerina of the Metropolitan Opera, both of whom studied at the Dunham School in New York, have since exploded Martin's biased and flawed views. In introducing Katherine Dunham at the Kennedy Center Honors ceremony in 1986, Agnes de Mille apologized for her own earlier comments to Turbyfill, similar to those of Martin. They represented "common opinion" of the times.

Because of such narrow views, Speranzeva prompted Dunham to focus on modern dance in her classes and develop her own style.[36] Dunham did not yet use African movement in her choreography, but she was searching for something "different."[37] She later recalled, "I was moving from Mark Turbyfill [in ballet] to Quill Monroe, once dancing partner of Argentina, to the 'maestra' who would lead me through her *Chauve Souris* variety show experience, her Kamerny theatre dramatic polish . . . her Russian gypsy affiliations and her own non-conformist attitudes into a style and decision of my own. I . . . practiced castanets with Quill Monroe and finger positions with Mirova."[38] As she began to move further away from ballet to her own dance forms and content, she encountered another challenge. Middle-class parents of the girls who were her potential students were not interested in "Negro" culture; ironically, despite the views of the white cultural establishment concerning their limitations, her students' parents identified with European cultural forms and preferred that their offspring learn ballet.[39] Consequently, she failed to recruit a sufficient number of students to the Negro Dance Group, the name of her reconstituted group.

Anthropology at the University: Beginnings

Dunham needed to discover her own artistic metier, and it was through her studies at the University of Chicago that she was exposed to materials and ideas that inspired her creative direction. She has given testament to this inspiration: "I could not have choreographed as I have or written the books I have written without the foundation of those early years at the University of Chicago."[40]

The university was at the center of much of the cultural ferment in Chicago. Its new president, Robert Maynard Hutchins, had a "towering reputation" and was in the avant-garde of educators.[41] He believed that the promotion of the intellectual life was the prime mission of a university, and he brought superior scholars and scientists to the University of Chicago to further that mission. Hutchins supported interdisciplinary studies, attempted to break down divisions between disciplines, and worked to diminish departmental politics and territoriality. Even more radical were his innovative ideas as an educator: he believed in giving students freedom to pursue independent projects and encouraged them to take a world perspective on topics.[42]

Writing about his experience at Chicago during Hutchins's tenure, a former student noted that the president kept the campus astir, constantly asking fundamental questions about the aims of education and the purposes of the university: "It was marvelous to be young in such a time and place. Freshmen and sophomores boldly set out to explore the great questions of human life and society, arguing incessantly, both within the classrooms and outside of them."[43] Katherine Dunham also recalled Hutchins's tenure with pleasure: "There was something great about Hutchins coming in. He swept in there so young, so handsome and so wise. He captivated all of us."[44]

In his speeches and writing, Hutchins clearly stated that the university was not to serve as in loco parentis: "Students will be educated in independence. They will be given all the advice they can stand, but their education will be up to them. . . . By breaking down the routine progression of students through the institution we break down the barriers that have separated some of them from an education."[45] The bulk of students' time was to be spent in independent study, with lectures by senior professors, small seminars on special topics, and counseling. These educational methods gave the University of Chicago its distinctive quality.[46]

Such an educational environment was in tune with Katherine Dunham's needs. She responded wholeheartedly to Hutchins's idealism and thrived in the educational system he promoted. She had scored high on her entrance examination and received a tuition scholarship, but her interests and activities were so varied that she would not have flourished in a more structured academic setting. She did not need to attend classes regularly, but she was required to write a paper at the end of the semester to show she knew what the class was about; in this way, she was able to work at the library, teach, and hold other part-time jobs while continuing her studies.[47] "The freedom that comes from substituting knowledge for formal education is what Hutchins contributed," she remarked years later.[48]

Albert, seeing the direction of her ideas and realizing that, unlike him, she liked working with people, suggested that she study anthropology. The anthropology department, which became Katherine Dunham's primary intellectual influence in subsequent years, was fairly new, having recently separated from sociology. Anthropology students were still encouraged to study sociology, distinguishing the department from others in the United States, which focused almost exclusively on non-Western peoples.

Certainly, the humanistic approach at the university is reflected in Dunham's emphasis on the human and personal in her own anthropological writing. While she is an independent thinker, as such she is also very much a protégé of the University of Chicago and her teachers. The influence of the anthropologists and other social scientists who taught her is apparent in her descriptions of Caribbean and other societies, in her teaching, and in her artistic presentation of these cultures.

Some of Dunham's teachers (Robert Redfield, Melville Herskovits, Edward Sapir, A. R. Radcliffe-Brown, Bronislaw Malinowski, and Lloyd Warner, in particular) played pivotal roles in the development of anthropology. A brief digression into the history of anthropology—especially at Chicago—is useful in identifying the intellectual traditions and affective influences of Dunham's teachers and mentors.

An anthropologist who studied at Chicago described the atmosphere of the anthropology department in the 1930s and 1940s as holistic, in tune with the interdisciplinary atmosphere at the university. Liberal humanism was the philosophy, and racial equality and cultural relativity were its first principles (*cultural relativity* referring to the equality of cultures, not to moral relativity).[49] After her visit to the anthropology department, Margaret Mead spoke of the "great excitement" and "real freedom" at Chicago.[50]

The linguist and poet Edward Sapir had been lured away from the University of Ottawa to strengthen the anthropology offerings in the Division of Social Sciences through the energetic efforts of Fay-Cooper Cole, who was teaching most of the anthropology courses. Sapir was a student of Franz Boas, the patriarchal figure in anthropology who had established the first American anthropology department at Clark University and who had since moved to Columbia University in New York. Sapir was considered one of Boas's top students and the most brilliant linguist of the day.

With the help of Rockefeller funds, the Division of Social Sciences had established a strong research program, and the emphasis was on hiring "research superstars," of which Sapir was an example. The combined Department of Sociology and Anthropology was the strongest graduate research department in the country; however, Cole and Sapir planned and petitioned for a separate anthropology department. Robert Redfield, who had received his Ph.D. from the combined departments, joined as the youngest member of the anthropology program, and the three submitted a proposal for a separate department to provide "a broad cultural background for students in the social sciences" to "bridge over the gap between the social and natural sciences," with primary emphasis on "fundamental research." They pointed out that anthropology differed from sociology in that it studied "human society and the human mind" through firsthand analysis of "the simpler cultures and the more primitive languages," which were rapidly disappearing.[51] The emphasis on the urgency of collecting information on cultures before they were lost was very much in the tradition of Boas, who sent students into the field with that explicit mission.

Katherine Dunham began her anthropological studies soon after the department was formed, in 1929. She found the emphasis on humanism congenial. The social liberalism at Chicago that produced such eminent African American scholars as the historian John Hope Franklin, the philosopher Albert Dunham, and the sociologist Charles Johnson, to name a few, also extended into thc anthropology department, where St. Clair Drake and Mark Hanna Watkins obtained Ph.D.s.[52]

Dunham was influenced by Sapir's contributions to cultural anthropology rather than to linguistics; adept in learning languages, she found his abstractions difficult.[53] Sapir followed his teacher Boas in his interest in cultural forms and the patterning of elements within a culture, looking at each culture as a unique system of interrelated elements—rituals, beliefs, customs, and art forms. His friend and fellow student Ruth Benedict developed these ideas even further in her classic work *Patterns of Culture*.[54] A biographer commented, "Sapir contributed, among other things . . . a remarkable, and iconoclastic, theory of culture—a theory that is structuralist in its analysis of formal patterning, but transcends structuralism in its concern for individual experience, creativity, and the possibility of change."[55] His interest in the effects of culture on individuals led him to write "Culture, Genuine and Spurious," a seminal paper in the study of the relationship between culture and personality.[56]

Sapir's influence was apparent in the work of Redfield, and both shared perspectives similar to those of Melville Herskovits at Northwestern University. Herskovits, also a student of Boas, analyzed the therapeutic aspects of African ritual, thereby contributing to the study of psychology and culture.[57] Both Redfield and Herskovits recognized elements and motifs of African cultures in African American cultural expressions.

Redfield, in the ecumenical spirit of the department, was interested in cultural forms in a variety of national and historical contexts. Dunham attended a lecture by him in which she learned about the relationship between dance and culture. He pointed out that black Americans had retained much of their African heritage in such dances as the lindy and the cakewalk. His presentation and subsequent counsel spurred her on to investigate this aspect of her heritage and, ultimately, to express it in her art.

Redfield, who was promoted to dean of Division of Social Sciences under Hutchins's reorganization of departments, was Dunham's greatest influence at the university. She wrote that he "opened the floodgates of anthropology" for her.[58] Redfield had gained a reputation through his work in a fairly isolated village in Mexico; he characterized such communities as "folk societies," cohesive communities with a religious orientation. This holistic view appealed to Dunham's artistic sensibility: "[Redfield] stressed the essential unity of activity—the cohesiveness of all elements—in a simple society."[59] For her, "[A]nthropology, which leads one to origins and the simple basic fundamentals of art which is made complex and esoteric by civilization, was the answer."[60] In turn, Redfield appreciated her art: "He would see the interior of what I was doing—the depth of it—what a man!"[61] He showed her the connection between dance and social life and gave her the impetus to explore a new area of anthropology, which she later called "Dance Anthropology."[62] An observer characterized Redfield as "more sophisticated" than most of his contemporaries, with a profound knowledge of art and humanities.[63] He collaborated with Milton Singer in developing a theoretical framework for the relationship between "little traditions"—that is, folk traditions—and the "great traditions" of the centers of civilization. The resulting paper, "The Cultural Role of Cities," stands as one of the few attempts to include literary and artistic expressions of urban centers in the scope of cultural anthropology.[64]

Redfield was a good listener, according to Singer, and responded quickly to students' communications. Moreover, he was "courageous in speaking out against racial and religious discrimination and for political and academic freedom, an idealist and optimist about the future of the human race."[65] He was asked by Hutchins to head the Committee to Form a World Constitution. The University of Chicago was at the time the premier midwestern educational institution with an international orientation.[66] Further, as Dunham stated, its "beliefs in social justice and individual freedom" made Chicago a "great school."[67] "I was," she said many years later, "inculcated with the idea of eliminating social injustice. Senator Paul Douglas told me that one day when he came [to East St. Louis]. He had been in the University with my brother—they were two or three years ahead of me . . . he came with a committee during one of the roughest periods here in East St. Louis, about 1969. . . . He came, spoke of the University of Chicago, and said, 'I see here an alumna of ours, of mine. I'm not surprised to find Katherine Dunham here because wherever there is social injustice, somewhere you will find somebody from the University of Chicago fighting it.' . . . It's true!"[68]

Dunham has referred to Redfield as her "moral sponsor" in her anthropological studies.[69] Her interest in other societies and cultures and her internationalist outlook were nourished through her association with Redfield and her other teachers. In 1993, discussing her membership in an organization promoting world citizenship, she commented, "I probably learned more [from these teachers] than I realized."[70] She has on many occasions voiced recognition of her debt to the discipline: "Without [anthropology] I don't know what I would have done. . . . In anthropology, I learned how to feel about myself in relation to other people. . . . You can't learn about dances until you learn about people. In my mind, it's the most fascinating thing in the world to learn."[71]

Dunham referred to anthropology at Chicago as her "haven from racial discrimination."[72] The position against racial discrimination for American anthropologists was established by Boas, a German Jew and trained scientist who was appalled by European racism. He argued that race and culture were independent of each other, the one being genetically inherited, the other learned. Consequently, to argue *innate* inferiority of one group over another on the basis of *learned* behavior was unscientific; furthermore, since all races had developed civilizations with the highest expressions of art and learning, all had equal inherent potential.[73] Boas maintained a cordial and fruitful correspondence with W. E. B. Du Bois, attended seminars at Atlanta University at Du Bois's invitation, and was an early member of the NAACP.[74] His students, especially Herskovits, Ruth Benedict, and Margaret Mead, actively carried on this tradition of antidiscrimination.

The anthropology department projected an urbane atmosphere that encouraged students to overcome parochial outlooks, and under Redfield's direction, the curriculum in the Division of Social Sciences was interdisciplinary, and ethnic and racial studies were promoted. Robert Park, founder of the "Chicago School" of sociology, had worked with Booker T. Washington at Tuskegee Institute; he had, according to Robert Bone, "a first hand knowledge of Negro life that could be matched by few white men of his generation."[75] As chair of the sociology department, Park advanced the life history and case study approach, which was in tune with both anthropology and the "literary realism" found in the works of Richard Wright and others.

In the years immediately following the split of Division of Social Sciences into anthropology and sociology departments, faculty and students often continued to identify with both disciplines. Redfield married Park's daughter, and he "moved easily," both socially and intellectually, between sociology and anthropology, although he is better known as an anthropologist.[76] Another student in the Division of Social Sciences, James T. Farrell, author of *Studs Lonigan* (from which Terkel took his nickname) and one of the "literary realists," later worked on Katherine Dunham's Federal Writers Project. St. Clair Drake, a student in anthropology, collaborated with Horace Cayton in sociology on the landmark *Black Metropolis*, a study of Chicago's Black Belt; Bone describes Cayton, a disciple of Park, as a "crucial link" between the Chicago school of sociology and the Chicago school of African American writers.

St. Clair Drake and Horace Cayton conducted research for *Black Metropolis* under the direction of W. Lloyd Warner, who held a joint appointment in anthropology and sociology. Warner studied Australian aborigines as well as communities in the United States, and he organized Latin American and black studies projects. Warner coauthored a study of Negro personality development that emphasized the importance of skin color to the African American. The research concluded that as a "badge of separateness" and as a basis for high or low social position and occupational success, skin color was the "most important single element" in the self-evaluation and self-concept of black Americans.[77] Warner sponsored

Katherine's study of cults, a Federal Writers Project, which focused on Chicago's Temple of Islam and the Moors, among other groups.[78]

In the introduction to *Black Metropolis*, Richard Wright wrote, "It is in Chicago's school of scientific thought that one finds a close affinity among the disciplines of sociology, psychology, and anthropology, and the men most responsible for this, Louis Wirth, Robert Redfield, and . . . Robert E. Park, were not afraid to urge their students to trust their feelings for a situation or an event, were not afraid to stress the role of insight."[79] Although he was not a student at the university, Wright stated that he drew the meanings for his novel *Native Son* and the inspiration for *Uncle Tom's Children* and *Black Boy* from the social research of Robert Park, Robert Redfield, Louis Wirth, as well as from the works of the sociologist E. Franklin Frazier and Drake and Cayton focusing on the South Side black area.[80]

The cosmopolitan atmosphere at Chicago led to visits to the anthropology department by such luminaries and international scholars as Bronislaw Malinowski, Margaret Mead, and Claude Lévi-Strauss (later, in 1941). Fay-Cooper Cole—department chair for many years—was described by Studs Terkel, who took an introductory course from him, as an Englishman with a "Bertrand Russell look" and a "delicacy" of manner and clarity in language.[81] During Cole's tenure as chair, A. R. Radcliffe-Brown, the "British" (actually, Australian, but a Cambridge scholar) social anthropologist, was employed to fill the vacuum left when Sapir left to participate in a research project at Yale. Since Sapir did not return when the Yale project was completed, Radcliffe-Brown remained longer at Chicago than anticipated. Having a European theoretical perspective, Radcliffe-Brown represented a sharp theoretical break, and he was strongly critical of the direction of thought in American anthropology.

Radcliffe-Brown was described by colleagues and students as "affecting an Edwardian Cambridge style."[82] A former student characterized him as a "challenging figure," while others described him as abrasive and highly superior in his attitude toward American anthropology.[83] Whatever his personal characteristics, he did establish Chicago as a center of social anthropology, based on a theoretical position that was critical of that of Boas. Boas's approach, stemming from a background in natural science, was more descriptive, less driven by theory. Distinguishing between social anthropology and cultural anthropology, Radcliffe-Brown contended that while culture was studied through historical, descriptive methods, the *functions* of social forms were studied ahistorically and by abstracting universal commonalities in social behavior. He was not interested in looking at unique cultural patterns but in establishing general laws of society by comparing social forms in different societies. He firmly believed that a science of society existed, and he debated Mortimer Adler, Hutchins's coeditor of the Great Books series, on the issue.[84]

Robert Park described Radcliffe-Brown's work as "sociology concerned with primitive peoples" and pointed out his debt to Emile Durkheim, the French social theorist who was the progenitor of the field of sociology.[85] Lloyd Warner, as well as others in sociology and anthropology, were greatly influenced by the "social anthropology" viewpoint. Redfield and Fay-Cooper Cole were early and strong advocates of including five fields—social anthropology, cultural anthropology, physical anthropology, archeology, and linguistics—in the discipline. Dunham would later refer to these five areas in her dance anthropology classes.

Dunham looked for areas relating to her interest in dance in all of her classes, including archeology and physical anthropology. She concluded, "Social Anthropology offered the best possible solution for joining my wish to be an anthropologist and the great physical urge to be a dancer."[86] Radcliffe-Brown "lectured in terms of function, so that I was always reminded to look for the purpose and the use of whatever I saw, as well as the form."[87] In a discussion of her Haitian fieldwork, Dunham noted that after a period of "happy participation" in dance, she became more scholarly in her approach: "I began to get seriously into the question of the choreographic form, psychological and sociological significance, organization and function of what I was seeing and participating in."[88] Her thesis proposal was entitled "Form and Function in Primitive Dance" and reflected her debt to Radcliffe-Brown.[89]

Redfield and other colleagues of Radcliffe-Brown were also influenced by his theoretical views. In his history of the Chicago anthropology department, George Stocking noted that Redfield "moved away from Boasian historicism toward a social anthropology with strongly evolutionary undertones."[90] The reference to evolution alluded to Redfield's view of the influence of urban development on folk societies. In his work on Mexican society, he traced a continuum ranging from simple, cohesive communities with sacred worldviews to complex urban centers that were secular and individualistic in orientation, with tendencies toward social disorganization. While this process of urbanization occurred over time, it could also be viewed synchronically as a "folk-urban continuum," made up of graduated changes over a given area. This evolutionary perspective informed some of Dunham's discussions of dance and society: "My desire was to see first-hand the primitive dance in its everyday relationship to the people; and anthropology . . . leads one to origins and the simple basic fundamentals of art [that are] made complex and esoteric by civilization."[91] She connected the theoretical concept of culture change with the moral imperative to see ourselves as part of the process, not merely as outside observers from the perspective of a "higher plane" of civilization: "We have somehow ... arrived at the conclusion that we are no longer to be measured by the same set of equations as govern peoples still living in a folk or primitive state. This is obviously a fallacy, and many of the intense crises of modern living when viewed from the vantage point of evolution or acculturation become less ominous and more amenable to solution."[92] The concept of the folk-urban continuum framed her comparison of the functions and forms of dance among Haitian peasants with urban, secular expressions, both in Haiti and in the United States.

Influenced by the Boasian tradition as well as by Radcliffe-Brown, Redfield distinguished between the "function" and the "meaning" of social forms. While such events as ritual dances function universally to bring about group cohesion, as Radcliffe-Brown held, Redfield saw that they also have a meaning or set of meanings based on the belief system of a people. For example, the system of *loa*, or spirits, in the Haitian *voudun* religion that Dunham investigated refers to aspects of African gods that are manifest in the dances and that govern the lives of initiates. They are reflected in peasants' character and personality and therefore penetrate deeply into their everyday lives. For Radcliffe-Brown, such symbolic systems were secondary, surface phenomena; he regarded psychological processes, such as beliefs and sentiments, as the outcome rather than the cause of social actions. The primary significance of such cultural forms as the *loa* rested on their effectiveness in organizing and unifying the group. Their African origin was merely an accident of history; it bore no intrinsic consequence, nor would the particular meanings attached to the *loa* in themselves have any significant effect on social organization.

Redfield's attention to the meaning of symbols reflected his debt to Sapir. Redfield defined culture, briefly, as "the conventional understandings, manifest in act and artifact, that characterize societies."[93] This view anticipated Clifford Geertz's view of culture as consisting of "public meanings."[94] Redfield's explanation simplified the profusion of definitions of culture existing at the time, many of them consisting of lists of such attributes as values and beliefs, ritual and social behavior, and categories of material items. According to the Sapir-Redfield view, such cultural traits provide the tangible basis for the study of culture as a system of meanings.

In recognizing the importance of both the function and meaning of social events and behavior, Redfield, along with Fred Eggan and other students at Chicago, synthesized the two radically different schools represented by Sapir and Radcliffe-Brown.[95] The synthesis is also seen in Dunham's approach to Haitian society. Her detailed study of the forms and functions of dance and the relationships between forms and functions (e.g., the connections among the *loa* and between the *loa* and the rhythms, movements, and ritual items associated with them), as well as the psychic and social effects of ceremonies and dance movements on participants, is a direct reflection of her work at Chicago.

In entering the discipline in that place and at that time, Dunham was at the leading edge of anthropology, and her subsequent teaching and intellectual development reflected this vantage point. Redfield's combination of the structure and meanings of cultural forms with social functions was a transitional link to later theoretical contributions of the Chicago Department of Anthropology, as influenced by the French symbolic structuralist Lévi-Strauss and found in the writings of Chicago anthropologists in the 1960s and 1970s.[96] Working in different field settings, these anthropologists assumed the fundamental importance of symbolic systems in social organization and analyzed in detail correspondences between ideas, values, and social acts. The seminal role of these anthropologists demonstrates the central position of the Chicago department in educating and influencing American anthropologists.

In the challenging intellectual environment at Chicago, Dunham found her professors—especially Redfield—to be supportive in her search for a theoretical and professional niche. Redfield suggested that she continue in both dance and anthropology when she began to experience a conflict of interests and felt she had to give up one or the other as a career. Fay-Cooper Cole, who stressed the importance of percussion as a unifying force in cultures, was also one of the influences in her development of the new area of dance anthropology.

Because of her characteristic disregard for social boundaries, Dunham was able to relate to her professors as human beings rather than as icons or figures of authority. In a passage describing the faculty at Chicago, Dunham recalled their personalities: "The personal appeal and dry wit of Robert Redfield, the crashing daring of a man like Robert [Lloyd] Warner, dapper, far-travelled Fay-Cooper Cole, Margaret Mead, who exposed sexual habits in the Pacific, Malinowski who exposed sex habits wherever he happened to be stationed, Radcliffe-Brown, an Australian being Oxford, a gaunt old yellow-toothed lion given to floating around the lecture hall dropping verbal bombs on tender blossoms—I being one of them—then retreating and grinning at the wreckage."[96]

Her professors came to the parties at Dunham's apartment, and she found them to be "a lot of fun." She did not realize at the time that this was unusual; her social world was, in her words, "strange" by most people's standards. In this informal setting, the cosmopolitan Malinowski, famous for his work in the Trobriand Islands in the South Pacific, taught her the beguine, bridging the gulf between academics and dance socially as well as in theory. A few months later, she observed the authentic beguine in Martinique and then incorporated it into her dance program.

While expanding her cultural knowledge, Dunham continued her explorations in dance. In Chicago, New York, and elsewhere, dancers, black and white, were experimenting with African and African American movement.[98] The strictures John Martin placed against black dancers performing European forms and white dancers doing African movements were not heeded by such white dancers as Agnes de Mille, Helen Tamiris, and Martha Graham, who were using African and African American themes in their choreography.

Ruth Page created and danced in *La Guiablesse,* based on a Martinique folk story recounted in Lafcadio Hearns's *Two Years in the French West Indies,* with music by the black composer William Grant Still. When Page became involved in other projects, she invited Dunham to dance the lead in *La Guiablesse* at the Chicago Opera House in 1934. Page wrote, "She remembered every single detail," and remarked that the ballet introduced Dunham to the West Indian material that later made her famous.[99] Although her claim was not entirely accurate, critical praise of Dunham's performance in *La Guiablesse* did reinforce her growing sense that her mission lay in seeking out and presenting new cultural forms.

The Inner Journey

Dunham's strength lay in intuiting feelings and motives and presenting them in organized, artistic form. Her empathy and astuteness in seeing into the essence of human character that enabled her to excel in anthropology and in the theater were the same skills that sustained her through life's difficulties. She has stated that she has relied on her "affective self" throughout her life in making important decisions.[100]

The turbulence of her childhood was echoed in her emotional life during the early Chicago years. Because of her alliance with her brother during those years, it is not surprising that her "affective self" was vested in Albert, who was a very attractive and successful young man. She perceived him as powerful; his illustrious mentors, such as Alfred North Whitehead, George Herbert Mead, Charles Moore, and John Dewey, protected him against racial and social prejudices at the university. Later, she would view him as something of a social and intellectual snob because he maintained an amused, critical attitude toward other, less favored black students at the university, but he remained a kind and devoted brother.

Albert Dunham's view of reality was probably somewhat distorted by the artificial social environment in which he moved. His experience at the university, where famous people recognized his abilities and brought him into their social orbit as an equal, gave him an unrealistic view of the academic world and his future in it. He was probably unaware of the extent to which prejudices were embedded in academe.

There was another side to the university that was obscured by the presence of such idealists as Hutchins, Redfield, and G. H. Mead. When Hutchins later parted from the institution, there was relief on both sides. After the United States entered World War II, his pacifism became unpopular and caused disruption among conservatives and humanists. Katherine Dunham wrote that their opposition "eventually would activate the resignation of the man responsible for abolishing the age limit, high and low, on learning, the man who, new, dynamic, daring, cultured [was] the first of those very young which have made themselves recognized in many ways."[101] He was also, indirectly, responsible for her great adventure in Haiti and all that followed. When she phoned Hutchins while on tour in California, he told her that the trustees had showed no confidence in him and that he had to justify everything he did. Many of his ideas were too progressive for them, and they were happy to find an excuse to let him go.

The university had originally been a Baptist institution, with a strong program of liberal theology and a sense of social service. A settlement house was established near the university, and there were strong ties with Jane Addams's Hull-House.[102] However, during the black expansion into the formerly white neighborhoods surrounding the university—a result of the "block busting" tactics of realtors—little of this idealism was expressed in positive social programs.

William McNeill, a recorder of Hutchins's presidential term at the university, wrote that actions by real estate managers to keep the neighborhood "lily white" were not supported by the administration, faculty, or students.[103] Hutchins detested discrimination and declined to use the resources of the university to put obstacles in the path of the black expansion. At the university, he made an effort to integrate the campus dining rooms; he was joined in this by Albert Dunham and his friends, with eventual success. The university hospital was open to blacks, as was university enrollment; however, in 1932, African Americans and Asians together made up less than 2 percent of the student population. McNeill asserted that it was "economic and behavioral differences" that excluded blacks.[104] Little effort was made to relate to the community or to develop social services, however, so that in the 1940s and 1950s, the university was surrounded by encroaching decaying neighborhoods and increasingly hostile citizens. Gradually isolated from its immediate environment, the university turned its focus to the international scene.

Katherine Dunham's positive view of the university was tempered by two incidents involving her brother, both reflecting unresolved racial conflicts. In one instance, he was with a white friend when they were attacked and robbed in a nearby black neighborhood. It deeply shocked and angered him, since it exposed the illusion of the enclave of enlightenment and culture the university represented in the midst of deprivation and discontent. Katherine perceived the significance of this experience to Albert and retrospectively described it as an omen of his later alienation and mental illness.

The second incident occurred when Albert's professional career was about to be launched. After working for a time at Harvard with Whitehead, he returned to Chicago, which accepted his credits and his thesis from Harvard and awarded him a Ph.D. He was to teach a class there during summer school, but half of the class walked out on the first day. Faculty and administrators exerted enough pressure to guarantee a full class for the rest of the summer, and ultimately the class responded favorably. Nevertheless, despite the efforts of his mentors, he could not obtain a position at the university and eventually joined the faculty at Howard University. In view of Albert's experience, the contention that racial discrimination at the university was merely by default and not actively practiced by students and faculty appears disingenuous.

W. E. B. Du Bois's insightful discourse on the "twoness" of the African American helps clarify Albert's predicament: "It is a peculiar sensation, this double-consciousness, this sense of always looking at one's self through the eyes of others . . . of measuring one's soul by the tape of a world that looks on in amused contempt and pity. One ever feels his twoness—an American, a Negro . . . two unreconciled strivings; two warring ideals in one dark body, whose dogged strength alone keeps it from being torn asunder."[105]

The internal struggle between a racist society's view of him and his self-image as an assured intellectual was intensified by Albert's failure to obtain a position at the University of Chicago. Caught in the dilemma posed by an oppressive system, he was unable to reconcile his potential with the limits placed on him. As pointed out in *Color and Human Nature*, "The more intelligent and sensitive . . . a Negro may be, and the more completely he assimilates and transmits the national ideals, the more seriously he is made to feel that his race, and race alone, bars him from enjoying the full rights of American citizenship."[106] For such a person, the paradox of discrimination and the American democratic ideal is explicit and acutely felt.

Albert had been strong for both Katherine and himself through the years. But in sight of his dream of total acceptance by his intellectual peers, he was rejected, and he ultimately succumbed to deep depression. Katherine's visit to him years later in a mental hospital was deeply painful. His illness and death were tragedies that weighed heavily on her, casting a shadow over her later successes.

Prior to the crumbling of her brother's dreams, he made a decision that had a more immediate impact on her: he married Frances Taylor, her best friend. Perhaps it was an expression of a need for emotional security on the brink of a change in his life. Shortly thereafter, the couple moved to Cambridge, where he studied with Whitehead at Harvard. Whatever the case, it was a crushing blow to Katherine, who felt abandoned.

She sought qualities in other men that she loved and admired in her brother: resolute purpose, intellect, and sympathy. She had experienced the "crushes" on teachers that idealistic young students often have for those they admire. She had fallen in love with Redfield when she first saw him walking on campus. She believed he was aware of her passion. "He knew I was dying for one glance from those blue eyes," she declared many years later.[107] She also liked a young student who was the son of Brigadier General Benjamin Davis, the first black general in the U.S. Army, but Ben Davis Jr.—"one of my first loves"—had his sights set on following in his father's footsteps and soon left for West Point. She wrote to cheer him up when no one would speak to him during his first two years at the academy. In her loneliness after her brother and best friend moved away, she married a young man, Jordis McCoo, who worked at the post office, one of the few opportunities for permanent work for black Americans and thus a symbol of security.

The two siblings, whose early lives had been desperately insecure, now appeared to have settled down to fairly normal lives. In 1933, Albert and his wife gave birth to a son, Kay Dunham. (Katherine was never very close to her nephew, however; when her stepmother died, she particularly resented the fact that he tried to assume part ownership of her parents' house.) Since her husband worked at night, Katherine was free to continue her pursuits in dance and anthropology. But this situation was short-lived; married life was not compatible with her aspirations. McCoo danced in some of her productions, but they gradually drifted apart. And Albert ultimately lost his ability to lead any kind of normal life.

With her brother's guidance no longer accessible, Katherine's need led her to Erich Fromm, the German-Jewish psychoanalyst, who was trying to raise funds to bring Jews out of Europe. She met him in 1933 when she was seeking financial support for her field research. She was in "good hands": he was a strong counselor, and she would turn to him many times during her life. She once remarked that he was "the closest I have come to having a guru."[108] Her brother had actually introduced her to psychiatry. One of Hutchins's innovations was to provide psychiatric counseling for students, and Albert advised her to take advantage of the services. When her psychiatrist committed suicide, Erich Fromm was concerned about the effect on her, though he would not take her as a patient since they had become close friends.

The most effective therapy for Katherine Dunham was the absorbing task of outlining her research plans and carrying them out. To advance her projected work, she needed to identify where she would do her fieldwork and how she would obtain support. Friends and mentors, impressed by her abilities as well as by her ambitious plans and the quality of her mission, came to her rescue.

She was anxious to leave Chicago, which had become like "being in purgatory," she later said.[109] She would return to Chicago after her fieldwork, but she would not remain there long. When she departed for the field, she was in many ways still a girl with dreams. Her work in the Caribbean would transform her into a woman with a practical vision, prepared to transmute her experiences into art and to interpret them on international stages.

3 *Fieldwork at the Cutting Edge*

> [Made] free of the open air, [my mind] breathed deeply
> and took on new strength . . . my astonished eye could
> hardly take in the wealth and variety of the scene.
>
> —Claude Lévi-Strauss, *Tristes Tropiques*

To COMBINE DANCE and anthropology, Katherine Dunham needed to study dance in a society in which it had a more central role than in the United States. In the Boasian tradition, the anthropology department emphasized field research, even for undergraduates. For the aspiring anthropologist, Malinowski's "mythopoeic" field trip to Melanesia set the standard for intensive fieldwork; his presence at Chicago stirred interest in the long-term, participatory experience he espoused.[1]

Dunham was prepared to immerse herself in her chosen area. She elected to go to the West Indies and particularly to work in Haiti, where the influence of African religions was evident and where there was a fusion of dance and religion. Cole referred her to Herskovits at nearby Northwestern University, who had done fieldwork in Haiti. Herskovits was an exponent of the view that African cultures had survived in many forms in the New World. In 1932, in her first contact with him, Dunham wrote to solicit books, articles, and reviews he might be willing to contribute to a library she was helping to establish for Provident Hospital on African American physiology, psychology, and culture. She also asked for his assistance in developing a plan of study and for his opinion on how she might combine anthropology and dance.[2] Herskovits replied that he needed all the materials he had for his own classes, but he did give her advice on how to proceed with her studies: "I feel that the best way to take up the study of any such special subject as primitive dancing is to become acquainted with general anthropological theory and field methodology."[3] Subsequently, in 1935, she worked with him to prepare for her first field trip.

To begin her quest, she needed financial support. Like other talented young African American artists and scholars at the time, she turned to the Rosenwald Foundation. The Rosenwald grants, initiated by Julius Rosenwald—onetime president of Sears, Roebuck Corporation—supported promising young artists and scholars, particularly African Americans. Upon reading Booker T. Washington's *Up from Slavery,* Rosenwald had been so impressed that he chartered a private train to take prominent Chicagoans on a tour of the Tuskegee Institute. The son of a penniless Jewish immigrant, he retained a feeling for the poor and a strong social conscience; his aim, like that of Robert Park, was to apply the principles of the Tuskegee Institute in a northern urban setting. To further this end, Rosenwald funded the Urban League of Chicago.

Charles Johnson, one of Park's students who later became the director of the National Urban League in New York, maintained a strong presence in Chicago through his work with the Rosenwald Foundation. He had received a Rosenwald grant and was the author of several studies of black communities; he was also a promoter and interpreter of the Harlem Renaissance in his capacity as editor of *Opportunity,* the Urban League publication.[4] He was strongly supportive of the young Katherine Dunham. Later, when he was president of Fisk University, he offered her a position at Fisk if she completed her M.A. degree and outlined her plans for future work.

Charles Johnson, Will Alexander of the New Deal's Farm Security Administration, and Edwin Embree, author of a popular biographical work on black authors, dominated the selection of the black recipients of the Rosenwald grants.[5] Black social scientists receiving awards included Horace Cayton, Allison Davis of Fisk University, St. Clair Drake, Katherine Dunham, E. Franklin Frazier, Charles Johnson, Zora Neale Hurston, and Ira Reid. All of these recipients except Hurston were trained at Chicago.

Social introductions were crucial to the prospective recipient. As a result of her growing reputation, as well as recommendations by teachers and acquaintances, in 1934 Dunham was invited to a Rosenwald reception, where she first met Erich Fromm. She believed he was instrumental in persuading a representative of the foundation to attend one of her dance recitals. Fromm and Johnson, who were enthusiastic about her combination of dance and scholarship, endorsed her application to the foundation, and Herskovits agreed to mentor her. When she was invited to present her research proposal to the board of judges, she demonstrated her interest in different dance styles by performing contrasting European and African movements. The startled committee funded her research, confirming at that early stage her effectiveness in communicating cultural differences through dance. Rosenwald support lent credibility to her attempt to combine anthropology and dance and was an important advance in her career.

The Rosenwald grant, which she received early in 1935, provided the opportunity to spend several months studying with Herskovits, learning about the Caribbean societies, the *voudun* in Haiti, and the material culture and living conditions.[6] He also taught her field techniques, including how to observe while participating in activities. Because of her egalitarian spirit, he warned her, she would have problems with the social stratification based on slight variations in skin color, as well as with the subordinate role assigned to women. He advised her to withhold judgment and not express opinions on such matters, to be patient and respectful. He informed her about clothing, medicines, and other supplies she would need and would not be able to purchase. He taught her how to operate a camera and a recorder, and he lent her his old Edison hand-operated cylinder recorder.[7]

Embree had informed Herskovits that the foundation would not have given the grant to Dunham, an undergraduate, had he not agreed to serve as her sponsor, teacher, and guide and that the grant was potentially far larger than that of any other candidate.[8] He stipulated that Herskovits inform them of her progress before they funded the field portion of the grant. On May 2, 1935, Herskovits wrote to Embree saying that her scholarship and class work were excellent and that he recommended the field trip.

Herskovits advised Dunham to have calling cards printed with her name, "The University of Chicago," and "dance" and "anthropology" inscribed on them. He also gave her letters of introduction to scholars and authorities in the countries she would visit, including Dr. Jean Price-Mars, a Haitian anthropologist; Colonel Simon Rowe of the Maroon people in Jamaica; President Stenio Vincent of Haiti; and other governmental officials and scholars in Haiti and the other sea islands.

Her time spent with Herskovits was an excellent preparation for the field; she learned how to use her senses as recording instruments as well as how to employ the necessary extensions of her senses—recorders, cameras—in recording information. Many years later, as an adjunct professor in the anthropology department at Southern Illinois University at Edwardsville, she used notes from her work with Herskovits in her classes in dance anthropology. She described him in *Island Possessed* as "a fantastic guide for getting to the bottom of things."[9]

Dunham's teachers introduced her to issues of fieldwork methods that were emerging in anthropology in the 1920s and 1930s. Herskovits impressed upon her the importance of presenting a balanced view and not imposing her own ideas on her subject of study. Redfield was ahead of his time in recognizing the inevitable influence of an anthropologist's personality and values on field observation and interpretations and perceiving the hidden questions that caused the fieldworker to focus on certain observations and overlook others.[10]

As a student of Park, Redfield had absorbed Ferdinand Tönnies's dichotomy of gesellschaft—secularized, heterogeneous industrial society—and gemeinschaft—coherent, small-scale community life. Redfield's folk-urban continuum includes these two as polar opposites in a constant process of acculturation as societies become industrialized and more complex. While Park saw the positive aspects of urbanization and industrialization, leading to freedom and the release of individual creativity, Redfield, having experienced some of the positive qualities of Mexican village life, saw urbanization as disintegrative. Katherine Dunham's outlook was inevitably influenced by Redfield's theoretical views, which he was developing during her period of study at the University of Chicago.

One of the classic theoretical discussions that emerged in anthropology of the 1950s, after Dunham had left Chicago, centered on different presentations of life in the Mexican village of Tepoztlán, as advanced by Redfield and as reinterpreted by the (then) young Oscar Lewis.[11] Redfield described an integrated community with a harmonious worldview, while Lewis focused on conflict and the oppression of poverty.

Because of the nature of most anthropological research, in which an investigator lives in and becomes identified with a particular community, discrepancies may occur when an observer with a different background and theoretical position restudies the same group and arrives at different conclusions. Similar challenges of bias have been brought against the work of other noted fieldworkers, including Ruth Benedict and Margaret Mead.[12] Scientists are human, and attacking giants is a path to recognition; at the same time, controversy is an inevitable result of scientific openness and can promote the advancement of a discipline. For these reasons, as in all fields of knowledge, progress in anthropological knowledge necessarily involves theoretical conflict, and it is often accompanied by a degree of sibling or generational rivalry.

In the public discussions with Lewis about Tepoztlán, Redfield did not assume a defensive stance but commented that Lewis's personality led to greater emotional involvement with the Mexican villagers than did his own and to insights and perspectives he had overlooked.[13] His intellectual sophistication led him to realize that interpretations were relative to the observers' viewpoints. Since the observer is relating to other people, not to inanimate objects, subjective responses are inescapable and do not necessarily result in error if they are openly acknowledged. Empathy can actually result in a more profound understanding of people, and it can be argued that it is an essential goal when one is studying a society in which one is an outsider.[14] As Redfield observed, "The anthropologist's own human nature is an instrument of work."[15] His grasp of the processes involved in the insider-outsider encounter reveals the qualities of Dunham's "moral mentor": "In coming to understand an alien way of life . . . the course of personal experience is essentially the same: one looks first at an incomprehensible other; one comes to see that other as one's self in another guise. . . . Slowly, for one or another of us, the vision and comprehension of humanity, both in its extraordinary variety of expressions and its fundamental sameness, is widened."[16] His viewpoint anticipated later critique of the "self-other" dichotomy expressed in some ethnographies, reflecting a psychic distance and lack of human connection afflicting the ethnographer's fieldwork.

As first pointed out by the philosopher Immanuel Kant, a crucial distinction exists between subjectivism, or personal bias, and intersubjectivism, which involves communication between subjects.[17] When, as with Redfield, the observer maintains an ongoing modification of interpretations, communicating, testing, and confirming them over a period of time, then subjective ideas become more than personal bias. In the same manner, Katherine Dunham's views have, over the years, evolved, paralleling the maturation of the observer herself. This will become apparent in comparing her earlier comments about Haitian society with those of later years.

Dunham's approach was shaped by all her teachers, but Redfield's influence was the most profound. From him, she absorbed a perspective that was in tune with her idealism, namely, a utopian folk society in which people were closer to nature and to one another and, though untutored when compared with urbanites, were also wise: a mirror image of the "wise innocence" she valued as an attribute in her own life. This view colored her early work with the peasant peoples of the Caribbean, and the extent to which it was an accurate view afforded her pleasure and rewarded her efforts to understand. Her faith in this assumption of simplicity—her "openness" to all experience—also gave her the courage and spirit to overcome the difficulties and negative influences she encountered.[18] While she recognized aspects of Haitian society that were repugnant to her values, she strove to be nonjudgmental. She has referred to herself as an "incurable optimist," which can be interpreted as the faith of an idealist.

While Redfield gave her direction, inspiration, and support, Herskovits at Northwestern University was Dunham's fieldwork adviser and guide. Her interest in the traditional roots of African Americans and her exposition of those connections on world stages owe much to Herskovits's pioneering work. On the basis of his studies in Africa and in Surinam and his work with other African American groups, Herskovits took the position, contrary to that of W. E. B. Du Bois and other proponents of integration, that black Americans shared many cultural expressions deriving from African cultures. Boas had consciously avoided such a position because of his support of social integration: he feared that as a result of uninformed views about Africa, segregationists would use identification with African cultures as an argument against integration. In the 1920s, Marcus Garvey's "Back to Africa" movement was supported by southern segregationists. Herskovits's strongest critic was the Chicago-trained sociologist E. Franklin Frazier, who held that African culture had been completely destroyed under conditions of slavery.[19]

Herskovits's views, with some qualifications, are currently supported by most students of African American culture. To Katherine Dunham, who found African rhythms and movement in her travels throughout the New World, his arguments were persuasive. In an early interview, she stated, "The African Negro is habituated to a certain kind of musical technique in which rhythm is basic. In America and the Islands we harbor an appreciation of this rhythm . . . but this appreciation is not based on any physical difference, nor is it psychological; we are sociologically conditioned by our constant contact with it."[20] Her comments reflect the Boasian view of the distinction between race and culture and recall Boas's reservation about distinguishing black Americans from other Americans. The rather careful admission that "we harbor an appreciation of this rhythm" reflects her painful awareness of the common assumption that black people were natural dancers and "had rhythm."[21] Still, she, like Herskovits, asserted the existence of *cultural* resonances between Africans and African Americans.

The influence of Bronislaw Malinowski was felt by all Chicago students in the social sciences, and his oeuvre informed the subsequent course of anthropological fieldwork. Dunham's approach to fieldwork was in the spirit of Malinowski's legacy. She, like other anthropologists, inherited his interior conflict between detachment and engagement in attempting to balance the "intimate view and cool assessment" of the participant-observer. This conflict was highlighted at the time of publication of his field diary, in which he revealed his personal struggles in relating to people in the field.[22] Such clashes are inherent in the participant-observer method, in which two fundamentally different processes—action and observation—occur simultaneously in the same person. While these processes occur together in all human behavior, in the scientific method there is an attempt to abstract observation from action in order to minimize observer effects on the objects of study. Participant-observation gives observers license to enter actively into situations, recognizing the fact that observer effects are inevitable when the "objects" of study are people. The inevitable consequences of the fieldworker's behavior should be openly acknowledged and attempts made to limit them.

Statements of the dilemma occur frequently in Dunham's writings, especially in her treatments of belief systems. Critics have claimed a similar breach between engagé and disengagé in her dance persona; they seem unable to reconcile her sensual and vibrant performance with her intellectual discussions of the relationship between dance and society.[23] While in the field, she was frequently able to resolve the dichotomy between scientific observation and human involvement through dance. The total commitment of intellect, body, and spirit she experienced in dance, together with its key role in the culture, and the social connections she experienced through performance gave her a special insight she could not have gained as a passive observer; yet, at the same time, she maintained a choreographer's objective eye.[24] The active nature of her research carried into her anthropological writing, in which she described in detail how her fieldwork progressed, including revelations about personal feelings and actions, encounters with named people, and individual participants in the events she depicted.

A rather commonplace, but to me revealing, event illustrates Dunham's approach to learning about another culture, as well as her unfailing urge to teach. During a visit to Residence Dunham at Habitation Leclerc, I tumbled down a hillside trail while on a walk, to the amusement of an audience of Haitians; I was unhurt but embarrassed. When told about this, Dunham asked, "Did you join in the laughter?" and advised that this would have been the best response.[25] Later, I was informed that I had won my Ph.D. from her when, years before, at her request I had gone to observe a ceremony and carry medicine from "Madame Dunham." This involved traveling in the back of an open truck on bumpy roads and by foot over several miles of rocky terrain, far into Haiti's countryside. She understood the import of the physical imprint of cultural experience.[26]

Katherine Dunham's fieldwork in the Caribbean took place about the same time as that of Zora Neale Hurston, who studied with Boas while she was at Barnard College. A comparison of the field methods and results of these women—both artists and anthropologists—is a study in the two prevailing schools of theory and methodology of the time. Hurston's anthropology mentors—Franz Boas and Ruth Benedict, among others—represented a traditional approach to fieldwork. Originally a physical scientist, Boas was primarily concerned that students collect information as rapidly as possible before simpler societies were swamped by contacts with industrial societies. He believed that theory would flow from the facts once sufficient and accurate materials were collected. His primary guidelines to students were that they focus on details of forms but also gather as much cultural context as possible for folklore, art forms, customs, and other cultural items so that integrative patterns among them could emerge. When Hurston was studying folklore in South Florida, he wrote, "Pay particular attention, not so much to the content, but rather to the form of diction and movements . . . methods of dancing, habitual movements in telling tales or in ordinary conversation," and he advised her to "describe practices relating to marriage, birth, death and other important events in life."[27] He informed her that the final goal was not merely collection but also interpretation of the materials in terms of cultural forms.

Boas recognized Hurston's mastery over the southern folk milieu and believed she was in a unique position to interpret its expressions. He noted her success in this enterprise in his preface to *Mules and Men*, her account of this first field trip.[28] Boas did not recognize the full implication of her achievement—that she had an inside perspective on southern black culture through her *participation* in it; the impact of this understanding on anthropological method awaited the work of Malinowski and others.

Dunham met with Boas at a "soirée" Erich Fromm held for her in New York on her way to Haiti; Margaret Mead and Ruth Benedict were also present.[29] Boas expressed his regret that he had not been a dancer while studying Northwest Coast Indians, and he predicted that she could discover cultural knowledge that was inaccessible to nondancers.[30] In suggesting that she possessed an advantage in gaining knowledge in a society in which dance was important, he implied the importance of participation. He also conveyed his primary interest in the theoretical question of whether rhythm was inherent or acquired—a matter relating to his position on distinctions between race and culture—which was not a focus of her study. However she returned to the subject in her later interest in "bio-rhythms," which she found to be universal.

A comparison of the writings of Dunham and Hurston is instructive in showing the ways in which personal history, cultural background, and theoretical discipline affect fieldwork results. In Accompong, Dunham followed her innate predilection as well as lessons of her mentors in assuming the role of a neophyte who was there to learn. By placing herself in the role of supplicant, she put the Maroons in the role of teachers to a benighted African American from the United States, one of a class of people whom they knew to be ignorant of their heritage. This allowed her to learn a great deal in the thirty days she was in Accompong. In *Journey to Accompong*, she sketched the daily activities and personalities of the villagers in a series of graphic vignettes. The recognition that her interest and insights were genuine was reflected in an invitation to participate in a celebration of Maroon culture in New York City more than fifty-five years later, in 1992.

In *Island Possessed*, Dunham described her growth as interpreter of Haitian society, documenting her progress in a denser series of vivid and detailed descriptions of the people and culture than she had presented in *Journey to Accompong*. As a dancer, she was able to enter into the dance ritual of the Rada Dahomey; her involvement in this important cultural activity helped transform her into an insider, much as Hurston's storytelling skills gained her an "in" for her work in the South. The relationships Dunham established in her "incorporative rituals" into Caribbean societies, including initiations into the various levels of the *voudun*, were not, as is sometimes the case with neophyte anthropologists, merely developed to gain information.[31] They were for life; her guardians and co-initiates became part of her spiritual family.

Hurston had more knowledge of West Indian religions, initially, than did Dunham. Throughout Hurston's childhood in southern Florida, she was conversant with spells, herbals, and stories of Caribbean origin. She grew up in an environment in which the "black magic" elements of voodoo or "hoodoo" were familiar; she was introduced to African beliefs and practices by Bahamian migrant workers at an early age. These influences are apparent in her novels.[32] As a student, she had collected folklore in the Bahamas, as well as in Florida and New Orleans; in her trip to New Orleans, she investigated the "two-headed doctors," or conjure men and women, and underwent initiation into their secrets.[33] In a note to her publication "Hoodoo in America," she informed the reader, "Veaudeau is the European term for African magic practices and beliefs, but it is unknown to the American Negro. His own name for his practices is hoodoo, both terms being related to the West African term *juju*. In the Bahamas as on the West Coast of Africa the term is obeah. 'Roots' is the

Southern Negro's term for folk-doctoring by herbs and prescriptions, and by extension, and because all hoodoo doctors cure by roots, it may be used as a synonym for hoodoo."[34]

Hurston despised the hypocrisy of the elite and the political leaders of Haiti, who lied about the *voudun*, calling it savage or even denying its existence while secretly believing in it and even using it for their own ends. She admired the growing nationalism of the young people of Haiti, who valued their own culture—including *voudun*—more than French culture.[35] She described *voudun* as an organized religion, stating that it involved "more detail of gods and rites than the Catholic church has in Rome" and that it fully understood its African origins.[36] Yet her written account of Arada Dahomey (or Rada Dahomey, to use the creole term), the more orthodox system, was brief and rather misleading, downplaying the power of its dominant spirits. She then moved on to the more destructive Petro and Congo cults and found the Petro gods "terrible and wicked" and more "powerful and quick" than those of Rada Dahomey.[37] She also devoted a great amount of space to a detailed account of zombies. By dwelling on the more sensational aspects of the religion without placing them in a social context, she tended to undermine her view of *voudun* as a positive force in Haitian society, thus playing into the hands of less sophisticated writers who described it in lurid terms.[38]

The practitioners of Arada Dahomey are primarily healers and harmonizers. Dunham noted that the destructive cults gain more prominence during periods of crisis and great hardship, when they serve to organize resistance or channel frustration. Hurston failed to appreciate the powerful integrative role played by Arada Dahomey in Haitian society during less contentious times; as a result, she underestimated the power of its *loa*, or spirits, and minimized the positive social role of the cults in Haitian society. However, her rather sinister view of Haitian religion (stemming in part, perhaps, from the fact that she developed a violent gastric distress while studying it) may also indicate recognition of covert malignant forces that erupt periodically in Haiti's politics.

Dunham's and Hurston's contrasting approaches exemplify the principles that were later brought forth in the Redfield-Lewis debates, as well as in other controversies about interpretations of fieldwork findings. In contrast to Hurston, Dunham adopted a more contextual view of Haitian religion. Her writings reflect Radcliffe-Brown's stress on social functions, as well as Malinowski's concern with social functions as the satisfaction of individual needs: she described not only the forms and patterns of dance but also the role of dance ritual in the formation of social groups, the transmission of values and worldview, and the well-being of individuals in the society. Her field report, published as *Dances of Haiti*, is a systematic treatment of the dances and the folk religion of Haiti, with analyses of the social and psychological effects of sacred and secular dances.

An unfortunate underlying rivalry between Hurston and Dunham developed because of a situation over which neither had control. The origin of their differences lay in the prior relationship between Hurston and Herskovits. They were both students of Boas who were tackling subjects related to his views that culture and race varied independent of each other. In the 1920s, Hurston was conducting physical measurements on African Americans to test Boas's hypothesis that head size and shape, as well as other measurements of all U.S. immigrants, including Africans, were influenced by environmental factors in the New World. This research was designed to refute the notion that the head size and shape of Africans and American blacks were genetically determined and indicated innate inferiority. Herskovits was looking at *cultural continuities* rather than physical affinities between African Americans and Africans.

Hurston corresponded with Herskovits concerning her work, and in 1935 when she received a Rosenwald grant to do fieldwork in the Caribbean, she proposed working with him at Northwestern. She decided to continue working with Boas, however, although the Rosenwald committee advised her to study at Harvard.[39] She did not depart for the Caribbean until April 15, 1936. On July 30, she wrote Herskovits that she was in Accompong and remarked bitterly that "Catherine [*sic*] Dunham had been here last year carrying out the program that I had mapped out for the Rosenwald gang."[40] In answer to her letter, Herskovits assured her that he, not the Rosenwald committee, had planned Dunham's itinerary and that there was nothing wrong in two people carrying out research in the same place, especially since Dunham's emphasis was on dance.[41] Hurston's response reflects her confrontational approach, which often alienated her peers. She wrote that she had criticized the president of Fisk University for running the school "like a Georgia plantation" and had referred to him as "Mr. Charlie" with his "good niggers," one of which was, presumably, Charles Johnson, who was on the Rosenwald committee. She had since heard that Johnson had boasted that he was "grooming" Katherine Dunham to take her place. She explained that she had nothing against Dunham and her work, but she obviously felt that Dunham was being used by the committee to punish her for continuing to work with Boas. The Rosenwald committee, she said, was "anti-Jewish" and anti-Boas, despite its establishment by a Jew.[42]

Although Herskovits acknowledged there were problems with the Rosenwald committee, he did not agree that Dunham was undermining Hurston's position. He pointed out that Hurston was a more experienced fieldworker when she went to the Caribbean than was Dunham and that she had already published accounts of her work in the southern United States.[43]

The personal exchanges that accompanied Dunham's and Hurston's intellectual differences were companion to their openness to the expression of feelings. When Hurston came to one of Dunham's parties during a trip to Chicago in the late 1930s, Dunham was affronted by her pose as the "senior authority" on West Indian society.[44] Hurston reviewed *Journey to Accompong*, Dunham's account of her fieldwork among the Maroons, and characterized the author as a keen observer. In a generally favorable review—she described the writing as "lively and word-deft," and entertaining—she remarked, "After all, thirty days in a locality is not much in research and hardly affords time enough for the field-worker to scratch the surface."[45]

In *Tell My Horse*, in which she described her Caribbean trip, Hurston cast doubt on whether Dunham had actually observed ritual dances; she noted that the Maroons' "real" dances occurred only once a year, while according to Colonel Rowe, "someone else had spent three weeks to study their dances."[46] Writing to Herskovits, she expressed surprise that Dunham had not stayed to see the important yearly ceremony.[47] In her review of *Journey to Accompong*, she referred to the "pert observations on the doings of the men, women and children of Accompong," but she did not indicate whether she had met any of them during her longer stay there.

Hurston did not achieve the same authority on Caribbean cultures that she did for the South because she apparently did not enter into the social life very deeply. In contrast to Dunham's description of her initiation into the *voudun*, Hurston's accounts, of both her Haitian and the New Orleans initiations, are relatively brief and bare of affect, providing a few rather sensational details. It should be noted that as in *Mules and Men*, Hurston's descriptions of Caribbean societies included personal reflections and her social encounters, suggesting discomfort with the standard "objective" approach. However, her insights do not penetrate very deeply, and her comments on her research in the Caribbean seem to indicate that during her stay she did not really become involved with the people. Her research focused on interviews with influential and knowledgeable members of the community and the more "picturesque" events, with minimal attention given to day-to-day activities. Of the Maroons, she named only two individuals, Colonel Rowe and his brother, and a sizable portion of her account was a detailed description of a hunt for a wild boar, in which the colonel allowed her to participate. She portrayed only one other individual in any detail, a man she referred to as "Medicine Man," with whom she spent much of her time. Her account reflected a fascination with healing and other rituals and magical beliefs to the exclusion of the "doings" of individuals, with which, as she noted in her review, Dunham concerned herself.

Hurston's writings sometimes express a distrust of West Indian people. In her description of her visit to Accompong, for example, Hurston stated that she did not reveal her purpose for being there—to gain information—so that she would not be misled, implying a distrust of her informants. She pointedly remarked that she did not want to see "staged affairs." Her strategy was to "just sit around and wait" for the desired experiences rather than to ask for help. According to these comments, she apparently adopted a strategy of gathering data in whatever way feasible, without attempting to establish the trust on which a reciprocal relationship could develop. The problem with such an approach is that the purpose of the research may be subverted, since people often discern one's sincerity or lack of it and may respond in kind with false information.

Lacking both method and motivation to enter deeply into the Caribbean worldview, Hurston remained an outsider to these cultures and apparently dropped all interest in the religions when she completed her fieldwork. The daughter of a minister, she maintained a lifelong identification with southern culture and, though appreciative of West Indian religions, remained an outsider to them. Dunham, springing from a more pluralistic background with moderate religious influence, came to adopt Haiti as her second home and understood it as few come to understand an "other" culture. Yet, for both Dunham and Hurston, West Indian cultures generally and Haiti in particular were important formative influences. Throughout Hurston's life, West Indian religions were in her subliminal awareness; as a Floridian, she seemed aware of the psychic forces emanating from the islands, and themes from her Caribbean experiences appear in her most highly acclaimed work, *Their Eyes Were Watching God*, written while she was in Haiti.[48] Perhaps her deeper insights into West Indian ethos found an outlet in her sensitive, moving novel.

Two eminent anthropologists with whom Katherine Dunham did not study—Ralph Linton and Claude Lévi-Strauss—commented favorably on her written analyses and evocations of Caribbean life. Linton, a social anthropologist and student of Boas, who taught at Chicago in the late thirties, commended her fieldwork methods in his introduction to *Journey to Accompong*, Dunham's account of her initial field experience among the Maroons of Jamaica: "[W]hile Miss Dunham's observation is that of a trained anthropologist, her method of approach was that of a sympathet-

ic participant . . . while many ethnologists go to a primitive group seeking proof for previously conceived theories, Miss Dunham seems to have
been completely open-minded. . . . Much of her own excitement and her
youthful response to the romance of the tropics color her story; without,
however, destroying the accuracy of her observations."[49]

Lévi-Strauss was also favorably impressed by Dunham's fieldwork
accounts. He wrote a foreword to the French edition of her ethnography,
Les danses d'Haiti, in which he described her "not only as a dancer and
choreographer, but also as a solidly trained specialist . . . [educated at the]
University of Chicago and Northwestern University, major institutions
that have long made their authority felt in the fields of observation, analysis, and ethnographic theory." He characterized the study as "an exem-
plary work of clarity and substance" and praised its "unquestionable originality": "Her book has the great merit of reintegrating the social act of
dance. . . within a total complex. Katherine Dunham proposed not only to
study a ritual, but also to define the role of dance in the life of a society."[50]

Lévi-Strauss was by then aware of Dunham's ongoing dedication to
field research and her presentations of Caribbean and other cultures on
the stage. She had met him in the 1940s, after she had launched her career in dance, at a school she had opened in New York. He came to Boule
Blanche parties—celebrations of Martinique culture—held to support the
Katherine Dunham School of Arts and Research on Forty-second Street.
Having spent time in Martinique and Brazil, he appreciated her promotion and interpretation of the dances and other cultural activities of those
countries.

Lévi-Strauss had taken refuge in New York during the war years and
worked for a time as cultural adviser at the French consulate. He was
sponsored by the anthropologists Robert Lowie and Alfred Métraux and
with their help obtained a teaching position at the New School for Social Research. Affirming his European intellectual heritage, Lévi-Strauss
claimed to be "nearer than any of my colleagues to the Durkheimian [so-
ciological] tradition"; nevertheless, unlike Radcliffe-Brown, he acknowledged a debt to American anthropologists, especially Boas and his students Robert Lowie and Alfred Kroeber, in whose writings he was for the
first time "confronted with an account of first-hand experience." He was
inspired through their work to study anthropology: "The observer . . . had
been so committed as to keep intact the full meaning of his experience.
My mind escaped from the closed circuit which was what the practice
of academic philosophy amounted to."[51] He coveted American anthropologists' practice of leaving the university and entering "primitive territory" with great ease, as well as their opportunity to do so.

Lévi-Strauss's account of his voyage to South America and the Caribbean, *Tristes Tropiques*, has been cited as an early example of "contextualized" ethnography, in which historical and personal details are interwoven with observational data.[52] His philosophy was doubtless highly compatible with Dunham's temperament and views. Lévi-Strauss's structuralism comprises symbolic systems relating a diversity of sense data—sight, taste, smell, feel, and sight—to cultural elements: kinship, language, and rituals. Dunham's concept of ethnographic description, stated in a 1957 interview, likewise reveals her dedication to the observation of a wide variety of cultural details: "It [anthropology] deals with the taste of the food and the quality of ecstasy during a religious ceremony and the inner community attitudes toward protocol and kinship and the visible effects of drugs and drum rhythms and the community attitude toward priests and artisans, and as to the dances, five minutes of participation might very well reveal more of truth and fundamentals than a 20 volume tome."[53] She was issuing a clarion call for the development of an expanded view of anthropology, linking a wide range of observations.

Dunham's written accounts are dense with sensory details and cultural insights, but her deepest perceptions are expressed in her dance and choreography. Her intellectual openness that Linton described, an essential aspect of her personality, gave her the qualities of sympathetic observer, but it was her choreographer's eye and dancer's memory that rendered her a peerless recorder of human cultural and social life. When she began her odyssey, she was prepared, psychologically, intellectually, and physically, to engage in the transforming experiences she would encounter.

4 *Katherine Dunham's Possessed Island*

> That I would come into their midst, able to worship
> these gods in dance . . . confirming to them that seg-
> ments of family, relatives known to have been separated
> from them and carried to some land vaguely north, oth-
> ers vaguely south, seemed to be of utmost importance.
>
> —Katherine Dunham, *Island Possessed*

In 1935, Katherine Dunham began her "Great Experience" in the Caribbean, with Haiti as the center of her intellectual and spiritual search.[1] Her
initial field trip lasted slightly less than one year; she returned in following years to perform, recuperate from strenuous tours, provide medical
services, and, at intervals, reside. Haiti was at first an outpost but later
at the heart of her spiritual home, which encompasses those places in
which her creative self lives and flourishes. On her first trip, she arrived
with great anticipation and hope and experienced the joys and excitement
of learning and relating to likable and gracious people. She also encountered the miseries of physical and mental ordeals and humiliations.

When anthropologists talk about their field studies, they often speak
in the possessive mode: "my village," "my community." The places they
refer to in this way are actually joint creations of fieldworkers and the
people with whom they work, reflecting the relative breadth and depth of
their connections in the culture. The island Dunham came to possess is
based on intense relationships with Haitians throughout an extended period of residence and visits and is shaped by dreams, plans, and hopes. Her
conception has been modified through the years as her knowledge has in-

creased, and it reflects much of the reality of the Haitian's homeland. Haitians understand this. Writing to her for published materials in 1937, Alan Lomax, who was collecting folk music for the Library of Congress, commented, "Cécile and Théoline [*sic*] and Cicerón and Dr. Reeser all seemed to think you were the only real collector who ever came to Haiti.[2]

Dunham has pointed out that in societies such as Haiti, with well-developed rites of passage, other members of the community routinely support individuals undergoing personal transformations and crises.[3] In initiation ceremonies, elders guide and advise acolytes through their passage into adult responsibility or into deeper wisdom and knowledge of cultural values. Dunham's practice of seeking out those with the knowledge and skills she desired and then listening to and following their counsel gave her a strong advantage in her fieldwork and led her into many initiation experiences, as did her ability to participate in dance.

Dunham's fieldwork began with an orientation period, a crucial time for the first-time researcher. In late May 1935, she made an initial visit to Haiti, where, as she informed Herskovits in a letter, she rode at the Jockey Club in Petionville, the wealthy district of the capital. She also reported attending a feast for the ancestors of a man who, she wrote, "allowed me to shake the rattle over them [bottles of water for ancestors] after a long discourse in creole to the effect that we were all of the same origin, and since I too was from African descent, he was glad to let me be present so that I would be able to tell the brothers in America."[4] She was already balancing the two worlds, one relating to her status as an educated American and the other to her association with the "less respectable" elements of society.

In July, she traveled to Jamaica, where she stayed for a month with the Maroon peoples in the village of Accompong. Here truly began her first stage of initiation into the status of anthropologist (in contrast to student of anthropology), that is, psychological separation from her accustomed environment. Traveling into the mountains on a little train winding through "tangled green forests" and "sharp, sudden valleys," she sat beside "a bandannaed old lady with a crateful of travel-sick chickens; two silent East Indian men; [and] a father in mourning with three little children," she reported. "[I] couldn't help but feel a strange ecstasy as though all of the steel-mill drabness of Joliet, Illinois, and the dark winter pinch of Chicago, and the confusion and bewilderment of New York City were sliding rapidly downhill and right off Kingston Bay into the ocean."[5]

With separation came culture shock. Her first night away from the tourist's Caribbean itinerary was a sleepless and terrifying one; she felt alone, alien, and unprepared. Herskovits had briefed her to some extent, but he himself had visited with the Maroons for only short periods, and no outsider to her knowledge had stayed with them for longer than a night.

The Maroons of Accompong have an ambivalent history of rebellion and loyalty in their relations with the English. A populace made up of captives who had escaped slavery, as well as slaves who had revolted and run away into the mountains, they have a tradition of fierceness in battle and independence of spirit. Through their guerrilla strategies, they forced the British to sign a treaty allowing them to live in peace in their own territory. To maintain their independence, they kept the terms of the treaty and supported the English during subsequent slave revolts. Largely as a result of their political caution, they were the sole surviving Maroon community.

This enforced fealty to their natural enemies had caused the people of Accompong to be very secretive and distrustful of outsiders. The performance of the Koromantee war dance may have been perceived by colonial authorities as threatening, even though many years had passed since their rebellion and radical political actions. As is often the case with isolated people under the constant threat of cultural and physical extinction, they were dominated by a strong leader. Spontaneous expressions of African rituals were discouraged. Through officially sanctioned performances, Colonel Simon Rowe attempted to control, legitimize, and thus render historically meaningless Maroon cultural expressions, a fact that Zora Hurston noted in her account.

In these circumstances, the beginning fieldworker was seriously challenged. Feeling her lack of experience, Dunham opted for a prudent approach: "The uncertainty of everything and the real lack of preparatory material . . . made me decide that I would simply examine what I could of their total life and recount each day as it happened."[6] She would "wait patiently for the music and dances and not get in the way."[7] The newcomer's response of lying low to avoid being humiliated, harming others, or jeopardizing one's mission is a tactic practiced by anthropologists, Peace Corps volunteers, or anyone who has been sensitized to cultural and value differences. Dunham had learned the value of patience from her mentors, as well as from her childhood experiences: "Though reports had it that the Maroon people were reluctant to reveal themselves to outsiders, and evasive about arriving at fact, I was sure that my childhood in Joliet, Illinois, had equipped me with enough patience to outwait them."[8]

Besides patience, other traits, including her love of dance, ultimately led to acceptance and the coveted opportunity to view the Koromantee war dance. Toward the end of her stay, the people she "could not imagine" dancing when she first met them, performed traditional dances for her, including the Koromantee. She had almost given up hope, having been promised by Colonel Rowe—to whom Herskovits had written a letter of introduction for her—that she would be able to see the dances, but with no results. Initially, she saw only the "set dances," social dances without the historical reference of the war dance. Apprehensive that she had not gained the confidence of the people, she worried that this was an omen of failure for her fieldwork in the Caribbean. But fate intervened in her favor. She had been promised a drum, which had not materialized, and following her instincts, she went to seek out the one who was making it. At his place, she found some of the villagers getting ready for a dance. The colonel—whom Dunham referred to as the "old curmudgeon" in a letter to Herskovits, was conveniently out of the village: "He was very vexed before I left because I was finding out too much."[9]

Such seemingly fortuitous circumstances as Dunham experienced occur as if by magic to those in the field as a result of deep involvement in a community, and they are invariably sources of the richest materials. At first miffed at apparent betrayal by her friends, since she seemed to have stumbled on their secret by chance, she rapidly overcame her feelings and threw herself into the most fulfilling experience a fieldworker can have: that of touching the deep roots of a people's life. "[O]n the eve of my departure all that I could have hoped for fell into perfect order, and in abundance," she later wrote. With the wisdom gained from years of relating to people of different cultures, she commented, "People and nature have a way of testing before giving up their secrets."[10]

Dunham's fieldwork account recorded the drama of her experience. Redfield commented on the draft she sent to him, "It is a vivid record of a personal experience. It is provided with two threads or themes, that give it some literary form, involving—almost—suspense and resolution." The two themes he mentioned were the successful search for desired knowledge and the growth of affection between researcher and people studied: "These are . . . the two perennial experiences of the field ethnologist that make the work exciting and human." He commended her for giving "the impression, bright and strong, of the look and smell and feel of Accompong," unconsciously, perhaps, breaking into rhyme.[11]

It is instructive to speculate why Dunham was more successful in tapping these African sources than Hurston, who also practiced patience. In Dunham—who candidly expressed a desire to learn about traditional ways—the people saw an opportunity to instruct one of the "lost" Africans of North America, and they also recognized in her a ready and apt student of dance. Behaving with characteristic African indirectness, they provided her with an exciting climax for her visit. In essence, they set the agenda of her future career when they directed her to share her knowledge with the other "lost people of Nan Guinée."

In choosing Accompong for her first entry into Caribbean society, Dunham was unquestionably plunging into a preserve of African cultural origins in a move that anticipated her venture into the challenging regions of the religious life of Haitian peasants. She had now seen something of the "real" Caribbean culture and would not be trapped by the surface that was a survival of colonialism, although she observed and wrote about that aspect of Haitian society as well. Her concern about falling short of her goals in Accompong suggested that she felt the journey was a trial effort for her work in the West Indies.

In the intensified learning situation that even a short time spent in a new culture can provide, Dunham absorbed many things in Accompong that contributed to her understanding of African culture and cultural differences generally. She learned that people in folk societies tend to communicate plans differently and less openly—especially where authorities are opposed—than do those in complex societies, where performances are widely advertised in advance. This knowledge would stand her in good stead as she sought out sacred rites throughout the world. She discovered that the people of Accompong danced for the sheer perfection of artistry; the old women were the most favored because they were the most accomplished. Segregation by age was unknown, with old and young mingling except when artificially separated by school or sports events.

Having learned about African societies from Herskovits and her other teachers, she was able to perceive African elements in Caribbean societies. She saw firsthand the social importance of work groups in Jamaica and Haiti, as in West Africa, and the storytelling skills in narrating the African "nansi" tales. Through her initiation into *obi* (*obeah*),[12] in a ceremony she induced one of her Maroon friends to perform, she learned about the African-based respect for the spirit world, especially ancestral spirits. The Maroon people, she believed, possessed a more African-oriented religious conception than did many of the other Jamaicans, who were influenced by revivalistic "possession" cults that had spread throughout the West Indies with the coming of Christianity: "The frank and friendly relationship between man and his gods reminds me of the more subtle side of the African religion. 'Me Cyarry me god inside me,' Simon Rowe said when I playfully chided him for not going to church."[13]

A practical attitude toward sexuality; customs surrounding birth, death, and naming practices, such as the use of day names; and the tendency toward polygyny all revealed an African background. While the Maroons were proud of some of their African traditions, they were ashamed of others, a condition that reflected their conflicting political and social experiences. They wanted to appear progressive, yet they were not quite ready to give up all the old ways, the investigator noted. Above all, the warmheartedness, the reciprocity, and the strong social supports she experienced caused her to recognize a collectivist spirit more akin to African than to more individualistic Western societies.

Herskovits was "thrilled with her diary," about the Accompong trip, which she sent to him from the field.[14] (She objected to his use of the term *diary*, preferring *journal* instead.)[15] Individuals Dunham came to know in Accompong were named and vividly characterized in *Journey to Accompong*, her published account. Her interest in people and her ability to describe something of their essential natures, so apparent in her memoirs and in her description of Haitian society in *Island Possessed* were already present in this early work. Ralph Linton noted in his introduction to *Journey to Accompong*, "Miss Dunham presents them as friendly and delightful people. . . . In this book one gets not only a picture of an interesting and unusual society, but of warm and living personalities."[16] This component is often missing from accounts of fieldwork that are tailored to fit academic requirements.

Dunham was able to film the Koromantee, as well as dances in Martinique and Haiti. She sent films to Herskovits, who commented that two or three of the dance sequences were "splendid" but that some were obscure. In her answer, she expressed dismay about his reference to "that picture where men are hopping about very fast," which was the Koromantee. Not being a dancer and unaware of the context, he did not see what she had experienced. In Martinique, where she traveled when she left Jamaica, she recorded the *Ag'Ya*, which Dunham described as "an acrobatic dance that much resembles the Dahomean thunder dance" and the beguine.[17] Herskovits commented, "I think the Ag'Ya is one of the most finished and exciting dances I have ever seen and you have enough of it so that you should have no difficulty in training people to do it."[18] He also felt that the film of the beguine had the "makings of an extremely interesting film."[19] These sophisticated dances were more familiar to him than were the movements of the Maroon peasants.

Dunham's objective was not merely to record dances and make good films but also to understand the social role of dance. She wrote to Herskovits, "Unless I'm dealing with purely social affairs, [I] must go easy on the equipment. I've seen the difference between something staged and something real, and besides people don't like [filming] . . . if they're doing something serious."[20] She remarked twenty years later, "In Martinique—I was all dancer and little scientist," being attracted to the festivals, dance halls, rhythms, and laughter of the island. She translated much of this excitement to the stage: "From Martinique came the ball L'agya [*sic*] with its creole gaiety, its vivid festival scene, of the Mazurka, the beguine, and majumba, its zombie Forest, its superstition and its tragic ending."[21]

In Trinidad, Dunham remarked on the active practice of Congo, Dahomey, and Yoruba religions and observed the *shango,* or eight-day sacrifice practiced to win court trials or to get well, dedicated to a Yoruba god. She studied the secular dances, as well: the calypso, with remnants of lewd songs and dances, and the *paseo,* showing Spanish influence.[22]

In one of her letters, she half-humorously commented on the opportunism required of the serious fieldworker: "[I am] a little ashamed of my tactics gathering data. [I] have become a regular gold digger for worming material and practical assistance out of men and old ladies."[23]

When Dunham returned to Haiti, she had accomplished the objectives she had set for herself. She had tested her courage and skill in the mountains of Jamaica and had observed dances rich in vitality and sensuality and exhibiting the eclecticism of Caribbean cultural life. She was ready for the supreme challenge, she told her mentor: "If all goes well in Haiti, I shall have a little controversy with you, I think. I shall try to be initiated which means that I will probably have to do away with the typewriter and picture machine for a while."[24]

Entrée

The first task confronting Dunham in Haiti was to identify the social group on which she would be dependent for her success and to gain the confidence of the people involved. She had been instructed in the various means of gaining entry and acceptance that are imparted to students of anthropology, namely, attention to political matters, including being introduced to leaders and maintaining neutrality when there are factions; the practice of reciprocity, providing services or other benefits in return for information and assistance; and respect for and interest in things important to the group. In the final analysis, however, Dunham had to use her own skills, common sense, and judgment in finding her role in the community.

Haiti was even more challenging than Accompong to Dunham because of the closed nature of its class system. In her 1969 treatment of her relationship with Haiti she stated—prophetically, in the light of more recent events—that the Haitian government was reluctant to support investigations such as hers that might reveal "the irreconcilable breach between the thin upper crust of the Haitian elite—who would have liked to be rulers of the land, participating in the revolution only to get rid of the French—and the bubbling, churning ferment of the black peasants, who really were by numbers and by historical content and character and humanness, I was to find, the true Haitian people."[25] She was carrying a letter to President Stenio Vincent given her by Herskovits, but she did not deliver it until the end of her stay. In hindsight, she believed this was largely because she intuitively perceived the ambiguous position she was in as a result of her research task, and she feared that she would be discouraged from completing it. Her academic credentials and letters of introduction to political and social leaders as well as her perceived financial status qualified her as a member of the elite. Yet, her independent ways and her interest in peasant life rendered her social position tenuous.

To reach the people she sought, she had to avoid being defined and limited by the social status in which she would be placed by birth, education, and economic criteria. The Victorian-style Hotel Excelsior—in which Dunham took a small room high in a cupola—was run by two sisters who were in straitened circumstances but were light-skinned and highly genteel in their comportment. They functioned as something of a "front" for her as she consorted with the peasantry. She met her peasant friends at the back garden gate or in the park to learn about important *voudun* ceremonies or personal news. She used the chauffeured car lent to her by a friend in the government to travel into the countryside in pursuit of religious rites and practitioners. She chafed under the restrictions and limits that others attempted to impose on her, because of her research needs as well as her opposition to social boundaries.

The class system reflected the historical circumstances of the island: the heritage of French colonialism and the revolution that overthrew it. The mulattoes were given privileges by their white fathers, and, if their parents belonged to the aristocracy, the bourgeoisie, or the military, the sons were educated in France. Since most of the landowners were descendants of "pirates" and other adventurers, however, they did not value education and were often extravagant, vulgar, and cruel to slaves. Some of the mulattoes emulated their behavior and values, feeling that this would place them on an equal social footing with whites. When they found that the divide and conquer strategy practiced by the white colonists—separating them from slaves and freed slaves—did not guarantee their social acceptance by their fathers' group, they joined in the peasant revolt. Yet they planned to be the "inheritors of French authority," according to the revolutionary hero Toussaint L'Ouverture, to "exterminate the whites and subjugate the blacks."[26]

During the first American occupation, which, like the recent short-er and more benevolent one, was carried out to stem the threat of anar-chy resulting from this unhappy history, the U.S. Marines, largely white and southern, ignored indigenous distinctions of skin tones, political status, and education. They observed the American caste system of black and white, causing the internal hostilities between classes to be direct-ed outward. As a result, to be white was to be hated and distrusted by all, including the mulattoes. In this environment, Dunham's skin color was an asset, if somewhat complicating. More problematic than her at-traction to the black proletariat and inexplicable from the point of view of her political friends as well as of her upper-class acquaintances was her friendship with Fred Alsop, an American who worked as a mechanic. In addition to being white, he had no pretensions to wealth and thus was considered "declassé."

The complications of social life were daunting. Rene Piquion, the internationally known intellectual who was one of Dunham's friends, was shunned by a mulatto friend because of his dark skin. Dunham's close companion and future president of Haiti, Dumarsais Estimé, was partic-ularly affronted by her visit to the former president of Haiti, a member of the upper class, who led the puppet government under the American occupation. Estimé also disliked her interest in the *voudun*, which he regarded as politically regressive. Obviously, she could satisfy no one, so she continued on her independent way, unpredictable, with "crashing naiveté," ruthlessly "trampling . . . customs and often . . . sensibilities," as she put it. "As the situation presented itself, I seem to have wavered or catapulted from mulatto to black, elite to peasant, intellectual to bo-hemian, in to out, up to down, and tried hard to keep out of trouble but didn't succeed."[27] Yet it was the peasants, finally, not the elite or politi-cal leaders, who were the source of the knowledge she sought. Further, as she pointed out, among the upper class, women were very much in the background, neither socially present in mixed company nor partici-pants in serious political or social discussions.[28] Conformity to these mores would have doomed her study from the beginning.

Dunham was accepted by the peasants, she commented, because of their common ancestry; her "love for babies and old people"; her medi-cal supplies and knowledge, which allowed her to treat minor ailments; her intuition; and "the flawless training in social anthropology field tech-nique begun by my professors at the University of Chicago and polished off by Melville Herskovits."[29] Years later, she remarked that she under-stood the Haitian peasants much better than the mulattoes, although she had friends in both groups.[30]

Her ultimate acceptance by the elite and the intellectuals came about through a dance performance at the Rex Theatre in Port-au-Prince. Although she was at first reluctant, feeling some conflict with her goals, she realized that she missed performing before an audience. She attempted to incorporate peasant dancers executing the *voudun* ritual dances into the program; however, this was forbidden by the management of the theater where she performed. She danced a ballet, a Russian Gypsy number, and Spanish dances, which were greatly applauded by the socially mixed audience. Cécile, her peasant friend who attended, mistook the opening act by a French singer for Dunham's performance and left early, convinced that her friend had been transformed into the goddess La Sirène, with long blonde curls and high, sweet voice. She spread the word, and the people with whom she had celebrated *voudun* initiation were greatly impressed. They did not understand the event, but they were exposed to an alien way of life and knew that their friend, Katherine, had included them, if only momentarily, in her world.

Dunham's description of this event provides a clear picture of Haitian class differences and her determination to override them. Her attempt to include all her friends and acquaintances in the program is predictive of later accomplishments, when, as director of a dance company, she would reach out to audiences and participants from the inner city and the village as well as from great metropolitan cultural centers. As a result of her presentations of Haitian culture on international stages, the dances she attempted to stage that night ultimately came to be accepted by Haitians as part of their cultural heritage. A student and former member of her dance company opened a studio in Port-au-Prince that featured Haitian dance, and Haitian dancers came to the United States to study Dunham dance techniques.

Dunham's enthusiasm for sampling all types of cultural experiences and dances led her to many parts of the island and to ceremonies in the company of Doc Reeser, a resident "expert" on the *voudun*. Herskovits rather pointedly suggested that she stay in one community and study dance in depth—to "dig in" somewhere—and remain independent of Doc Reeser, whom he respected, but who was interested in the religion more for personal reasons than for scientific ones.[31] Dunham followed his advice in cutting down on her travels, but she "settled down" in her own fashion. She respected and understood the exigencies of scholarship, but she also followed her personal needs and inclinations to become a novice in the *lavé-tête*, the first level of the *voudun*.

In her eighties, in answer to a question about fears of participating in the *voudun* during her fieldwork, Dunham replied, "Being aware of

[them] makes you less susceptible to the dangers of this life."[32] Her description of her *lavé-tête* was written more than thirty years after the fact, with the benefit of a long-term acquaintance with the people and religion.[33] Because of the difficult nature of much of the material and the common misunderstandings surrounding the *voudun,* she waited until she had grown in understanding before she committed it to print. Consequently, it is a prolific account, rich in associations and replete with historical and personal insights and cultural and social details.

As one with African ancestry, Dunham was from the beginning a possible candidate for the *voudun;* however, she was not allowed to petition for admission, nor were followers free to approach her on the subject of initiation. In fact, there was no membership as such: one either believed or did not; it was an individual decision rather than a group concern. She developed close bonds with Téoline and Cécile, *voudun* followers; the women danced together, exchanged personal items, and ate from the same pot. Still, her friends did not directly broach the matter of *lavé-tête,* but they observed her interest and desire to learn, her skill in dancing the *yonvalou,* and other intangibles, such as her personal needs and inclinations.

She noted that gradually commonplace events began to become "full of meaning." Unobtrusive signs, such as a special chair set at ceremonies for "one about to belong," and detailed explanations of ritual and warnings about the *loa,* or spirits, steered the hopeful toward the declaration of intention.[34] Even then, a ceremony at which the spirits manifested themselves might merely have involved a participant's promise of a later ceremony, or an appeasement of ancestors, or the opportunity for a *loa* to give instructions or make demands. It might have been an occasion for fixing a date for initiation, or, finally, it might have become an actual initiation rite or marriage to a *loa.* For all of these purposes, certain preparations and cash outlays were necessary, but the differences in expenditures, demands, and commitments were great, depending on the needs and status of participants. Because of the requirements of her research, time restrictions, and her enthusiasm and predilections, Dunham's involvement was at the highest level of intensity, including both initiation and marriage to Damballa, the supreme god of the Rada Dahomey sect of the *voudun.*[35]

To be initiated, Dunham was required to give evidence to the community that a *loa* had chosen her.[36] Téoline, the priestess of the temple, or *houngfor,* where she underwent *lavé-tête,* observed her affinity with the movements of the *yonvalou,* the undulating movement often associated with Damballa, the serpent god; she concluded that he would reveal himself as Dunham's spiritual ruler.

The *lavé-tête* would serve as a protection against unwanted appearances of the *loa* or *mystères,* since in the *houngfor,* such manifestations were guided and controlled by experienced practitioners, such as Téoline. In describing Téoline, Dunham commented, "Most of her time was spent controlling *bossale,* divining, taking care of services for ancestors and family and individual crises," and receiving various *loa.*[37] The *bossale* were the uninitiated who did not heed the calling of the *loa,* who then singled them out, demanding ritual acts. Dunham saw what happened when they were "ridden," for example, by Gèdé, god of the cemetery, who forced them to commit painful, humiliating, wild, and sometimes obscene acts. The possessions of initiates were much more ordered, which appealed to the young spiritual pilgrim and scientist.

Dunham was fascinated by the African-derived beliefs and rites but was, in her words, on the "border of belief and disbelief" regarding *voudun* practices. Damballa, she would later concede, was a powerful and jealous god; she almost regretted her decision to become "married" to him, made partly in the interest of science and partly, half-hopefully, for benefits in the form of career successes and the well-being of her brother. On her brother's well-being, she was highly vulnerable. A *houngan* informed her that it was a *loa* "running loose" that was causing her brother's self-destructive behavior. Since her family was not performing the correct rituals, he consulted the *loa* to find what actions on her part would appease them.[38] The *lavé-tête* was a common prescription for well-being.

Dunham wondered if her seeming ability to see with "startling clarity" the meaning of the marriage to Damballa "without loss of self" during the ceremony was because of drugs administered in sacrificial foods, the incense permeating the air, the hypnotic effects of fasting and drumming, or other influences. "Then," she noted, "the sensation would leave me, and instead of feeling the god in possession of me, the calculating scientist would take over, and I would be making mental notes on clothing, social organization, speech habits, associated traits. . . . This split in attitude I have always found difficult to reconcile in any sort of research."[39] She is expressing the dilemma posed by participation in activities, on the one hand, and the scientific requirements of ethnography, on the other. She recognized that as an outsider with special entitlement, she had to respect the system and those who followed it, even though she was unsure of her own position vis-à-vis the basic structure of beliefs: "I am there to believe or not believe, but willing to understand and to believe in the sincerity of other people in their beliefs, willing to be shown, to participate, and where the participant begins and the scientist ends, I surely could not say."[40]

Dunham took her obligation to science very seriously: her research commitment was prior to her initiation vows. Yet her relationships with her *voudun* mentors, as well as with her research community, led her to treat her privileged position with circumspection. In some instances, she decided that neither scientific curiosity nor "self-examination" justified revealing details that were "best left within their sacred environment where for those who experience them they represent truth."[41] In other cases, she candidly admitted that some things did not lend themselves to investigation, such as how the *houngan* (male priest) or *mambo* (female priest) decide the order of rhythms summoning *loa* and determine which *loa* are to be dominant in a ceremony and which are to be sent away. She decided that the answer lay in a "marriage of extra-sensory perception, personal taste, custom, and the multi-theistic mysticism that makes the voudun what it is."[42]

Those who officiated at ceremonies were adept at observing even slight or intangible signs of appearances of an individual *mystère*. Dunham, the novice, was not able to discern such indications; the mature author of *Island Possessed*, who had studied many religions and encountered African and other spiritual manifestations throughout the world, showed confidence in reading and interpreting spirit indications. She could identify, with some certainty, a necrophage in an African drummer, a member of the Diola tribe that was rumored to continue the practice of ritual eating of the dead.[43]

Dunham did not personally experience possession. Such manifestation was neither necessary nor exclusive to the initiate. The *loa* of initiates appeared at the ceremony but entered other participants as well, including a drummer. DéGrasse, a powerful priestess—possessing the second highest degree of the *voudun*—who assisted Téoline, did not become possessed at the *lavé-tête;* she embodied the "abstract" essence of Damballa while not being controlled by him. Detached, in full command of her powers, she served as spokesperson of the most powerful of the gods. With the example of DéGrasse and other authoritative priests before her, Dunham developed into an observer who could see and impartially consider herself, other people, and gods. She became one who does not close her mind to others' beliefs but who is discriminating in who and what she follows.[44] She commented that "when man is looking desperately for salvation he shouldn't turn his back on doorways. That is not to say that he should follow each 'call' or every soothsayer, who sensing his need, approaches his horizon, but with discrimination should keep seeking, and should not find one structure of beliefs serving well another human being to be outside the scope of his own credibility."[45] She grew into mysticism, recognizing different cultural manifestations of spirit without limiting herself to one form.

While Dunham's research and personal inclinations fueled her relationship with the *voudun,* another, more submerged but nevertheless strong motive also was evident. The Iphigenia theme again emerged, this time referring not only to her brother but to the entire black race as well. Writing about her thoughts during the physical and mental trials of initiation, she half-wryly, half-seriously referred to herself "as Iphigenia tied to the mast, as Erich Fromm had pointed out in friendly conversation, and all the while the black race broiling on hot coals below."[46] According to her Haitian mentors, as a North American, separated from the customs of her ancestors but still able to worship the gods through dance, she had to "carry the meaning of the true *voudun* to [her] people." She suppressed her reservations regarding this instruction: "I made no effort to disillusion these well-meaning informants about what might be expected of the children of Guinée dispersed to the north."[47] Still, the *voudun* adherents, like the Maroons, provided the social justification for her venture. She was acutely aware that her work was funded by philanthropic grants. She would not be able to convince many North Americans of African descent of the truth of the *voudun,* but, in the wider sense of their charge to her, she would not disappoint the expectations of her Haitian mentors. In her dance and teaching career, she was committed to reveal to African Americans, along with other races and nationalities, the value, dignity, and beauty of African expressions.

The Rada Dahomey is based on spirits and rituals of West Africa, especially those of the Kingdom of Dahomey. A somewhat abstract sky and creator god (Mawu-Lisa) with male and female aspects forms the apex of the pantheon; other divinities take many forms, corresponding to natural phenomena, cultural entities, and individual identities. These deities consist of three categories: ancestral spirits; gods of earth, water (Agwe), and thunder (Shango); and personal deities. Among the personal deities are Damballa, who supports the universe and is represented by a snake holding its own tail in its mouth; Aida Ouedo, his wife and the earth mother; Erzulie, his mistress, who personifies and directs love in all its forms; Legba, who takes and delivers messages to and from the gods; Ogun, representing iron and warfare; Asaka, god of farmers; Gèdè, in his many expressions; and scores of others. The personal deities, referred to as *loa* or *mystères,* have proliferated, and there is no general agreement on the names and attributes of the more recent additions. The rival Petro cult, reportedly started by a black man of Spanish descent, includes a different series of gods, with a few overlapping, such as the Gèdés and

Baron Samedi, who are not particularly welcome at Rada ceremonies since they consort with the dead. Petro is, by tradition, much more given to blood sacrifice and magical practices than is Rada. Congo gods, said to demand human sacrifice, also make appearances in Petro rites.

All of the *mystères* are associated with special foods, colors, scents, movements, behavioral traits, and functions. These accouterments and characteristics allow the *houngan* and *mambo* to identify the spiritual affinities of individuals and the devotees to express their *loa* affiliations. Dunham commented on "how simple it was to associate a given personality with the behavior patterns, diet, colors, mannerisms, characteristics, potentials, predictabilities of the loa whose alter ego, identity, personification, they were to become."[48] She likened the process of identification to a complex and rapid computer operation and depicted possession as akin to an electrodynamic process, with *loa* and "abode" attracting each other. Those officiating were deft analysts, discovering the basic personalities of novitiates under the layers of social conditioning.

While the spirits are African, the entire Rada Dahomey system assumed many attributes and practices of the Roman Catholic church. This was not surprising, since the church in the French West Indies baptized the slaves en masse and turned a blind eye to many of their religious practices, as long as they maintained a facade of Catholic ritual. The *mystères* are pictured as Catholic saints: Damballa as St. Patrick, Erzulie as the Virgin Mary, Legba as St. Peter, the gatekeeper and messenger of God. The opening ceremony in the peristyle, or outer chamber of the *houngfor*, begins with Catholic liturgy, complete with bell ringing; *actión de grace*, including prayers and hymns; and the use of censers. However, soon the drumbeat, the symbol and driving force of African religion, drowns out the Christian interloper.

The Haitian drums, Dunham wrote, are more like those brought by slaves than present-day drums in urban Africa. The drummers are knowledgeable about the *loa*; they reinforce and enhance the actions of the officiating priests, calling forth and banishing spirits through associated rhythms and "breaks" that clear the air and give respite from intense participation. Many of them are initiates, some to two or three levels.[49] The initiation ceremony could not continue, she noted, if the drumming stopped.

In the opening dance in the peristyle, or public hall of the *houngfor*, the qualities of the drums and the power of the drummers help induce the mental state essential to the ritual. The '*zépaules* movement, involving "a spasmodic hunching forward and releasing of shoulders," is, according to Dunham, "driven by the piercing beat of the kata, enriched by the broken rhythms of the seconde, and eroticized by the deep, insistent tones of the mama drums." The forced, repetitive deep breathing this movement induces, along with the hypnotic beat and rhythmic movement, causes a mental state conducive to possession. The drummers play a commanding role in the introduction of "breaks," which occur at the point of high intensity among the dancers: "The drummers take complete control of these feints once the dancer has indicated, consciously or not, that he is ready for them, breaking the rhythm, sucking air in and hissing it out, ejaculating glottal sounds which are supposed to beat the 'broken' or out-of rhythm dancer or group of dancers back in line and to show that it is they, the drummers, who dominate the rhythms."[50] Since her initiation, drummers have played a key role in Dunham performances, and she has a great respect for them, working closely with them as she directs master classes.

Dunham collected two sets of the three drums used in the *voudun*, one at her initiation and another, older set that she believed was among those hidden to protect the secret rituals during the U.S. Marine occupation. The older set, which she used in dance performances, was destroyed in a boxcar fire during a tour. A Haitian associated with the company as a consultant advised her that this was a sign of Damballa's jealousy, since profane hands, including Brazilian and Cuban drummers, had touched them. She preferred to interpret it as the god's protection over her enterprises, because the insurance collected on the drums came at a very lean time for the company. Since she had spent considerable funds on the "care, feeding, ritual bathing and anointing, customs duties, and preservation" for these and all of her sacred percussion instruments, she considered the considerable insurance claim justified.[51] Dunham's pragmatic approach to this supernatural matter was not disrespectful; rather, it reflected the "frank and friendly" relationship with the gods she described as the essentially African approach.

The dance movements, music, and language are powerful African ingredients of the ceremony. *Langage*, a mixture of African dialects, is used in invocations. In usual circumstances, Dunham could not comprehend it, but in the trancelike state induced by the drums and narcotic effects, she felt she could grasp the meaning of the words. The songs are primarily in *Langage*, and in them the tribes, kingdoms, and historical events of the Africans who were enslaved and shipped to Haiti are identified and explained accurately, those who know this history have claimed. The nonverbal communication of the dances reinforces this verbal knowledge, making cultural memories visible. Even the postures of participants record cultural history. The folding up of the *houngan's* body with his head parallel to the earth as he prepared the *vévé*—floor paintings made with the pouring of colored meal—recalled the carriages of women sweeping African compounds and African farmers planting and harvesting. The function of the *voudun* as a repository of historical and cultural knowledge has attracted the interest of anthropologists. As a living expression of such knowledge, it has enabled Haitians to survive, physically and psychically, throughout a history of slavery, rebellion, tyranny, and poverty. The ritual sacrifice of chickens, goats, and other small animals is African in origin, although it is less central to Rada Dahomey than to Petro or Congo. Other African elements of the *voudun* include the use and symbolic value of iron. Traditionally, the *ogan*, a percussion instrument accompanying the drums, is made of iron. Iron is associated with Ogun Feraille, the god of war, and plays a significant role in West African society. Some contemporary archeologists believe that iron was originally discovered in Africa and later diffused to the Middle East and Europe. The calabash gourd, originating in Africa, is a utilitarian object in Haitian homes and is used as a chamber pot for the initiates.

For Dunham's initiation, the small containers—*pots tête*—holding various foods, sacrificial blood, and other relics associated with *lavé-tête* and decorated with trade beads and snake's vertebrae were white china pots formerly used in pharmacies. All the initiates had such containers, which they were admonished to keep, unopened, throughout their lives. They each wore a head cloth covering the foods, oil, incense, blood, and other items placed on the head; these offerings functioned to purify the head—the seat of the spirit—of the initiate. The ritual purification included the ceremonies in the *houngfor*, as well as mild ablutions in consecrated (polluted) water at the altar. The novitiates left the inner temple, in Dunham's words, "clean in body and spirit, purified of whatever *bossale* or tormenting spirit" had prevented them from meeting with their *loa* "on friendly terms."[52] The purification was purely symbolic; the physical cleansing was postponed until after the ceremony, creating a delay during which the magic continued to work. The kerchiefs were taken off a week later, the hair was washed many times to remove traces of the offerings, and the remains were placed in a second *pot tête* on the altar of the *houngfor*.

Dunham's *pot tête* was later misplaced, and she wondered about its effects on one who might find and open it. In collecting the ritual objects needed for the ceremony, she observed, "I began to feel in the personal care and effort in the choosing of each object its inherent '*mana*,' its mystic power, as different from the object next to it—similar in appearance but utterly profane and unmystic."[53] She realized that her relation-

ship with these articles was not as intimate as it was for other participants, who were familiar on a day-to-day basis with the items and who
often had to save and scrimp for years to purchase them. But her instant
appreciation of the efficacy of such material objects and essences, as well
as others used in ceremonies of crisis and social identity throughout the
world—many of which are on display in the Katherine Dunham Museum in East St. Louis—stemmed, perhaps, from her childhood experience
with her uncle, the cosmetician and masseur/chiropodist, and her other
encounters with healers and with pharmacopeia, herbal remedies, and
cosmetics. She speculated that it was to a great extent the sensuous impact of physical objects—the constant drumming, ringing of bells, and
rattling of the ason, or gourd rattle; the smells of burning charcoal and
incense; and the intonations, along with fasting—that gradually changed
bossale into *hounci*, or initiates.

Knowledge of the use of dance and ritual and the material objects
associated with them in physical and mental healing is fundamental in
anthropology. The *mana*, or supernatural power, of objects and rituals
associated with the *mystères* and the belief in their influence in various
human enterprises and crises are universal. The Western medical system,
as well as other traditions, developed from efforts to heal using herbal and
ritual remedies. Further, most religions make use of rites and fetishes.
Dunham commented that the fact that she was not christened in an organized religious belief system allowed her to be receptive to her initiation experience. In addition, her African American heritage—a legacy
transmitted largely unconsciously but perhaps effective in generating an
attitude of acceptance toward the socially unorthodox—rendered her
mind open to the mystical and healing aspects of the *voudun*. For the
captive slaves and their descendants, Dunham reported, the food offerings were believed to carry the spirits of those cut off from the mother-
land, who could not hope to return to Africa.[54] Perhaps the recognition
of her empathy with these ideas, even her predisposition to believe in
unconventional appearances of the sacred, influenced the people of Accompong and Haiti to entrust her with their secrets.

Dunham's intense and graphic account of the participants of the *lavé-
tête* sets her description apart from most anthropological treatments of
the *voudun* and other religious rites. Except for "unsavory" ritual foods,
she shared with them three days of fasting, during which they all lay on
the floor of the *houngfor*, "spoon-fashioned," turning over together at
determined intervals. Dunham's highly developed sense of smell and her
sensitivity to sound and touch led to an awareness of the physical personae of her co-initiates and to a feeling of union with them. Her empathy

informed her detailed physical and psychological profiles of them. She described the processes by which they came to be participants and the personality traits that led to their association with particular *loa*, as well as her own connections with her co-initiates. She noted that they were male and female, old and young, financially well-off and very poor. Some of them she liked quite well; others she did not particularly admire, such as the woman next to her who became possessed and acted out in an uninhibited manner during the confinement, urinating on Dunham's dress. She also felt uncomfortable around a woman, a lesbian, who was possessed by Gèdé. She thought the woman was not deeply affected by the initiation but used her identification with Gèdé as a social sanction for vulgar behavior. Despite some feelings of distaste for some of her fellow initiates, the close confinement led her to identify with them: "I was beginning to feel at home with them, to sense the tie of kinship that must hold together secret societies the world over."[55] She mused on the fact that she had never joined sororities and clubs, "all forms of belonging" that involved ritualistic processes of joining, and that her intellectual mission demanded she be involved only as a scientist; yet here she was entering into a secret pact with her fellow *hounci.* While such involvement was perceived as an aberration according to her internal compass, it led her to a revelation of the social as well as the sacred nature of dance.

In the public dance after the confinement in the sacred part of the temple, she felt, in her words, "[t]he sheer joy of motion in concert, of harmony with self and others and the houngfor and Damballa and with all friends and enemies . . . and with whatever god whose name we were venerating."[56] Her account of leaving the *houngfor* after the period of fasting reveals that this profound experience was based partly on a psychic unity flowing from her physical closeness with her fellow *hounci.* She reported the same emotions that she felt when leaving Joliet and the Maroons of Accompong and that she would experience many times in her life when leaving behind close ties, "a part of oneself walking through the exit, another part staying behind for eternity."[57]

Dunham expressed admiration for the two *mambos* who officiated at the ceremony. They were very different: DéGrasse was elegant, subdued, and subtle while authoritative; Téoline, who had identified Damballa as Dunham's potential spouse, was earthy, powerful, and outgoing. Dunham felt that Téoline understood her needs, intellectual as well as spiritual, and that she would help her "to the full extent of her vast matriarchal intelligence." She represented the "authentic African woman, undefiled by colonialism, untouched by the inroads of Western civilization . . . and enriched by the experience of slavery in the New World."[58]

She sought such an exemplar when she was in Africa but found that African women had been undermined by external forces, including Islam and Christianity, that weakened their positions and that they had not experienced the liberating experiences literally forced on black women in the New World.

The descriptions of the two *mambos* foreshadow elements of Dunham's stage persona. During her performance career, many critics commented about, on the one hand, her detached, suave, and subtle approach to her art and, on the other, her sensual, earthy aura. Because of her impressionability and her aptitude in learning from role models, it is perhaps not far-fetched to see the germ of her own stage performances in her perceptions of these women. The authority of the women in the ceremony, Téoline exerting leadership through "the sheer power of her robustness" and DéGrasse directing by "sharp, fine, birdlike movements," provided patterns to emulate in her career as director of a dance company.[59]

Dunham also paid attention to the costumes painstakingly made especially for the ceremony and the entire mise-en-scène, which she creatively reproduced for theater performances. The music, drama, pictorial art, costumes, chants, and energy generated from dancing and drumming—when conjoined in a vibrant art form—had a hypnotic effect, just as in the peristyle.

Dunham's introduction to the *voudun* was not a wholly positive experience, however. The discomfort of the cramped position on the floor, which exacerbated the incipient arthritis in her knees; the repugnance she felt toward the messy substances in her hair—purifying only in the sense that the polluted Ganges River purifies Hindu worshipers; the distaste for the sacrificial foods, for animal sacrifice, for foul smells; and her qualms about drinking unclean holy water all reminded her of Fay-Cooper Cole's stories about dog-eating ceremonies and other disagreeable repasts and his counsel to hide her disgust at such unaccustomed viands. Some of the more indecent actions of the possessed were offensive to her. These distressing conditions led her at one point to totally reject her mission, condemning, in her words, "all mysticism, all research, all curiosity in the ways or whys of other peoples, all 'cults,' all causes."[60] Suffering severe culture shock, she nonetheless endured and found the climactic dancing to the drumbeats of the gods to be "good in every sense of the word," and the "feeling of the rightness" of the *voudun* dances remained with her.[61] She discovered that her knees allowed her to assume postures and movements that she ordinarily would not have attempted.

The French anthropologist Alfred Métraux, who studied Haitian religion, wrote a tribute to Katherine Dunham in which he said, "How often have I heard people talk about 'Miss Katherine' . . . who was dancing on the peristyle of the temple as if she had been brought up in voudun."[62] Unquestionably, her love of dance and her dance skills provided her with a key to an appreciation of the power of Haitian religion. Viewing her experience from a broader religious perspective, in 1969 she wrote about her initiation dance, "We danced, not . . . with the stress of possession or the escapism of hypnosis or for catharsis, but as I imagine dance must have been executed when body and being were more united, when form and flow and personal ecstasy became an exaltation of a superior state of things, not necessarily a ritual to any one superior being."[63]

At the time she wrote this passage, Dunham had begun the study of Zen Buddhism. She regarded possession and animal sacrifice as problematic at best and was reluctant to use her initiation status in *voudun* except to protect someone possessed. During a class at the Dunham Technique Seminar in 1988, with the assistance of a Brazilian dancer, she had occasion to control a participant who showed signs of possession. Although she called upon other spiritual traditions and techniques, Dunham functioned in the spirit of the ministrations of DéGrasse, Téoline, and other sacred practitioners who were highly judicious and skilled in their handling of novitiates and *bossale.* She recalled when, helped by experienced Brazilian, Haitian, and Cuban drummers, she had subdued a male dancer in the Dunham Company who went into a seizure while performing "Shango." Since she regarded the situation to be dangerous— the youth could do injury to himself—she did not take him on tour. Dunham used these experiences to educate students in her master class about such psychic phenomena and advised the one who had become possessed to develop his own center of energy as a protection against unwanted spirit invasions.[64]

On her first trip to Haiti, Dunham met Louis Mars, a Sorbonne-educated psychiatrist who was the son of Jean Price-Mars, the Haitian anthropologist. Together they devised a plan to determine whether the inmates at Pont Beudette, where the French had built an institution for the insane, were truly "insane" or merely possessed. They tested the theory with two young men: one gained his sanity through *voudun* ritual; the other was profoundly ill, they concluded. Despite this 50 percent rate of success—better than leaving them in limbo or, worse, as zombies, as the rumors portrayed the unfortunates—President Vincent interceded and asked them to stop the experiment.

Although she has distanced herself to some extent from the practice and belief system of the *voudun,* Dunham maintains an attitude of respect toward it, and much of its essential content is preserved in her worldview and in her conception and execution of dance. She honors Damballa, her spiritual mate, as an expression of the spirit world, evidenced by her restraint with regard to snakes (though not her natural affinity with them) and in her preference for his colors, pale blue and white, and for his dance, the *yonvalou*. She has lost the ring that was part of the marriage rite, but the Dahomean god in his capacity as "symbol of continuity, the roundness of time, of indestructibility by time" is surely a vital ingredient in her life and philosophy.[65]

Dunham's attention to Damballa and to the Rada Dahomey precluded an intensive study of the Petro cult, the Congo Moundong, zombies, and even the *bocors*, magicians. She did attend a wake and succession ritual of a Congo *bocor*; she was amazed that when she arrived, the *bocor's* followers were expecting her, since she thought no one knew she was coming. She consulted a seer who was a member of the cult; he spoke of her family situation, including her brother's plight, and brought messages from him and her dead birth mother, although she had talked to no one in Haiti about these family matters. He also predicted her marriage to Damballa, his future jealousies, and those of others around her. The accuracy of these predictions and observations convinced her of the authenticity of some of the "bush priests."

On a later trip, she visited a powerful priest of the Congo Moundong cult, who was rumored to control zombies and even to partake of human flesh. Surprised when she found herself discussing with him her study of cults in Chicago, she found he understood and agreed with her theory that the power of these organizations was based on deprivation of people's needs and that the rumors of cannibalism among them were caused by their victim status, in an especially virulent expression of the "blame the victim" syndrome. The two reached a high degree of rapport, and, as he instructed her in some of the Congo lore, she felt a tinge of regret that she had decided to devote the large share of her field study to the Rada Dahomey sect. She found him to be charismatic, with skills of "unusual clairvoyance, divination, highly developed extrasensory perception." It was not difficult for her to believe that his reputation for controlling zombie wives and supernatural spirits reached Haitians of all social classes, though she could not vouch for either.[66] Whatever his agents or powers were, however, she felt he would use them for both good and evil.

Because of her Protestant upbringing or her university education—she was not sure which—she left this charismatic figure without becoming a convert of Congo Moundong. She was never able to obtain direct evidence of zombies or human sacrifice, although at various times in her research she was teased by hints and clues of one or the other. Her moral scruples precluded her involvement in a cult that focused on magical practices pursued for personal benefit, to say nothing of one that was oriented principally toward blood sacrifice, human or otherwise, as in the case of the Moundong. Her attraction to the Congo cult lay in the fact that it was more purely African than other sects in that it had little Catholic or other Christian influence. Her curiosity was piqued, but her allegiances and her personal inclinations lay elsewhere.

Both the Congo and the Rada Dahomey were organized religions, with priests, rituals, and personal codes. Some priests were more powerful than others, and some were more inclined to use magic than others were, although the two attributes were not necessarily present in the same person. If an individual believed that magic was being practiced against him or her and the protective ceremonies of priests were not successful, then *bocors* or herbal "doctors" were consulted. There was a predisposition among Haitians for magical and animistic beliefs and a constant searching for benefits and protection through their employment. Dunham recounted, "Periodically . . . Port-au-Prince will fall into a state of hysteria over the report of some incident impossible to be measured by any standard other than mass hypnosis."[67] Such an incident might be a talking cow or fish or a metamorphosis from one animal to another. The rapid folk communication system, together with the predisposition to believe, has resulted in a mass hysteria. As Dunham's views on cults suggested, the extreme poverty of Haitian peasants, as well as the many disasters that have been inflicted on them historically, likely contributed to these outbreaks.

Dunham has consulted seers and healers and has collected various amulets throughout her adult life, following her dictum of not closing doors to any possible source of enlightenment or spiritual help. Yet, her source of power, her greatest font of well-being, is in rhythmic movement. It was, after all, dance that guided her into the Rada Dahomey.

Commenting on Maya Deren, who served for a time as her secretary, Dunham recalled that Deren had found a key in the performance of the Dunham Company that caused her to gravitate toward a life-transforming religious expression in the *voudun*.[68] Deren offered her services free and came to understand and identify with the *voudun* to the extent that she adopted some of its basic conceptions and feelings. She expressed a desire to go underwater when she died, for example; those with a strong belief in the *voudun* believe the soul comes from the water, and they long to go back to their spiritual home. A ceremony is performed for acolytes who voice this wish, in which family and friends gather to coax them back to life.

In contrast, Dunham identified with the religion primarily through dance. Erich Fromm introduced her to Nietzsche's assertion, "I should only believe in a god who would know how to dance."[69] She did not fully grasp the meaning of the statement until her *lavé-tête*, when, dancing the *yonvalou*, she felt "out and above and beyond" herself: "I felt weightless, like Nietzsche's dancer, but unlike that dancer, weighted; transparent but solid, belonging to myself but a part of everyone else. This must have been the 'ecstatic union of one mind' of Indian philosophy, but with the fixed solidarity to the earth that all African dancing returns to, whether in assault upon the forces of nature or submission to the gods."[70] This affirmation of mysticism, made in later life, interpreted profound emotions that she felt during her initiation. They came toward the end of a ceremony in which *voudun* priests acted in an autocratic manner, supervising all proceedings through their assistants and preventing any deviation from the rules. This discipline served to protect and direct the initiates, who were considered to be in danger. Paradoxically, the resulting intense, constricted atmosphere gave participants the freedom and ability to experience and express sensations of power to which they were not accustomed in ordinary life. It was as though the authority and force of the priests and their associates were conveyed to the *hounci*. This transfer of power, together with the psychic bonds among initiates, led to the apotheosis Dunham described, in which freedom and fundamental connection with humanity were simultaneously celebrated.

Some contemporary writers have likened the anthropological fieldwork experience itself to possession, in that the line between observer and observed may be transcended, occasionally leading to an ecstatic experience.[71] Although Dunham did not succeed in her youthful desire to undergo possession by *loa*, the intensive quality of her involvement in the *voudun* induced a mystic communion that she had not known in the religion of her native culture. Likewise, her participation in dance enabled her to embrace the contradictions and differences thrust upon her by fieldwork and to reconcile her own emotional and intellectual striving.

5 Anthropology and Dance

I have . . . tried, always unsuccessfully, to put on paper
this rhythmic progression taking place always and all
around, whether near sea, in mountains, or on plains, to
capture the ebb and flow of its tide.

—Katherine Dunham, *Island Possessed*

IN *Island Possessed*, Dunham described Haiti as being in constant motion. The complexities in the study of its sacred and secular
dances were overwhelming: the many rhythms and movements, social
contexts, and social and psychological functions could be accurately described and analyzed only by someone who, like Dunham, participated
in the dances. Her presentations of her findings, in written form, in
teaching, and in performance, form the foundation for her work in dance
anthropology.[1]

In her field report, *Dances of Haiti*, she distinguished between sacred
and secular dance by having memorized distinctive drumbeats and movements during hours of recording, watching, performing, and listening.[2] She
considered the social organization and functions of different dance categories and judged the dance events of the *voudun* to be the most organized.

The primary social functions of dances in the *voudun* were religious:
preparing disciples for the reception of the gods, petitioning the *loa*, clear-
ing the air of unwanted spirits, providing relief ("breaks") to participants
in periods of intensity, and indicating possession by a *mystère*. Here, form
and function of dance movements were interrelated. The *'zépaules*, with
its rapid pumping movement of the shoulders, served to clear the air and
bring about a semi-hypnotic state. It was usually directed to Legba, the
intermediary for the *mystères*, and prepared the participants for their re-

ception. The *yonvalou*, involving a flowing motion along the spinal column, induced a state of complete relaxation and ecstasy associated with prayer. It caused the worshiper to be completely open to the *mystères*, especially, Damballa, Erzulie, and Aida Ouedo, although others also might appear. The *maison*, involving grinding of the hips, was deliberately sexual in effect, acting as an emotional cathartic to someone who was possessed.

Besides these special purposes, the dances enhanced group solidarity, a function critical in maintaining the African traditions for which Haiti has remained the center in the New World. The authority of the priests and the unity among acolytes resulted in different local styles, Dunham noted, as dances assumed the artistic mark of particular priests and priestesses. She could not only identify religious groups by dance movements but also determine from what part of the island a dancer came.

Stylistic variation and artistic expression were present in secular dances as well. The rhythms of Haiti often materialize in social dances in the countryside, *bamboche*, in which small groups performed couple dances—such as the *meringué*, *rumba*, and *bolero*, all *pou' plaisi'*—for pleasure. Intent on learning as much as she could about dance, Dunham attended and participated in as many of these as possible. Escorted by Haitian officers, she also spent many evenings at a Port-au-Prince bordello, which was operated and staffed by Dominican women. Here, dance was focal, and older women, who were experts of the popular dances, were favorites among clients. The women became her "professors" of popular dance while her escorts slipped away upstairs for other pursuits.

Other secular dances, such as the Mardi Gras, were for large crowds, with the impetus of the crowd creating the movements. The *rara* bands of carnival were often temporary groups, but sometimes they were made up of members of a *combité*, or work group. The *chairo-pié*, a moving step to carry the *combité* quickly from field to field, was also the step used in carnival. *Raras* occasionally appeared during Lent as sacred processions; the *banda*, a funeral dance, occurred as a private, sacred ritual or as a secular performance, depending on the wishes of the family. Obviously, here the distinction between sacred and secular was one of function rather than form. Only in the *voudun* were special movements— particularly those associated with *mystères*—and instruments restricted to sacred rites. And only in the social gatherings of the elite (with the exception of carnival) were "vulgar" and sexually suggestive movements prohibited. On the whole, sacred and secular dances shared similarities in pattern and body movement. Haitian religion had little of the sexual puritanism usually associated with Christianity; as in African religions, the spirits permeated all of life's activities.

Dunham identified social functions of secular, as well as sacred, dance groups and described the relationships between dance forms and their social purposes. She noted that among secular dances, Mardi Gras was unusual in bringing together Haitians of all social classes and that, on this one occasion, people were grouped according to age and sex rather than on the basis of skin tones, providing opportunities for cross-class encounters. In the heat of intense activity, peasants might curse someone of the elite class toward whom they would ordinarily show only respect. Likewise, the upper classes were freed from polite inhibitions of the gentry, sharing the release of sexual and other energies with commoners. The work groups forming the *rara* were brought together with other members of their trades in strong bonds of occupational and recreational communion. Competition between the societies as to costumes and quality of dance and music also brought about more unity within the membership. For individuals of all groups and classes, externalization of emotions—joy, grief, anger, or sexual stimulus—and recreation and play were psychological benefits of the crowd dance.

Although the identifying mark of the Mardi Gras was its uncontrolled sexuality, Dunham observed that the primary goal of that sexuality was not physical consummation. The movements were symbolic, perhaps reflecting origins in agricultural and fertility rites. When she followed the crowd, finding herself carried along by its motion and performing pelvic movements with people of both sexes and all ages, she did not mistake sexual gestures or close physical contacts for direct sexual advances. Real sexual overtures among Haitians, she noted, were made with characteristic African indirection.

The *bamboche* were country parties involving courtship dances, with emphasis on skill in executing dances and agreeable appearance to attract the opposite sex. The audience, including old people, judged the relative merits of the participants. The well-trained, proficient dancer was recognized and appreciated as a true artist. Since the participants were neighbors and acquaintances, the gatherings functioned as community theater, as well as sexual selection. The pleasures individuals experienced and the skills and confidence they developed in dancing, singing, and playing instruments and in constructing instruments and creating costumes taught her lessons she would use in many contexts in later life.

Dunham was able to show in detail how both sacred and secular dances brought Haitians together, locally as well as nationally, reinforcing and promoting cooperation in other areas, such as politics and business affairs. Temporarily, at least, dance events transcended irreconcilable differences in a historically volatile society. At times, the unity of the *voudun* has resulted in the uprising of the masses, although it has also caused them to submit to tyranny, both circumstances illustrating its power and the power of its rituals. Petro rituals, for example, are credited with the success of the revolution of 1804, unifying the people and giving them the courage and adrenaline to fight against colonial oppression. She noted that more recently Haitians had not been disturbed by appearances of Petro gods at Rada Dahomey ceremonies, although when she was initiated, such unwelcome invasions were not infrequent.[3] She was hopeful that conditions in Haiti would eventually improve to the point that Gèdé and similar gods would be driven away from Rada ceremonies.

The fieldwork and analysis Dunham accomplished on this first trip were significant in advancing the conception of the anthropology of dance. The work is also of interest in anthropologists' ongoing debate about methods and assumptions of the discipline, including the nature of ethnography. It appears that in simply and consistently following her ideals and her feeling for human relationships, as well as the examples of her teachers, Dunham solved many of the theoretical problems in ways that anticipate current proposals and prescriptions.

Ethnography, literally, "cultural writing," is anthropologists' primary means of communicating their findings, and, for the most part, it is styled in a straightforward, "factual" manner. Recent ethnographers question the nature of "facts" and point out that a neutral, expository manner may disguise considerable biases, inadequate field data, or an inability to relate to people of other cultures. Since, the critics assert, the validity of cultural knowledge rests on the accuracy of the fieldworkers' observations, the quality of their conversations and interviews, and the extent of participation in social activities, we need to know more about the ethnographers and their relationships with the people they encounter to evaluate and understand their findings.[4]

The texts of *Journey to Accompong* and *Island Possessed* are encrusted with details relating to Dunham's web of relationships with individuals through time, how she came to learn from them, her intellectual and social background, her indispositions and feelings of culture shock, her ethical concerns, her social placement, the historical and contemporaneous political situation, and numerous other descriptive elements. For example, we learn the importance of the *voudun* initiates' slow and careful planning in collecting the items for the ceremonies when Dunham contrasts this with her own accelerated preparations, made with less personal sacrifice. She informs the reader that while her knees—which troubled her throughout her dance career—pained her in the cramped position in the *houngfor*, she did not dare reveal this because she was

afraid it would show disrespect for the *loa*. In this single descriptive detail, she demonstrated the authority of the priests, the deep devotion of
acolytes, and her transcendence of her own weaknesses to obtain her
desired goal. We learn of the complications—emotional and social—that
result from being a woman in the field and the attitude of some profes-
sionals toward women anthropologists.[5] In learning about these conditions, we are presented with her understanding of a culture in the broader context of her experiences, and the pretense of unconditional authority
is exchanged for the contingent knowledge shared by all humans.

George Devereux, a psychoanalyst and anthropologist, has pointed
out that scientific objectivity is impossible in the study of human societies, because research conditions cannot be replicated but can be only
approached by reproducing a fieldworkers's methods and the quality of
their relationships with people.[6] A radical critique of traditional approaches depicts ethnography as a dialectical process, involving the people the
anthropologist is studying in the creation of a statement about a culture.[7]
The contextual information Dunham provided is valuable to those who
aspire to understand another culture because she openly portrayed her
problems and tactics in relating to people. We see that she related to the
people upon whose cooperation she depended in *their* terms, not by imposing her own conditions, and she exposed her own vulnerabilities in
writing about her encounters. In this, she differed from her predecessors
and contemporaries, who recorded such matters in private journals, not
for publication, or else they published them under pseudonyms. Many
of the best-known cultural accounts that include autobiographical details
are by women authors. These techniques may be more comfortable to
women, who are less apt to project an authoritative image, either while
in the field or in writing ethnography.[8]

Dunham's attention to the nuances of relationships with people gives
the potential researcher the opportunity to emulate, at least in spirit, her
research strategies, with the hope that similar perseverance can bring
comparable results. Her accounts illustrate the delicate balance continuously maintained between persons as friends and as counterparts in the
creation of ethnography, as acquaintances and as sources of information,
and they show how these functions and roles were related in her day-to-
day encounters in the field.

The reappearance in ethnography—at least openly—of the anthropologist as a person, revealing nationality, gender, cultural, intellectual and
disciplinary heritage, social status, and personal temperament, requires
an expansion of the media available to the ethnographer. New ways of
communicating knowledge and insights across disciplinary, social, and

cultural boundaries have been proposed. Dunham experimented with many forms: autobiography, essay, discursive text, choreography, drama, including community theater, and poetry. She employs literary devices and dramatic techniques. Her style in *Island Possessed*, for example, is literary, and the allegories of "the lost people of Nan Guinée" and the myth of Iphigenia are effective as devices to raise methodological issues, as well as to underscore the meanings and significance of her findings.

As James Clifford points out, standard field accounts are based on a "hierarchy of senses," with vision predominant, providing few details relating to touch, odors, or sounds, and with the observer "buried" in the neutral exposition.[9] In the field, however, anthropologists learn through *all* senses and kinesthetically, through their bodies, as whole beings.[10] Dunham has shown that in the *voudun* dances, the entire body, as well as material objects, signifies, and *all* senses—sight, sound, touch, and smell—receive messages. Her accounts quiver with her sensuous responses: sights but also smells, tastes, sounds, and somatic and kinetic experiences.

Kinesics, the study of body movements, demonstrates that humans constantly communicate through ritualized body movement, for example, gestures, facial expressions, the use of space. The activity we call dance is an elaboration of that communication process, dramatically heightened and consciously framed as performance. Dunham's involvement in dance sensitized her to total body response and the translation of culture through movement. She understood the significance of gesture. For example, hand expressions among Haitian peasants may have a different meaning than gestures of Javanese and Balinese—as influenced by East Indian dance—though elements of their movements may be similar.[11] In their sacred and social dances, both African- and Indian-derived movements employ dance isolation: moving one part of the body independently of others, communicating with complex vocabularies and syntax.[12] She credited Herskovits with alerting her to the study of the meaning of the use of the body. According to Dunham, "Very few think of [dance] isolation in terms of the culture from which it comes," its history and values.[13]

To appreciate the use of gesture, she studied the culture and the total vocabulary of bodies in motion. The emphasis of different body parts discloses something about a culture, if one knows how to interpret it. For example, in African dance, emphasis on the movement of the middle of the body, of pelvis and abdomen, is related to the importance attached to fertility and childbearing in African social life.

In many forums, Dunham has stated goals of promoting and enabling communication among peoples of different cultures, using a wide variety of media, including dance, drama, music, plastic and decorative arts, and different writing styles. An explorer of performance styles noted that when one group wants to communicate with another across cultural or political boundaries, the rapprochement is often an exchange of theater, dance, music, and ritual, which need no literal translation.[14] The Maroons and Haitians displayed their recognition of the centrality of performance in intercultural communication, as well as shrewd judgment, in recognizing Dunham's potential to act as an emissary in that domain.

As is vividly present in her ethnographic accounts, Dunham had a special affinity for the dramatic character of fieldwork. Clifford Geertz has characterized the participant-observer role as one of dramatic irony, in that none of the participants takes it literally or considers the fieldworker as a cultural participant in the same sense that members of the community are. Fieldwork has been portrayed as a drama in which the script is continuously being written by participants and in which the performers believe in the emotions and values expressed while recognizing that the participation is not "real" in a literal sense.[15] This theory explains the exceptions that are often made for researchers—in Dunham's case, for example, allowing her to play drums ordinarily taboo for women.[16] Dunham, the *mambos* and others understood, was not going to become an ordinary member of their community. They did know that they had imparted important values and meanings to her that would change her life, just as dramatic performances, sacred and secular, influence peoples of all cultural backgrounds. The high level of intensity in her case stems from the nature and extent of her involvement.

Dunham's appreciation of the power of drama and the communication it affords, both in the field and on concert stages, led her to provide an effective "frame" for her ethnographic presentation. Speaking of her research, she stated, "I lived a sort of dual existence of having my intellect absorbed in searching out and annotating the real and authentic steps and movements and an eye trained to see all of this color and movement translated into theater idiom."[17] She has given wide scope to dramatic values in her dance performances, pointing out that she attempted to express the meaning and values behind the dances by employing a variety of staging techniques rather than merely reproducing "folk art" on the stage. As the dance scholar Millicent Hodson wrote, "Working with John Pratt and others, she set a new level of design for dance theatre, extending the lines of dance movement through the cut and color of costumes, using the tropical context of her dances to awaken the kinesthetic sense of the audience."[18]

Colin Turnbull, who has extensively studied and written about African societies, recommended that anthropologists investigate connections between "ritual, drama, and entertainment" as the key elements of rites of passage and that they need to concern themselves seriously with alternative modes of awareness.[19] Dunham's dramatic, kinesthetic, and possible psychic gifts expand the potential of ethnography, in power of presentation and in effectiveness in intercultural encounters.

Exponents of performance as a form of ethnography posit a postmodern exchange, in which distinct cultural expressions are fused into a self-conscious interculturalism, for example, pan-African, pan-Indian, pan-Pacific.[20] Dunham dance technique, as it has evolved through performance, represents a fusion on an even larger scale, basically African but incorporating North American, Latin American, Caribbean, European, and South Asian patterns and movements. Communication based on such varied expressions calls on the existence of widespread psychic and biological resonances, which Dunham has referred to as "universal rhythms." She has elicited these kinesthetic responses in many contexts: in theaters, ritual ceremonies, and dance therapy classes and among children and inner-city gang members. Dunham technique is an organized medium of intercultural communication.

Her fieldwork in the Caribbean transformed Dunham's professional and personal life. She has educated a worldwide audience in cultural differences through her dance and theatrical presentations, and she has inspired those whom few others in "art dance" have attempted to reach: African American youth. Her recognition of the role of dance in the survival of Haitian culture and her use of it in individual therapy and for social remedy in inner cities reveal her debt to Malinowski's view of the vital, even biological functions of cultural expressions.[21]

Dunham continued her research during her dance career, in Africa, Asia, South America, and urban North America. She published books and articles and lectured on dance anthropology at Yale, the University of Chicago, Stanford, the University of California at Berkeley, and Case Western Reserve University, among many others, and anthropological societies in London, Paris, and Rio de Janeiro. She established the School of Cultural Arts in New York and the Performing Arts Training Center at Southern Illinois University, East St. Louis Center, where she taught the course "Dance Anthropology" for many years. She has received innumerable honorary doctorates, which in reality were earned. Métraux remarked that in the *voudun*, "Katherine Dunham attended a school that was even stricter than all the departments of anthropology."[22] And she adhered to a tradition of discipline and rigorous standards in teaching and performance.

At a presentation arranged by the anthropology department at Yale University, Dunham elicited cultural universals with a performance of "Rites de Passage," one of her most famous pieces. The warm response was notable in what many considered a bastion of academic stuffiness. Geoffrey Gorer called the presentation "revolutionary"; George Murdock, regarded as conservative in his writings and views, wrote that he found the presentation "pleasant and profitable" and a "genuine treat"; and Donald Horton, the department's chairman, wrote, "Few of us have been so deeply stirred by any dancing as we were by this return to simple, universal human experience."[23] Recognition by these respected anthropologists was no doubt gratifying to Dunham, but her example did not lead to an immediate acceptance of the study of dance as integral to anthropology. A limited approval granted to dance research would occur much later.

Katherine Dunham and brother, Albert, Joliet, Illinois, 1930, perhaps earlier.
(Courtesy of the Missouri Historical Society)

Katherine Dunham (center) and Ballet Nègre in "Fantes/ Enegre," circa 1933–34.
(Photograph by Dorien Basabe; courtesy of the Missouri Historical Society)

Katherine Dunham in a solo Spanish dance, Chicago, 1937.
(Photograph by Dorien Basabe; courtesy of the Missouri Historical Society)

Katherine Dunham and her company in "L'Ag'Ya," 1938.
(Photographer unknown; courtesy of the Missouri Historical Society)

Costume sketches by
John Pratt for "L'Ag'Ya"
and poster for *Ballet
Fedré*, 1938.
(Courtesy of the Library
of Congress)

John Pratt and Katherine
Dunham, 1938.
(Photograph by Valeska; courtesy
of the Missouri Historical Society)

Garland Wilson and Katherine Dunham as Georgia Brown in *Cabin in the Sky*, 1940.
(Photographer unknown; courtesy of the Missouri Historical Society)

Eartha Kitt (far left) performing with the Katherine
Dunham Company and
Katherine Dunham (far
right) directing in her
well-known red plaid
dressing gown, circa 1947.
(Photographer unknown; courtesy
of the Missouri Historical Society)

Lucille Ellis performing
in the Katherine Dunham
Company 1950 production
of "Choros."
(Photographer unknown; courtesy
of the Missouri Historical Society)

John Pratt, Katherine Dunham, and their daughter, Marie-Christine, Paris, 1951. The photo was used in their 1951 Christmas cards.
(Photograph by Studio Iris; courtesy of the Missouri Historical Society)

Katherine Dunham and Vanoye Aikens in "Floyd's Guitar Blues," circa 1955.
(Photograph by Roger Wood, London; courtesy of the Missouri Historical Society)

John Pratt and
Katherine Dunham
backstage in Hamburg,
1954.
(Photograph by Nicolaus
V. Gorrissen; courtesy of the
Missouri Historical Society)

Katherine Dunham
at work on *A Touch of
Innocence* in Tokyo,
December 1957.
(Photograph by Matsuga;
courtesy of the Missouri
Historical Society)

Katherine Dunham and Eubie
Blake in the finale of the
Treemonisha premiere, 1972.
(Photographer unknown; courtesy
of the Missouri Historical Society)

Glory Van Scott and Darryl
Braddix in "Floyd's Guitar
Blues," *Winston-Salem* (N.C.)
Journal, April 27, 1973.
(Photo by staff photographer, Jim Keith;
courtesy of Darryl Braddix)

Katherine Dunham with
East St. Louis mayor
Carl Officer and children
in front of the Katherine
Dunham Museum, 1977.

Katherine Dunham and
Talley Beatty at a fund-
raising event for the 1979
Carnegie Hall production
celebrating the Albert
Schweitzer Music Award.
(Photograph by Ayoka Chenzira;
courtesy of the Missouri Historical
Society)

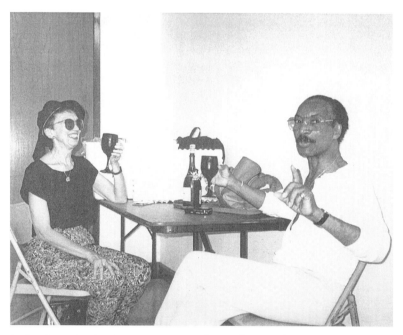

Author interviewing Tommy Gomez at the Dunham Technique Seminar, 1991.
(Photograph courtesy of James D. Parker, photographer)

Katherine Dunham receiving a city proclamation from the mayor's aide,
June 2000, on the occasion of her ninety-first birthday.
(Photograph courtesy of Roscoe Crenshaw, Panacea, Inc.)

6 *Ethics and Politics*

> Anthropology . . . is the outcome of a historical process
> which has made the larger part of mankind subservient
> to the other.
> —Claude Lévi-Strauss, "Anthropology: Its Achievements
> and Future"

IN A 1966 ESSAY, Claude Lévi-Strauss asserted that to gain the
trust and cooperation of those they study in a postcolonial era, anthropologists "must undergo a deep transformation." He noted that many
peoples "have had their resources plundered and their institutions and
beliefs destroyed," while they themselves were killed, enslaved, and subjected to diseases against which they had no resistance. Characterizing
anthropology as the heir to this "era of violence," he maintained that the
objectivity claimed by some ethnographers stemmed from the fact that
"one part of mankind treated the other as object." He affirmed that "the
so-called primitive societies exist in history" and that they undergo transformations embodying specializations different from those of industrialized societies.[1] Ethnographic depictions of societies implying that they
are self-contained and essentially outside of history fail to reflect the
sometimes disastrous, often overwhelming contacts they experienced
with Western colonial powers.

Lévi-Strauss's forthright political statement and his charge to anthropologists reflected postcolonial realities that compelled a reappraisal of
ethics in the discipline. His views were prefigured in Katherine Dunham's
approach to fieldwork. In *Island Possessed*, Dunham's "thick description"
of her initiation and other experiences involved digressions and associations that provided the historical, political, and social contexts of the

events she depicted.[2] Faulting Dunham's inclusion of "anthropologists, Haitian Presidents and politicians," world figures, and various dancers and theatrical personalities in her account, a 1970 review of *Island Possessed* in the official journal of the American Anthropological Association reflected the narrow views of ethnography that Lévi-Strauss abjured.[3] While Dunham's knowledge of the *voudun* stemmed from her relationships and identification with peasants, she also developed close friendships with intellectuals and politicians and described the political history of the island in her treatment. She was aware of the privileged position she held as a representative of a formerly occupying power, as well as some of the resulting problems she would encounter. Her sensitivity to such issues, stemming from her own experiences and her awareness as a "new Negro," enabled her to relate to Haitians of all social and political persuasions and to describe Haitian lifeways with authenticity.[4]

In early (and some later) ethnographic accounts, Africans and other non-Western peoples were objectified as "the other" and made exotic and potentially exploitable for the titillation of the senses and imaginations of the "Western world," or they were used to further questionable theories.[5] Dunham pondered some of these issues before they became current in the literature. During the First World Festival of Negro Arts at Dakar, Senegal, in 1966, she joined Wole Soyinka, a Nigerian writer, in opposing the concept of negritude promoted by her friend Léopold Senghor, the poet-philosopher and president of Senegal. She stated she did not believe categories should be used that in some way placed a people outside the human race. To her chagrin, while her company was performing in the United States and Europe, audiences and critics stressed the "exotic" nature of its materials, often failing to recognize the creativity of the choreography and the innovative synthesis of Western with non-Western forms.

The review of *Island Possessed* in the *American Anthropologist* questioned Dunham's credentials as an anthropologist and expressed disdain for her stated desire to believe in *voudun* spirits. Such a limited view reveals an insensitivity to humanistic concerns. Rather than treat Haitians and *voudun* as exotic "others," Dunham exhibited respect for Haitians and their belief systems in her openness to their rituals and *loa.*

Shortly before Dunham left Haiti, she experienced a personal crisis that revealed her ethical sensibility in matters of belief. She decided to perform a ceremony in which she would promise the *loa* to consummate the *kanzo,* or second *voudun* initiation, at a later date. She wanted to perform the *kanzo* rite itself before she departed, but Herskovits had written her warning against it; he had been cautious about tackling things that were beyond his reach while working in Dahomey—the place of origin of many of the *voudun* mysteries. After observing the *kanzo* several times, she felt uncertain about undergoing the trial by fire. She was concerned about her "moral position" in making promises for future initiations. Questioning her own motives, she asked, "Could Herskovits tell me, could Erich Fromm, could Téoline or DéGrasse tell me what part of me lived on the floor of the houngfor . . . and what part stood to one side taking notes? Each moment lived in participation was real; still . . . without conscious doing or planning or thinking I stayed outside the experience while being totally immersed in it."[6] She longed for an indication of possession to prove to herself that she was sincere. She had few precedents to follow, and many of her predecessors had expressed little ethical reservation about their involvement in ritual life.[7] In later years as a world traveler, she could smile at her earlier anxieties: "I can now observe with some pity, even amusement, the newly traveled, ethnic-saturated, homesick-for-Chicago Iphigenia wondering [how] to prove herself a scientist to her Alma Mater . . . [and] the selfless sacrificial maiden to her people."[8] Still, it is to her credit that she was aware of the ethical issues arising from her initiation. By the time of her later comment, she was more attuned to the give-and-take of relationships, and she had paid back with interest the trust invested in her by her Haitian mentors. Her lifetime commitment to Haiti and its people and her respect for and transmission of their culture to the world represent an ideal applauded by contemporary anthropologists, if not always emulated.

Recognition by the anthropology establishment was auspicious, if belated. In 1986, the American Anthropological Association awarded Katherine Dunham, along with Pearl Primus, the Distinguished Service Award. At the 1991 annual meetings, at the prompting of the Association of Black Anthropologists, a session in honor of Katherine Dunham and Pearl Primus was held.[9]

Dunham has persevered in her attachment to Haiti and its people through tyranny, revolution, and exile of friends. She credited her friend Dumarsais Estimé for heightening her political awareness. Estimé's ambition to serve his people made her realize that she needed to "turn this thirst for knowledge to a way of service."[10]

Estimé was a man of the people. Although his family was able to secure at least primary schooling for him, he was largely self-educated. Like Dunham's brother and her other role models, he was an intellectual, but his primary motivation for knowledge was social action. He entered politics at a young age and represented St. Marc, his place of birth, in the Chamber of Deputies, of which he was elected president, a position he held during Dunham's first field trip. He later became minister of education and finally president of the Republic of Haiti, from which seat he was forcibly ejected and exiled, in a move reminiscent of the ouster of Jean-Bertrande Aristide.

Estimé was opposed to the *voudun* and Dunham's interest in it because he felt that the belief in spirits held the people back, leaving them ignorant of many modern advances in education, hygiene, finance, and economics that he believed were necessary to the future of the country.[11] Like most of his compatriots, he was angry about the U.S. Marine occupation and distrusted white people, but he realized the advantages of economic and cultural arrangements with the United States and other countries and the emulation of their successes. He was preoccupied with social problems, such as the exploitation of children as virtual slaves, and he worked to provide children with shoes, clothes, and education and to promote public sanitation. He was also deeply troubled by the class system, which prevented Haiti from uniting on such pressing problems as mass poverty.

Dunham had never separated her emotional from her intellectual life, and, predictably, her affections became involved. She idealized his physical image, calling forth such African icons as Benin bronzes and Bambara and Baule masks: "the head large for the body, because there in the head the artists of the ancient kingdoms of Benin placed the spirit and soul and intelligence of a man, which should overshadow his earthly, corporeal self."[12] In her mind, he was associated with Toussaint L'Ouverture, the liberator of Haiti. Both were self-educated and thoughtful; they were similar even in the fact that they were ultimately overturned because of attempts to hold onto their power: L'Ouverture threatened the French by naming his successor; Estimé attempted to extend his term and, worse, sided with the masses against fellow politicians.

Above all, both Estimé and L'Ouverture were men of culture and compassion. In this they differed from two presidents she came to know who also left imprints on Haiti: Paul Magloire and François Duvalier. Magloire was president during the period when she spent much time in Haiti, and she maintained a cordial, if distant relationship with him and Madame Magloire. Magloire was physically charming, with great personal dignity, but he loved the "good life" and was vain and ostentatious, Dunham remarked.[13] While he accomplished some advances in agriculture and construction projects during his six years in office, he was corrupt and exploited the peasants.

Magloire's successor was Duvalier, or "Papa Doc," the only president in Haiti's history, Dunham remarked,[14] who was successful in extending his term of office. This he accomplished by forming his own personal militia, the notorious Ton-ton Macoute, literally, "uncle big-stick," allowing them freedom to pillage and intimidate, so long as they remained loyal to him. He distrusted the army, which had betrayed Estimé, in whose cabinet he had served. His militia was made up of unemployed laborers, rootless and angry; he gained their allegiance by permitting them to loot the property of the wealthy and enrich themselves. Unlike Magloire, he had no personal ambitions of wealth and extravagant display; he was primarily interested in power and in continuing to hold it.

Duvalier controlled the elite through physical fear; he ruled the masses by psychological intimidation. While he undermined conventional religion, he did not oppose the *voudun* and was rumored to be possessed by Baron Samedi. He did not discourage these suppositions, although he was an intelligent, educated man, with a medical degree from Cornell University. Despite this background, he was anti-American and anti-white and hated the mulatto elite as well. He identified more with the laborers and peasants, although he trusted no one.

Dunham's first meetings with Duvalier, in 1956, were pleasant, involving discussions about anthropology and national health. Duvalier was an admirer of Estimé, although he did not follow his policies. Estimé had conferred on her the post of chevalier in the Haitian Legion of Honor in 1949; Duvalier arranged for her promotion to commander grand officier in the legion. Her friend Louis Mars, a psychiatrist and statesman who was minister of foreign affairs and later ambassador to the United States and France, placed the ribbon and medal around her neck.

When she later saw Duvalier at a public affair in 1962, he was, she felt, a changed man. He appeared morally, spiritually, and physically ill, and she recalled his reputed diabolic possession. He did not acknowledge her at that time or later, but her property was not touched by the Tonton, although most plantations, villas, hotels, and businesses were plundered. She wondered whether this favor was by order of the president or through the protection of the small band of Estimistes, followers of the former president, who were the only opposition group that existed in Haiti.

Dunham was able to maintain a foothold in the beloved country in which she was an "adopted daughter" through the policy of nonalliance that she had established in her fieldwork. While she did not excuse Duvalier's acts, she did not publicly censure him. Some criticized her for her lack of open condemnation of the Duvalier regime.[15] She was the "outsider within" and felt obliged to remain politically neutral. The position gave her some misgivings, but she saw it as the only one possible for a sympathetic non-Haitian. Many who were critical of her were particularly angry at Duvalier's anti-Americanism, a not uncommon posture among Haitians as a result of the occupation and one with which she could sympathize.

The striking exception to Dunham's neutrality was her allegiance to Estimé, although she had very little contact with him during his presidency. She was fairly secure in this preference, since most Haitians admired him, even if they did not support him. Still, she was troubled with guilt and anxiety when she smuggled a letter from him into Haiti while he was in exile. He lived under protection in Jamaica, under surveillance and hunted and harassed by his enemies. He needed money desperately and asked her to take the letter to his relatives, who could handle some financial transactions for him. She was aware of the consequences to her and others if the letter was discovered; still, she knew she had to help her friend. Three years later, in 1953, he died in New York. Although there were rumors of assassination, she believed he died of a broken heart, separated from the country he loved and in which he had invested his dreams, hopes, and life work.

Dunham noted that the acts that brought the downfall of Haitian leaders, through exile or assassination, and sparked rebellion of the people invariably centered on threats to the constitution, especially as it related to elections or lengths of presidential terms. Because of the violent history of the Republic and the limitless ambition of some of its leaders, the only alternative to tyranny appeared to be mass revolt. In this atmosphere, she believed, democratic processes were extremely problematic.[16]

Her remarks are illuminating when applied to political events after the publication of *Island Possessed*. Although Duvalier was able, through brutal methods, to extend his tenure and obtain leadership for his son, "Baby Doc," who was not as strong and ruthless, was forced out. Elections were held, and Jean-Bertrande Aristide was elected with the overwhelming support of a coalition of liberal intellectuals, communists, peasants, and the urban proletariat.

Although she had not been directly involved in, or even aware of, some of the post-Duvalier (senior) political happenings in Haiti, Dunham was closely in touch with national events during and after the removal of "Baby Doc." Commenting on the corruption in the capital, she declared, "Michelle [his wife] was Baby Doc's downfall. Her 'Ladies from Paris,' God knows who they were. She installed air conditioning in the palace; they wore their fur coats."[17] After "Baby Doc" was forced out, a political vacuum existed. Free elections were held under the auspices of the United Nations, and Marc Bazin, who was a friend of Dunham, declared his candidacy for president.

During the election in 1990, she was residing in her home in Port-au-Prince; she followed the election closely, as well as the interim presidency and the inauguration of Aristide, through her many contacts. Again breaking with her position of neutrality, she supported the U.S.-backed Bazin in the election. She had met him in Morocco, where he was financial consultant to King Hassan II. He had helped her assemble Royal dancers for a New York production. Impressed by his abilities and his cosmopolitan background, she thought that after the disastrous Duvalier reign, he might lead Haiti into international acceptance. "Mark Bazin was the only one I could understand," she remarked. "After he came back to Haiti [from the World Bank] he said he was 'totally scandalized' by the way money was used."[18]

Bazin had married the daughter of a former president. He was a member of the elite class and had inherited money that originally came from white ancestors. The Bazins had held an affair in Haiti for Katherine Dunham when she won the Kennedy Award. Dunham held a preelection party for the Bazins so that they could meet diplomats and other influential people.

In the weeks before the election, she concluded that the only way to settle the issue between Bazin and Aristide was to create a prime minister. She wanted to have them meet two weeks before the election to decide that one should be president, the other prime minister: "I was all set to give a dinner so they could talk. . . . The American ambassador said, 'You can't do that.' I didn't know why not." "Aristide," she continued, "taught peasants to sign their names or to vote using fingerprints. But when they tried [to vote], the army came in and shut down the election."[19]

An interim president was appointed while the international community tried to sort it all out. Finally, the election was judged to be democratic, and Aristide was declared the winner and sworn in as president. Dunham attended the inauguration, along with Jimmy Carter and others who had monitored the election. Dunham still felt that Bazin would have made the best president, that he was knowledgeable and a realist; he would clean things up, except for the market in drugs, which he would be wise to ignore. Aristide, she feared, would try to institute a kind of "prehistoric communism."

The class system, which Estimé so deplored, operated to subvert the election. The elite, aligned with the military leaders, opposed Aristide's attempts to attain economic justice for the peasants and arrested him, sending him into exile. The situation was, in many ways, reminiscent of Estimé's downfall. Aristide is considered neither a communist nor even a socialist but a populist, and the coup leaders feared his alliance with the people. They blamed him for some of the excesses of the poor, who sought revenge against individuals they believed had wronged them. The Haitian peasants and the poor revolted when he was ousted, confirming the fears of the coup leaders and leading to a brutal crackdown.

After the coup, Bazin took the de facto job of prime minister under General Raoul Cedras, and Dunham was disappointed when he appeared weak in relation to the military leaders. She knew he was in favor of having democracy restored, but his brief tenure did nothing to advance its cause. She felt that the situation in Haiti was impossible to set right without forceful intervention, and she petitioned the U.S. government to act. She believed that the legacy of past mistakes of U.S. policies in Haiti imposed a moral obligation to right the situation.

In the meantime, she had finally met Aristide, and while she had been skeptical because of his appeal to the populace—she recalled that Duvalier had mass support at one time—she decided that he was a straightforward and good man. The meeting occurred after she had returned to her home in East St. Louis, Illinois, and was in the midst of a fast in support of Haitian refugees. Mark Silverman, an independent filmmaker and supporter, included the meeting in a film he made about her fast: "In the film, *Forty-seven Days of Fasting*, Aristide and I were holding arms. . . . He is a spiritual man and I'm afraid for him."[20] She felt he was innocent of the atrocities his followers had committed. "He thought the world democracies would support his action against drugs. . . . The CIA controls drugs and wouldn't put up with that," she declared.[21]

The setbacks to democracy in Haiti—the assassinations and the reneging on agreements by the ruling oligarchy—were not unexpected to Dunham. She had warned the administration and the Congressional Black Caucus—Representative Charles Rangel, who was actively attempting to influence policy, in particular—that General Cedras and the oligarchy would not give up without a fight. She was familiar with the mind-set of the Haitian elite and the unscrupulousness of its thugs.

Dunham's backing of both Bazin and Aristide illustrates her dual loyalties in Haitian society and her disregard for social distinctions. While her proposed political solution appears idealistic in the face of the political realities of that beleaguered country, it was based on her deep desire to further the social reconciliation she deems necessary before any solution to Haiti's economic problems can be found.

In the meantime, she acted in the only way she felt was feasible to support the Haitian peasants caught up in the political conflict. Dunham's fast in support of Haitian refugees in February and March 1992 was a singular phenomenon in a lifetime of dramatic events. For forty-seven days, she refused food to dramatize the plight of the refugees who were fleeing political repression by the army and were being repatriated or incarcerated by a U.S. government indifferent to their suffering. She was concerned about the imprisoned Haitian refugees, some of whom joined her in fasting. "Those Haitians at Guantánamo Bay are too feeble to fast," she exclaimed. These were the people with whom she had identified in the early years and from whom she had learned about the *voudun.* She had only her body and her life as media for expressing her grief and despair at what was happening to them, she asserted, since she had no money and no longer led a dance group that could dramatize and call the world's attention to the crisis.[22]

Dunham's fast became a national media event and gained the support of people throughout the country, including such notables as Jesse Jackson, the screen director Jonathan Demme, Dick Gregory, Harry and Julie Belafonte, Representative Charles Rangel, and Mayor David Dinkins of New York, and such organizations as the American Friends Service Committee, Haitian refuge associations, Jewish groups, and Catholic and Protestant churches. A reenactment of the social movements of the 1960s occurred, with rallies, sympathetic fasting, marches, and civil disobedience occurring throughout the country. Several people, in moral outrage, chained themselves to federal buildings in East St. Louis and were arrested. Candlelight vigils, with prayers and drumming, in eclectic Catholic-Baptist-Jewish-Voudun services, were held on the doorstep of Katherine Dunham's East St. Louis residence. It was a spectacular expression of intercultural communication. Neighbors joined in, and a graduate of the Dunham program in East St. Louis brought his young singers and dancers as well as his drums to celebrate in African American mode. Dunham was hospitalized in East St. Louis and during her stay was provided with a pressroom, into which poured calls, telegrams, gifts, and other messages from all parts of the country and the world. She called, wired, and faxed political leaders, including presidents Bush and Clinton, as well as members of Congress, black leaders, fellow artists, and anyone she thought might have some influence. It was truly a Dunham-style event, tapping into many cultural and social domains and associations.

Weakened by lack of nutrients, she nevertheless kept up her fast as well as efforts to persuade political leaders to change policies toward the refugees. But her strong will to survive prevailed, and she finally took food after forty-seven days, feeling she had at least alerted others to the situation. Her health was permanently damaged by the fast; she has not regained her ability to walk and now uses a wheelchair. Celebrated as a local hero, she was presented with a humanitarian award at a 1992 recognition ceremony at Washington University in St. Louis.

The culmination of the fast was a birthday celebration in her honor in New York City, hosted by Jonathan Demme. Fittingly, it was held in the garden of the Episcopal church in which his social activist cousin was pastor. He was the subject of Demme's social documentary, *My Cousin Bobby*, dealing with the minister's work in an inner-city pastorate. The party was attended by celebrities from the entertainment and art world. Dunham had been asked to invite a special guest from anywhere in the world; she chose Danny Glover, whose acting she admired. He reminded her that he had visited her in Port-au-Prince years earlier, a fact she had forgotten, she later admitted. Her apparent chance selection of an actor whom she had met when he was a young unknown is an expression of the "synchrony," as she terms such felicitous accords, that recurs often in her life. Characteristically, she did not passively accept "fate" but turned it to her advantage: she persuaded Glover and Harry Belafonte to visit East St. Louis to plan strategies for economic and cultural development.

In a radio interview, Dunham explained that her actions during the fast were part of the "architecture" of her life, that given her former experiences and actions, this act of protest was predetermined.[23] Her action was intelligible to those who were aware of her long association with Haiti, but others expressed perplexity. An unnamed source commented to a journalist that Dunham had never previously been involved in anything of a political nature.[24] The assertion overlooked Dunham's unpopular public stands on human and civil rights in the 1940s, 1950s, and 1960s. These reactions caused her to remark, "It's surprising how few people know me."[25]

Louis Farrakhan visited her and supported her during her fast in 1992. "They [Nation of Islam] ran half-page ads about the fast and the situation in Haiti," she noted. Farrakhan's anger at the American establishment resonated with Dunham's feelings about the government's treatment of Haitian refugees, and she found him to be a sympathetic partisan. He shared her view of the kinship between the oppressed in Haiti and the oppressed in the United States. She listened to his radio program and remarked that he is the only black leader who speaks to the "down and out." As a result, he cannot reject his followers, although some are strongly anti-Semitic and give voice to the rage of the "throw-aways" in U.S. society. She felt that he could accomplish some of the things necessary for black Americans to pull their communities together, but not everything. She pointed out that in Elijah Muhammad's and Malcolm X's Islamic societies, at least no one went hungry.[26]

Dunham's views about Farrakhan and the Nation of Islam are similar to those of many African Americans. They welcome their program of guarding and cleaning up the housing projects and respect the young men dressed in suits and polished shoes who perform a valuable service instead of hanging around on the corner, mugging people or selling drugs.[27] A leader pointed out that African Americans are perfectly capable of sorting out the wheat from the chaff in Farrakhan's message. Most focus not on the negative parts of his message but on the positive statement that African Americans need to shape their own destinies, and they admire him for being independent of white organizations.

While Dunham does not view white people as the enemy, she deeply relates to the frustrations arising from racism and their expression by such leaders as Louis Farrakhan and Malcolm X. She also understands the rage of the Haitian masses. She did not condemn President Aristide for exhorting them to recognize their oppression and to overcome hopelessness and apathy, although she did not sanction the violence he released.

Dunham was later disappointed in Aristide's failure to accomplish much when his presidency was restored. He was unable to extend his term to the full six years in a move to compensate for the period of his exile. Embittered, he retired to a "million dollar" mansion in the mountains, built, Dunham suspected, with funds that were intended for restoring infrastructure and property destroyed during the anarchy surrounding the coup. He maintained his political organization and succeeded in regaining the presidency in a subsequent election.

Dunham's political involvement was complicated by the fact that she had become a property owner and therefore had a social and material stake as well as a moral one in the outcome of any political actions. She had first been made aware of Habitation Leclerc by Papa Augustin, a Haitian whom she met on her first trip to New York to perform at the Young Men's Hebrew Association (YMHA) in 1937. He joined the company later, as cultural consultant and drummer, and became a teacher at the Dunham School. She had much respect for him as a "bush priest." He accompanied her to Haiti in 1949 when she received her decoration from Estimé; at that time, he told her about Habitation Leclerc and took her to view it. She felt strong misgivings about the property, a combination of fear and dread. Papa Augustin informed her that she was destined to own it, so she needed to take steps to overcome the negative aura that was affecting her. He suggested she consult Kam, a priestess.

Habitation Leclerc was reputedly a temporary residence of Pauline Bonaparte, Napoleon's sister, who married General Victor Emmannuelle Leclerc, the military commander of the colony. General Donatien Rochambeau, Leclerc's successor, was sent to squelch the slave rebellions; he did so with great cruelty and brutality, and some of the midnight parties at which he conducted these barbarities, including burying slaves alive, were said to have taken place at Habitation Leclerc. The place was secluded, and structures and amenities had been constructed by later owners. Apart from its baleful history, it was an ideal spot, Dunham felt, for the rest and rehabilitation of company members in the midst of their world tours.

During her 1949 visit in Papa Augustin's company, Dunham had renewed her bonds with *voudun.* After she purchased Habitation Leclerc, she decided to consult Kam, who had impressed her as having power, about troubles there. Company members were expressing fears of snakes they encountered on the property, and she continued to have her own apprehensions. Even more compelling than these concerns was the experience of her mother, who had accompanied them. She awoke them with her screams one night. She had seen a black man, bare-chested, with hands tied behind him and wearing ragged trousers, who knelt at her doorway and asked for help. Her mother knew nothing about the history of the estate and thought it was a thief or vagabond. She saw the man run toward a building that was supposed to be a prison in which slaves had been starved or asphyxiated. Later, iron rings attached to short lengths of chain were dug up, giving credence to the claim.

Convinced of the need for exorcism, Kam consented to come to Habitation Leclerc and was installed in the "slave house." Dunham was ill with fever and missed the exorcism, but when Kam informed her that the unhappy spirits had departed, Dunham's fever also lifted. Habitation Leclerc experienced other visitations and more rituals were performed, but Dunham's uneasy feelings about the property have never completely disappeared.

During Duvalier's time, she opened a clinic for sick Haitians at Habitation Leclerc, treating malaria, influenza, internal parasites, yaws, and other illnesses. She received sample remedies from Max Jacobson, her trusted physician in New York, for the clinic, and several doctors and a nurse assisted her at various times. Duvalier visited the clinic but seemed unimpressed. Dunham felt that it was because her efforts, while desperately needed and successful for some ailments, were amateurish. When the clinic was discontinued because of competing demands, she received an offer to revive it but refused. She later discovered that her instincts were correct; the offer was from opponents of Duvalier who wanted to use it as a "front" for a munitions station.

The clinic was merely one way in which Dunham has attempted to put Habitation Leclerc to use to benefit Haitians. In the interests of tourism, which had drastically declined during Duvalier's rule, in the 1970s she leased part of the property to a syndicate that built a luxury hotel. Members of the jet set, including Jackie Onassis and Richard Burton, stayed there. When conditions in Haiti further discouraged visitors, she resolved to establish an international cultural institute, using guest villas of the hotel as hostels for dancers and other students who attended classes and seminars. Financial shortfalls, lack of backing, and the political situation in Haiti prevented this. She recalled that a Haitian once said to her, "The master of Leclerc will never be happy."[28]

Residence Dunham is a hillside villa in the tropical style, consisting of rooms arranged around a pool, with Dunham's suite at the top of a flight of stairs at one end and a tropical garden ascending the hillside to the side. Opposite the garden is a courtyard, with a *houngfor* at the rear. The layout of the rooms and gardens, the kitchen facilities and shopping requirements in a tropical climate, as well as social demands, call for a permanent, year-round staff. The financial support as well as personal problems of these Haitians are a constant worry to "Madame," who takes a personal interest in their well-being.

The shanties of the Haitian poor have gradually crept up to the property, and pedestrian traffic is constant on the nearby road up the hill, which separates Residence Dunham from the rest of Habitation. Many of the travelers are women on their way to the spring on the far side of the property to launder clothes, which constantly hang—blindingly white or in faded colors—from any available projection. Before the recent political upheaval, visitors to Residence Dunham were frequent, and Haitians of all classes and occupations appeared for various business or professional purposes or to offer respects.

The protection of Residence Dunham extended beyond Duvalier's death, until the social upheaval during Aristide's exile. A group of religious sect members, she conjectured, who were angry because Rosie Rubenstein, Dunham's manager, had berated them for "barbecuing cats on the property," took advantage of the unrest and retaliated by burning two rooms, along with files, paintings, materials from company tours, deeds to property, notes, scripts, and photographs. Again, during the publicity surrounding her fast, marauders she believed to be a gang of *zenglindo*—soul mates of the Ton-ton Macoute—looted her villa, bringing in a truck and taking everything of value, including furniture, linens, mattresses, et cetera, leaving only two beds. They were not common hooligans, she believed; they knew which things were valuable and stole with discrimination. The *zenglindo* were apolitical and were believed to join the gang by eating human flesh. However, she felt the action was deliberately promoted by those who resented her fasting. Many Haitians, in Haiti and in the United States, as well as Maroons, had watched and applauded her actions and statements. "I didn't want to tell anyone about this latest disaster in Haiti," she admitted. "They'd say, 'I thought you felt safe there.'" She mourned the loss of the security she had for decades: "It's not the material things that count. . . . Are they setting a pattern for posterity?" She had been trying to promote Haiti's entrance into the international community on a positive basis, and she felt this personal attack deeply. She recalled, "In 1944–45 Fromm said, 'Be careful that you don't become an Iphigenia.' I said, 'No, it's not for the race, it's for humanity.'"[29]

Heartbroken, she nonetheless decided to return to Port-au-Prince, repair her home, and renew her plans and dreams. "I want to go to Haiti. I have not been able to see the residence as it was," she declared. She did return twice for brief periods. However, since she did not receive benefits from U.S. agreements of restitution to property owners on the occasion of Aristide's return, she has not been able to finance the restoration of the residence, although she does retain a limited staff there.[30]

When Dunham left Haiti in 1936, she knew she would return, but she did not realize that her future would be so intimately tied to the island. Her personal loyalties and the indebtedness to Haitians incurred in her fieldwork led to an ongoing relationship with the troubled country. From her field trip, she had gleaned the ideas and materials for a stunning career, as well as the ideals and visions for a dedicated life. She carried elements of the theater—fabrics, costume items, drums, and other instruments—in her trunk. She would never forget her spiritual debt to Haiti; however, her immediate challenge was to organize a dance company and shape a choreography to build a career, as well as to seek out those who would assist her in creating a new dance form and way of life.

7 *Creating the Company*

With the arrival of Katherine Dunham on the scene,
the prospects for the development of a substantial Negro
dance art begin to look decidedly bright . . . for certainly
never before in all the efforts of recent years to establish
the Negro dance as a serious medium has there been so
convincing and authoritative an approach.

—John Martin, *New York Times,* 1940

KATHERINE DUNHAM'S PRIMARY creative achievement was
the founding and artistic direction of a dance company, composed main-
ly of African American dancers and performing, for the most part, dances
based on themes from Africa and the "black diaspora." Springing from
an idea and a dream, it was realized through her ability to enlist others
in her mission, and it generated her spectacular career.

On her return from the Caribbean in 1936, she was confronted with
a choice between continuing an academic career or becoming a professional dancer. At first she followed a traditional path; she graduated in 1936
and received a grant from the Rockefeller Foundation to complete her graduate work at Northwestern, with Herskovits as her adviser. Since she felt
that the University of Chicago was more in tune with her temperament
than "bourgeois" Northwestern, she proposed to Herskovits that she continue at Chicago with him as her adviser. He pointed out the impossibil-
ity of this and also discouraged her in her proposals to travel to Paris and
Brazil for further research. Advising her that the foundation would not
favor such a deviation from her study plan, he pointed out that if she completed her master's degree, the foundation could help get her placed in a
university "with an assured income." He represented anthropology as "a

way of making possible your study of dance."[1] His advice earned from her the adjective "single-minded," although she felt indebted to Herskovits and acknowledged his help and his expertise in Caribbean cultures.

Herskovits attempted to persuade the Rosenwald committee to support her in her intention to communicate her fieldwork findings through dance. He wrote, "Although I have been in constant contact with her during the period of her fieldwork, I do not think that I myself realized what remarkable material she had obtained in the field until on her return everything was put together and there was an opportunity to discuss her findings with her." He went on to describe her as "one of those rare persons who continues the finest aesthetic perceptions with an intellectual capacity of the highest order." He felt she had "to an almost unprecedented degree" understood the inner significance of the dances.[2] Nevertheless, the committee felt she had already received more support than other recipients and wanted to extend help to new scholars.

Dunham turned to Redfield, whom she viewed as a kindred spirit, and chose to continue her work at the University of Chicago. Redfield also suggested that she pursue both anthropology and dance, but she felt that he had a deeper understanding of the importance of dance and theater in her life. He asked her, "Why can't you just do both? . . . If you're sincere in both, you'll never stop being one or the other, anyway, so go right ahead. . . . You can always do anthropology whenever you want to."[3]

But her decision to become a professional dancer rather than an academic was made with much soul-searching and guilt because of those who had supported her in her studies. She even felt a certain resentment that her teachers did not allow her to pursue academic studies on her terms, and she experienced a letdown after her successful fieldwork in the Caribbean. She complained to a friend, who wrote, "Why shouldn't Redfield allow you to continue on to a PhD?"[4] She protested to Herskovits, "By stressing the artistic do you people mean to discard a scientific approach? I have an uncomfortable feeling that it is merely a polite way of telling me that I'm too stupid to be an anthropologist!" She added rather plaintively, "I could be made into a good field worker."[5] Herskovits replied that neither he nor Redfield felt that she should give up the scientific approach "but that your most important contribution, because of the nature of your abilities, must be through your choreographic work."[6] Her mentors likely believed that her uncompromising independence would cause her problems in an academic setting and that her creativity would be better nurtured through an artistic career.

Without a source of income, she faced the continual problem of how to support herself and her dancers in pursuing a dance career. At a Rosenwald reception held when she returned from the Caribbean, she met Al Smart, who was one of the owners of *Esquire* magazine. He agreed to publish an essay telling the story of the ballet "L'Ag'Ya," which she later staged. The illustrations were by the black cartoonist E. Simms Campbell, who drew the popular "Little Sultan" cartoons. She said of another essay, "Les Pecheurs," later titled "Promenade to the Ocean," "I was so charmed by the sight of women [of Martinique] carrying bowls on their head in the morning to the ocean; later I found they were carrying slops."[7] These stories and another about Martinique, "La Boule Blanche," were the first to be published in *Esquire* either by a woman or by a black writer; they appeared under the name Kaye Dunn, and they earned a little money for the hard-pressed young writer. But any real financial security was elusive.

She needed a place to work with her dancers, and Ludmilla Speranzeva and Ruth Page assisted her in obtaining studios. She also needed to mount productions that would attract participants: dancers and musicians. While she was at the University of Chicago, she was able to give yearly presentations at the Abraham Lincoln Theater, which was near the university, on Oakwood near Cottage Grove Avenue. Talley Beatty, who had joined her group before fieldwork took her to the Caribbean, reminisced, "[I was doing] street dancing, like everybody else, which was tap, soft shoe. In Chicago, I lived at 46th and Vincennes. Then Dunham had a studio [in a] carriage house at 48th and Vincennes [and] a friend of mine took me by . . . they were doing La Guiablesse, [for] Ruth Page, and she [Dunham] asked me to participate in it as a mise-en-scène . . . extras, I guess you call them."[8] They did three performances at the Civic Opera House, with Page's Chicago Ballet.

Beatty's relationship with Dunham was, in his words, like "sister and brother"; she took him to his first ballet and modern dance performances. "She taught me everything I knew," he declared.[9] He became a principal dancer with the group and received sufficient recognition so that when Dunham left for the Caribbean, he was offered a scholarship to study dance by the art critic of the *Chicago Tribune.* He worked with Edna McCrae and Kurt and Grace Graff during Dunham's absence, then resumed his place as a lead with her when she returned.

While Beatty was studying with the Graffs, he remembered, "I had to do my work in the dressing room or in the office before anybody came, so it was a very unpleasant experience." It is not surprising that he preferred the very different atmosphere of the Dunham classes. The group she assembled when she returned continued to give Chicago performances, and they were invited to appear at the Young Men's Hebrew Association (YMHA) in New York in the spring of 1937: "She took us to New

York in about 1936 [*sic*]—at that time I was in Junior High School. She drove all the way across the country. We only had about 20 minutes on the program with all these New York dancers!"[10] He called it a "splendid performance," with excellent reviews, but it did not result in further work. "I just think it's amazing that anyone could be so sensational and then be out of work," he remarked.[11]

Edna Guy, a student of Ruth St. Denis and a former member of Hemsley Winfield's black dance group, and Massey Patterson had arranged the "Negro Dance Evening" at the YMHA, which was to be the company's New York debut. Patterson was the aunt of Rita Christiane, who later joined the Dunham Company. Dunham met Archie Savage, who studied with Patterson, and the drummer Papa Augustin on that trip; both later appeared in the 1940 Dunham Company production at the New York Windsor Theater. She later called both artists to Chicago for a series of presentations at the Sherman Hotel. Beatty recalled, "That's when she did 'Barrel House' with Archie Savage, which turned into 'Floyd's Guitar Blues' and the 'Bahiana' . . . 'The Woman with a Cigar,' which was just so glorious. All those things, they just stopped the show, you know. She just had to repeat [them]. Subsequently, those things always remain in the Rep, so that it was like she found a center then."[12]

The company danced at the Goodman Theatre in the Chicago Art Institute and on other similar stages, with artistic and critical, though not financial, success. A *Chicago Tribune* review of a benefit performance at the Goodman Theatre, sponsored by the American Friends of Spanish Democracy for "child victims of the civil war," described the audience as large and Katherine Dunham and her group as "sensational": "She is the young colored woman who went to Haiti on a Rosenwald travel fellowship to study and collect the native dances of the island. These dances are of such a singularly exotic character and were so superlatively well executed Wednesday that they constituted for the majority of the audience nothing less than a revelation."[13] However, here, too, there were few follow-up performances. The group was stalled at the level of occasional performances with fairly limited public exposure.

By this time, the Haitian materials were incorporated into the presentations: *congo paillette, yonvalou, 'zépaules*, emphasizing movements of, respectively, hips, spinal column, and shoulders. Beatty and others responded enthusiastically: "It was so new and so different, and [other dancers] were tap dancing, you know, making all that noise and chorus girls in lines, and we were doing 'Rara Tonga.' . . . I knew I probably won't make a living off this, but every time there was a rehearsal I was there. It was this completely new concept and it was absorbed by all the dance world, and now they call it jazz ballet." Beatty noted that the basis for such later works as *Tropical Revue* and *Carib Song* had been established in the first concert in New York.[14]

Dunham's productions were not the first to include African-based movements on the North American stage. Zora Hurston had presented a collection of dances and songs from the Bahamas in the early 1930s, employing a group of dancers from Bimini.[15] Asadata Dafora, from Sierra Leone, wrote and choreographed an opera, *Kykunkor*, which appeared in New York in 1934; it was described as colorful, spectacular, "complete with stimulating African drum rhythms, costumes, songs and dances."[16] Other artists, such as Hemsley Winfield, who danced in a Metropolitan Opera production of *The Emperor Jones*, and the Creative Dance Group at Hampton Institute included African themes in their performances.[17] However, it was Katherine Dunham who introduced a systematic technique incorporating African movement; she and her company launched a series of dance programs that changed the course of modern dance and provided opportunities for black dancers.

In a lecture in 1992, Dunham noted that some choreographers made more use of the African and Caribbean "steps" and choreography than she did, attempting to copy the ceremonies: "What I observed was an inspiration. . . . I don't like the copying of what someone else does. . . . You filter it through your own imagination."[18] She does not like the category "ethnic dance," which any style other than European or Euro-American is often labeled. As Beatty characterized Dunham performances, "They did it universally."[19] In floor work and work at the barre, she broke down movements for purposes of pedagogy. Working with Uday Shankar, she was inspired by the systematization of East Indian dance to establish a system of prototypes.

While it could be used in choreographing ballets of many styles, Dunham technique had its own dance vocabulary. The dance scholar and critic Millicent Hodson wrote, "The Dunham technique makes available to the 'modern schools' of dance the liberation of knees and pelvis that is fundamental to African dance. . . . Her choreography, evolving from the same principles, established for the modern dancer a new vocabulary of movement for the lower body."[20]

Agnes de Mille and Eugene Von Grona had attempted to found black dance units, and Helen Tamiris and many other dancers had used African and African American themes and movements. But, as de Mille wryly observed, "Directly Katherine Dunham came along with authentic material," and such experiments ended.[21]

De Mille described her own black dancers as without dance technique or rehearsal discipline: "This was before Katherine Dunham established her school, and Negroes did not train for serious dancing because there was literally no opportunity for them to practice. . . . They came late; they absented themselves; they came so hungry they fainted. They couldn't remember; they caught every sickness conceivable."[22] These were the conditions under which Dunham, too, was working. Her students had the same problems as de Mille's: financial difficulties, lack of discipline, high dropout rate, and, above all, the need to overcome the stereotype that Negroes were natural dancers, with little or no training necessary. Talley Beatty commented, "Dunham really did a magnificent job training us, so we were really top-rate dancers. We went right into Broadway shows when we left the company." Nevertheless, they had problems of surviving on their art: "They reduced us to such a low level economically that we couldn't think of anything but trying to get food on the table."[23]

Beatty admired Dunham's resourcefulness: "If anybody has any native talent, that Chicago University education can really hone you. . . . I don't know how she did it. It was just her genius; I asked her, but she didn't really know. I asked Dale Wasserman [company manager] why it was and he said perseverance, but I think it was more than that."[24] Dunham's goals were clearly stated in an early interview: "To establish a well-trained ballet group. To develop a technique that will be as important to the white man as to the Negro. To attain a status in the dance world that will give to the Negro dance-student the courage really to study and a reason to do so. And to take *our* dance out of the burlesque—to make of it a more dignified art."[25] She had to achieve a miracle, and like all miracle workers, she used her innate skills and all available resources to achieve a transformation. A means soon presented itself, and she was prepared to take advantage of it.

The Federal Writers and Theatre Projects

For Dunham, as for many other artists in the 1930s, the New Deal projects provided a significant career break. Franklin Roosevelt and his advisers realized that the Great Depression was as disastrous for artists and writers as it was for laborers and other workers. When Roosevelt put his friend Harry Hopkins in charge of developing the Works Progress Administration (WPA), designed to provide jobs for unemployed workers, he suggested that a writers' and theater project be included. From the outset, these projects were political creations and were closely identified with the Democratic party agenda; like other programs of the WPA, they were subject to the vicissitudes of politics. Because some products of these units were controversial and even threatening to powerful politicians, they were relatively short-lived.[26]

The Federal Writers Project, the Federal Artists Project, and the Federal Theatre Project were the first governmental measures to support the arts in the United States. While they were brief in duration, their value is apparent in the large number of notable writers and artists whose careers were established and advanced through the programs. Because the Roosevelt administration supported equal opportunity for Negroes—though not necessarily integration—African American writers, playwrights, dancers, artists, and actors were a part of the effort, although they often worked in separate units directed or supervised by whites.[27] For black and white artists alike, the rosters of the WPA projects read like a Who's Who for writers, artists, directors, actors, and dancers throughout several decades of cultural life in the United States.

The writers' projects combined social research and literary works. Much of the research carried out by Horace Cayton and St. Clair Drake for *Black Metropolis* was funded by a WPA project. Lloyd Warner's study of the social effects of skin color was supported by the Federal Writers Project, as was the historical treatise *The Story of the American Negro* by Ina Corrine Brown, a graduate student in social anthropology at the University of Chicago.[28] Arna Bontemps supervised a project entitled "The Negro in Illinois," which included historical investigation of black Illinoisans in politics, economics, the arts, education, and theater, as well as treatments of northern migration and social history.[29] Among writers employed in the unit were Richard Wright and Jack Conroy; others who worked in this and other Chicago writers' projects were Margaret Walker, Frank Yerby, Nelson Algren, Willard Motley, Studs Terkel, Katherine Dunham, and Saul Bellow. Bontemps credited the WPA Writers' Project with the Chicago Renaissance of black writers, spearheaded by Richard Wright, which introduced a new note of realism supplanting the—in his words—elitist "primitivism" of the Harlem Renaissance writers.[30]

In his preface to the second edition of a joint study with Jack Conroy, based on the Illinois project, Bontemps painted a memorable picture of the work setting: "Not far away . . . was a serious young supervisor . . . Nelson Algren. Across the big room, in an area assigned to the radio unit, one occasionally saw the energetic and personable young figures of Studs Terkel and Lou Gilbert. . . . Katherine Dunham, Richard Wright, Frank Yerby . . . had worked at these same desks just weeks or months earlier, and some of them returned occasionally to see how things were going."[31]

At Redfield's suggestion, Dunham took her manuscript for *Journey to Accompong* to John T. Friedrich, the director of the Federal Writers

Project in Chicago. On the strength of her writing, she was hired to supervise a project investigating religious cults in Chicago, Detroit, Pittsburgh, and New York. Friedrich was also instrumental in getting her manuscript published. According to Dunham, it was apparently a very simple process: he merely recommended to Henry Holt that they publish it. In the meantime, she recounted, "He was courting me madly; he gave me these huge bouquets of flowers," bringing them to her apartment on South Grand Boulevard.[32]

Nelson Algren, Mary Fuji—a fellow student—Frank Yerby, and Robert Lucas, a well-known writer for radio, worked on the project. They employed anthropological research techniques, including participant observation. Yerby became an associate member of the Muhammadan sect, a group of "pure followers of Islam," who did not identify as Negro or "black."

Dunham's group investigated followers of Aimee Semple McPherson and Father Divine, as well as the Temples of Islam No. 1 and 2, founded in Detroit and Chicago, respectively. Bontemps wrote, "We discovered . . . that Katherine Dunham . . . had directed a bit of research toward a study of Negro cults in Chicago, and that this had led her writers to collect information about the groups that later became widely known as Black Muslims."[33] At that time, Dunham met Elijah Muhammad: "I have a special place with them [the Nation of Islam] because I knew Elijah Muhammad." During World War II, when members of Temple No. 2 refused the draft and Elijah Muhammad was arrested, all of Dunham's notes on the project disappeared from her file cabinet; at the same time, agents of the Federal Bureau of Investigation pressured her for information, which she refused to provide. She "lectured" the FBI on the reasons such cult groups are formed.[34]

The paths of Dunham and the Muslims crossed repeatedly during later years. Malcolm X, then known as "Big Red," called on her in her dressing room in 1947 before his conversion and while he was still a procurer. Even then, he was an impressive personage and expressed a "contempt for white men and their low-down ways."[35] On his way to Mecca in 1964, he stopped in Haiti, where he preached faith, discipline, and economic development.

The outcome of the project she supervised was a report, "The State of Cults among the Deprived," which she presented several years later (in 1948) at the Royal Anthropological Institute in London and also in Paris in 1949 and in Rio de Janeiro in 1950. In it she defined a deprived person as "one who has had taken from him some precious substance necessary to the wellbeing or to fulfillment of ones social role, or of some-

thing never possessed but which . . . is essential to the community structure, since to live life fully one must play a useful role for oneself and in
the community." Deprivation can result from refusing a group the opportunity "to consider itself an integral part of the community, or even
as part of the human race," or from dissolving a traditional way of life
while "withholding the values of the dominant culture."[36]

Dunham was very conscious of the negative effects of deprivation;
her work with Robert Redfield and her acquaintance with the "radical
humanism" of Erich Fromm influenced her perceptions, as did her discussions with Estimé. She applied the same theories years later, when
she established her cultural program in East St. Louis. She recalled her
explanation for the development of cults in the 1980s and 1990s, when a
series of disastrous encounters between officials and cult members—
including the disaster involving the Branch Davidians in Waco, Texas—
revealed the government officials' continuing lack of understanding of
these social phenomena.

Dunham has said that she was "tempted to become a writer" through
her work on the Federal Writers Project. She had been the class poet at
Joliet High and contributed to the *Child Life* magazine; she published
stories and articles in *Esquire* and other magazines, as well as books. But
the stage "became a physical and spiritual necessity" to her, and life as a
writer or as an academic would not satisfy her deep needs for communication to an audience.[37] Her involvement with the Federal Writers Project
may seem a detour from her attempts to form a dance company, but she
has explained that because her sign is Cancer, the sign of the crab, she
often travels sideways rather than straight ahead toward her goal. In this
case, the work with the WPA not only provided financial support but also
promoted the social activism that would set her and the Dunham Company apart from other dance groups.

When the dance component of the Federal Theatre Project was acti-
vated in Chicago, Dunham was prepared to produce dance programs based
on her Haitian research. According to Talley Beatty, before her work in
Haiti, the main discipline and practice was ballet: "then when she came
back from Haiti, she incorporated the Haitian material into the dances
and songs and into her concert presentations. . . . We did the *baule,* the
danse, the dance of the hips—[Congo] *paillette.* We did them purely at
first, but very simply, you know, she has this talent for cutting things to
the simplicity, the essence, that's so impressive to me."[38] Expertly done,
with trained dancers and with a complex understanding of the meaning
of the dances, their performances were well received by audiences and
critics.[39]

The performances earned Dunham an appointment as director of the Negro unit of the Chicago branch of the Federal Theatre Project group. She staged dances in several projects, including the Chicago productions of *Run Li'l Chil'lun, Swing Mikado,* and *Emperor Jones.* Ruth Page and Kurt and Grace Graff also participated in the Theatre Project, which had the avowed intent of developing dance as a form of theater. A dance that Dunham had presented to the Theatre Project, "L'Ag'Ya," was accepted and became part of the *Ballet Fedré* at the Great Northern Theater in 1938. The performance led Hallie Flanagan, the national director of the Theatre Project to make the following brief comment: "Katherine Dunham, a young choreographer of the Negro group, in *L'Ag'Ya* dealt with folk material from Martinique, shaping with authority the native grace of our Negro dancers."[40] Flanagan, a playwright and theater producer, was apparently unaware of the revolutionary aspect of this performance, in which a young African American woman, outside of the cultural center of New York City, choreographed a well-trained group of dancers. Flanagan was more impressed by the ballet *Frankie and Johnnie,* a performance by Ruth Page, to which she devoted several paragraphs in her memoirs. Her reference to the "native grace" of the Dunham dancers reveals the common misapprehension of the time, that African Americans were "born" dancers, that they did not require the difficult, intensive training that other dancers had to undergo. Dunham fought this misunderstanding throughout her career, as she struggled to produce disciplined, committed dancers and worked with students whose artistic expectations were not only low but often misguided as well.

In "L'Ag'Ya," Dunham combined Caribbean research with the thematic principle she had absorbed from Ludmilla Speranzeva, producing a ballet based on a tragic love triangle set in a village in Martinique; it included movements based on the martial arts of that country. Dunham wrote the script. She chose Henry Pitts, who later taught philosophy in a Kansas school, to play the lover, Alcide: "I thought he'd look terrific on the stage, and of course I was right."[41] Woody Wilson played Julot, the other member of the triangle. A critic for the *Chicago Daily News* described the dance: "L'Ag'Ya is . . . based upon the folklore of Martinique, and concerns love theft by witchcraft with a tragic and powerful ending. The real strength of the action lies in the long sustained dance in which Woody Wilson, aided by a Zombic charm, forces Miss Dunham (an exquisite figure) to yield him her clothing item by item until Henry Pitts, her rightful swain, suicidally intervenes. There is delightful movement throughout the ballet. John Pratt's costumes are brilliantly done."[42]

The group performing "L'Ag'Ya" included people off the street: maids, cooks, typists, and chauffeurs. Dunham perceived their presence as "solid and reassuring": "The non-professionals gave the stage the dimension of reality which made the folk myths believable." They were able to help bridge the cultural gap between the "hip swinging, shoulder shaking," and "lusty enjoyment" of the Martiniquan dances and the nervous stuffiness of churchgoing black Chicagoans.[43]

Central to the dance was the fight between the rivals, based on the martial arts of the Caribbean. Dunham had filmed such an encounter between sailors in Martinique. Tommy Gomez, who danced the role of Julot, the villain, on tour, had not seen the film, but viewing it later, he remarked that she had given them the feeling of the action, so that they were able to portray the duel with authenticity. It was a dangerous dance, he asserted; when the company danced it on tour, he sprained both thumbs when Vanoye Aikens, who was playing Alcide, threw him on his back.

Years later, Studs Terkel still remembered the "excitement" of the Dunham group in the performance, the "exquisite" Katherine Dunham and the "crazy, wonderful costumes" of John Pratt.[44] Pratt, who was to become Dunham's husband, was a graduate of the University of Chicago and the Chicago Art Institute; he had been active in Chicago's cultural life and was an intimate of Inez Cunningham Stark. Stark lectured on poetry and literature on the South Side and sponsored a poetry contest that the young poet Gwendolyn Brooks—future Pulitzer Prize–winning poet laureate of Illinois—won.[45] Dunham attended parties at Stark's North Side apartment, where she met the composers Prokofiev and Darius Milhaud and the actor Paul Schofield. She met John Pratt at a party at Schofield's home. Enchanted with Dunham, Pratt soon strayed from Stark. He became Dunham's partner and lover. "It was rare," Dunham wrote in her memoir, "for anyone to correct or criticize me in any of my creative [works] . . . or that I would listen and consent to changes. . . . He was someone special, someone with whom I could take wings and fly."[46] They achieved a "glowing fusion" in their creative partnership, begun in the Federal Theatre production, and they married in 1941.

John Pratt was an established artist and designer, collaborating with such dancers as Agnes de Mille and the Graffs. His father's family was descended from Enoch Pratt of Baltimore, who founded the first free library. His mother was related to the Balls of the Ball and Mason Jar Company, who endowed Ball State University.[47] After they married, Pratt's parents moved to Canada, where his father established political connections and published a newspaper. They returned to the United States in the early 1920s, where Pratt's father continued his career as a promoter and publisher.

Although there was a strong business orientation in the family, Pratt's mother was a musician—an accomplished organist and singer—and when the family moved to Chicago, she joined the Lake Shore Musical Society. An aunt sang and gave readings at Chautaqua events. Pratt's younger brother, Davis, also became a designer and taught art and design at Southern Illinois University at Carbondale.

Many among their family and acquaintances did not accept Pratt and Dunham's relationship: mixed marriages were not common. By virtue of his family background and his artistic accomplishments, Pratt was an established member of Chicago society; his marriage to Dunham was a sensation to many of his peers. Annette and Albert Dunham opposed the marriage, especially Annette, who was shocked by what she felt was the impropriety of the relationship. She gradually came to accept Pratt as a son-in-law, and they became close. He visited her and cared for her during her illnesses when Dunham was performing, and he was with her at the time of her death.

Dunham would only wear costumes designed by Pratt; he also designed her street clothes. Eartha Kitt spoke of other company members' envy of the "beautiful clothes Miss Dunham always had": "Handknitted tights, with a hand-knitted sweater to match, or a skirt and blouse effect with long tights underneath. She always looked like the essence of success to me. Her husband, Mr. John Pratt, was always there, cheering her on, seeing that she dressed properly, making new clothes for her, or maybe just for moral support."[48] Bernard Berenson, with whom Dunham shared a long friendship, reflected on her couture in his memoirs; he did not, however, acknowledge the originator but instead resorted to stereotypes: "Katherine Dunham, looking like an Egyptian queen, like Queen Ti, dressed in stuff that clings to her . . . draping rather than clothing her. Whence this sureness of color and its creative use, bold, and not negative as in most of us, that seems a birthright of the Blacks? . . . Katherine Dunham is herself a work of art, a fanciful arabesque in all her movements and a joy to the eye in color."[49]

Dunham recognized the critical importance of Pratt's designs to her stage presence and was always insistent that his contribution be recognized. Her respect extended to the work of other costume designers; her handwritten note on a program layout for a 1987 opening of a performing arts center at Buffalo State College strongly advised recognizing the costume designer.

The artistic alliance with Pratt had deep roots in Dunham's childhood fascination with theater and costume and her interest in the details of Caribbean ritual and social dress, which culminated in her theatrical dance performances. The costumes of "L'Ag'Ya," though imaginatively conceived by Pratt, included authentic hats, designs, and materials she had brought back from the Caribbean. The movements, including the fighting dance for which the ballet is named, were based on her field observations in Martinique. The union of art, theater, dance, and text, validated and realized through their marriage, was the powerhouse that carried the Dunham Company through world tours for thirty years of successful professional performance that irrevocably altered the character of dance theater.[50]

The response of Chicago critics to "L'Ag'Ya" was more effusive than Flanagan's; after briefly mentioning the compositions of the Graffs and Berta Ochsner, a *Chicago Tribune* reporter commented, "Miss Dunham's dance drama, "L'Ag'Ya" carried off the evening's first honors. Her large troupe of colored dancers moved with admirable ease and lack of affectation. John Pratt's handsome tropical costumes and Robert Sanders' pointed and danceable score shared the distinction of Miss Dunham's choreography."[51] The reviewer in the *Chicago Daily News* echoed this assessment: "The Ballet Fedré, presented by the dancers of the Federal Theater at the Great Northern last night turned out to be a program of five ballets, all clamorously received by a sold-out house. The show was clearly stolen, however, by "L'Ag'Ya," a fiery folk ballet from Martinique, choreography by Katherine Dunham . . . and an excellent score by Robert Sanders of the University of Chicago music department.[52] Another writer in the *Tribune* called her "[o]ne of the most important and aggressive artistic geniuses of Chicago";[53] and a commentator on a subsequent performance sponsored by the Urban League wrote in the *Chicago Defender:* "Few of us will ever see enough of this great artist and somewhere in the recesses of collective consciousness . . . lurks always the fear . . . we are enjoying in borrowed time a contribution intended for world acclaim."[54] The prediction reveals the clear understanding in the African American community of the scope of Dunham's achievement.

Although Dunham's material was Caribbean, she was already moving away from the simple, "pure" folk material toward the development of a basic technique. In a 1938 interview, she stated that while early on she had aimed to present "ordinary folk material," now she planned to develop a system of "primitive pattern" that would be as articulate as "anything either modern or classical."[55] Dunham technique was evolving, and with it, a praxis that would reflect the complex and diverse society in which she lived, as well as the international world in which that society made its influence felt. While incorporating Caribbean materials, her work was becoming universal in scope, and it was in the spirit of the Federal Theatre Project that extolled the variety of cultural expressions and the ambitions of a nation.

Interestingly, it was the women commenting on her work—Consuelo Young-Megahy in the *Chicago Defender* and June Provines in the *Tribune*—who responded to and remarked on the strength of her drive for perfection. They could fully appreciate her achievement as a black woman and what it entailed in personal effort and sacrifice.[56]

The immediate goal of the Federal Theatre Project was to employ people on relief; the long-term goal was, in Flanagan's words, "[t]o set up theatres which have possibilities of growing into social institutions in the communities in which they are located . . . and to lay the foundation for the development of a truly creative theatre in the United States with outstanding producing centers in each of those regions which have common interests as a result of geography, language origins, history, tradition, custom, occupations of the people."[57] The aim was a theater of the people, with little or no admission charged. A program of the *Ballet Fedré* announced three price ranges: twenty-five cents, fifty cents, and eighty-three cents.[58]

While the aims of the Federal Theatre Project were lofty—to produce "free, adult, uncensored" theater, according to Hopkins's stipulation—politicians and moralists felt threatened by the social realities portrayed in drama. Throughout its duration, various productions were closed, were never produced, or were undermined through administrative decisions because individuals or organizations objected to the political or moral content. The watchdogs objected to *Big White Fog*, by Theodore Ward, which dramatized a Chicago labor dispute in which some characters advocated a merger of black and white labor for their mutual benefit. This was seen as a potential danger to race relations, since integration was not an accepted doctrine at the time, and Flanagan had to fight to get the play produced in Chicago. After a run of less than two months, local Federal Theatre Project authorities transferred it to a black neighborhood school, supposedly to encourage more black attendance, but it soon closed from lack of support. *Model Tenement*, a play by Meyer Levin that showed some of the problems of landlord-tenant relations, was never produced, nor was *Liberty Deferred*, by Abram Hill and John Silvera, a historical account of African Americans based on factual cases. *Black Empire*, by Christine Ames and Clarke Painter, which portrayed Haitians and their religion in a negative light, was staged, while Langston Hughes's more thoughtful *Troubled Island* was not.[59]

Standard works produced with all-black casts were very popular, though. These included *Swing Mikado*, based on the Gilbert and Sullivan operetta, and Orson Welles's "voodoo" *Macbeth*, in which the Haitian president Henri Christophe was represented as a black Macbeth. Canada Lee played Christophe, Archie Savage was among the dancers, and William Grant Still composed the music. *Macbeth* was a production by the Harlem unit, led by John Houseman and Rose McClendon, who, before her early death, was the best-known black actress of the time. When, in 1938, Katherine Dunham attempted to create a ballet based on the life of Henri Christophe, with music by Still, she was discouraged from doing so because of Welles's *Macbeth*. What surely would have been a more authentic presentation was rejected, while a European interpretation of African American experience was embraced by cultural "authorities."

Dunham staged and choreographed *Tropical Pinafore*, which was one of the many Gilbert and Sullivan takeoffs that were produced, along with *Swing Mikado* and *Hot Mikado*. *Tropical Pinafore*, produced by the American Negro Light Opera Association of Chicago, opened in March 1940. John Pratt designed costumes for both *Pinafore* and the Chicago production of *Swing Mikado;* the latter employed Dunham dancers as well. Dunham also choreographed the Chicago presentations of *Run Li'l Chil'lun* and *The Emperor Jones*. *Swing Mikado* was so successful in Chicago that it was taken to New York. Some of the adjectives critics used to describe the Chicago production indicate its fresh and spirited character and reflect the high quality of the work: "startlingly good," "gorgeous," "a colored convulsion," "sultry," "endlessly alive," "superb," "electrifying."[60] Dunham's touch and the skilled Dunham dancers, as well as the imaginative character of John Pratt's costumes, doubtless contributed to the effects.

Despite the positive reviews of the Dunham performances, Dunham had to struggle to keep the company together. Her goal was to establish a permanent group under her direction; but after the *Ballet Fedré*, she was released from her contract, and her dancers were put into other productions, such as *Swing Mikado*, under white direction, a move she did not endure without protest. Ignoring the bureaucratic hierarchy, she went directly to the top, thus establishing a protocol for her subsequent artistic and social projects. She tried to arrange a hearing with Eleanor Roosevelt about the unfairness of a situation in which Ruth Page and the Graffs were kept as directors of intact units while her group was dispersed to be absorbed into other productions as needed. She also wrote to Mary McLeod Bethune, then head of the National Youth Administration, asking her to bring the matter up with Hallie Flanagan, and to Arthur Mitchell, an Illinois congressman, saying, "The tremendous success of the ballets, produced under great difficulties, the widespread community interest, as well as the interest of the dancers themselves, convinced me that this unit had the same justification for continuing as the white units under white directors . . . those people who should rightfully be training in the dance as are the white units have been separated through other projects in which they have a very minor part and very minor interest. They are dancers and they want to dance." She asserted that productions directed and danced by African Americans were "vitally important to the community," and she cited the tenets of the WPA, insisting that the dancers be given the full benefits of working on a dignified basis.[61] While the policies of the federal programs reflected the racial biases of the times, the careers of individual black artists were undeniably advanced by the federal productions.

As a result of the success of "L'Ag'Ya," Dunham and her group were invited to participate in the 1939 Broadway production of *Pins and Needles.* Louis Schaefer, who was production manager of *Pins and Needles,* came to Chicago and saw the group perform at the Goodman Theatre. A rival to the popular *Swing Mikado* in New York, *Pins and Needles* was first presented on the Labor Stage by the International Ladies' Garment Workers Union. Its popularity resulted in three productions: one performance in 1936, a long run in 1937, and then, moving to Broadway in 1939, it became, in the words of one critic, "the most popular musical of the decade."[62] It was a light antifascist satire. Mary McCarthy wrote that although the actors were "clearly proletarians," it was the creation of a union that had "made its peace with the New Deal."[63]

Dunham took part of her company to New York for the production of *New Pins and Needles,* in which she employed New York dancers as extras: "I tried to use out-of-work people in New York in *Pins and Needles* rather than the Cotton Club crowd."[64] One of the numbers she choreographed was "Bertha the Sewing Machine Girl."

Talley Beatty recalled, "Dunham got us sent to New York to [appear in] a show called *Pins and Needles,* three of us: a girl by the name of— her name was Lily May Butler then—Carmencita Romero. And Roberta McLauren. And we were in the chorus of extras in *Pins and Needles* while Miss Dunham prepared her first concert—that sensational concert at which she did *Tropics* and *Le Jazz Hot.*"[65] Carmencita Romero and Roberta McLauren were with the company for only a short time. Romero went on to teach and perform in the Latin style after she left the company. McLauren, according to Lucille Ellis, was a beautiful, streetwise black woman with an African body, the type Dunham admired, but she was "crazy," with a violent temper.[66] She did not fulfill her promise as a dancer and eventually became a nurse.

While Dunham was in New York, she left part of the company in Chicago. When she returned to choreograph *Tropical Pinafore*, Lucille Ellis and Tommy Gomez joined the group. Ellis recalled, "I didn't audition, she asked me to come up on the stage."[67] Dunham returned to New York, leaving part of her company to perform in *Tropical Pinafore*, which had a six-week run.

The versions of classics that employed black artists were excellently done, but they challenged few stereotypes. An exception to the pattern of white productions in black face, Hall Johnson's *Run Li'l Chil'lun* was written, directed, and performed by African Americans. It included African-influenced dance and music—Dunham choreographed and staged the 1938 Chicago performance—and was "overwhelmingly 'authenticated' by the black community," according to one writer: "[*Run Li'l Chil'lun*] contributed enormously to black consciousness, dignity, and pride. . . . Hall Johnson . . . contributed positively to the dawn of white understanding and greatly enhanced white respect for black capabilities. . . . In the crucial decades preceding The Supreme Court's historic decision on desegregation, such positive influences on white public opinion cannot be discounted."[68]

African American music and dance played transformative roles in U.S. society from early beginnings. Black minstrels, vaudeville performers, and Broadway productions and performances by such artists as Noble Sissle and Eubie Blake, Miller and Lyles, James P. Johnson, Rosamunde Johnson, Florence Mills and Josephine Baker, Bill Robinson, and Bert Williams had acquainted white audiences and critics with superb black artists. However, for the most part, they did not truly acknowledge the genius and artistry of the participants, nor did they realize the disciplined craft of these performances or those in the popular Federal Theatre presentations.[69] White audiences and critics generally were not receptive to black-produced dramatic productions and choreography. Thus, the significance of such creations as "L'Ag'Ya" and *Run Li'l Chil'lun* was not fully recognized by many writers and critics. Nevertheless, the seeds for the later blossoming of black drama as well as dance were planted in the Federal Theatre projects.[70]

The Federal Theatre Project came to an end in 1939 as a result of activities by the House Committee on Un-American Activities, which spread alarm—for the most part, unfounded—about communist infiltration into the projects, as well as through the lack of support by other members of Congress. Despite a groundswell of support by artists, critics, and producers, the program was a convenient scapegoat for dissatisfaction about spending on federal programs and fears of racial integration.

The idea of a theater for the people was too threatening and idealistic for some politicians; however, it, like other artists' projects that were also soon to be cut, spawned a generation of creative output and influenced the course of American cultural development.

The most important outcome of Dunham's work in *Pins and Needles* was that it gave her artistic freedom to prepare for her entry into the New York dance scene: the 1940 appearance on the Labor Stage at the Windsor Theater, arranged by her manager, Mary Hunter. Because of union restrictions, there were no Sunday performances of *Pins and Needles* so Schaefer allowed the Dunham Company to hold stage performances on Sunday. Since these were not included in the contract, there were no union difficulties. Most of the materials in the Sunday performances had been presented in Chicago, but they were reworked, and new dancers had to be trained. Responses to the opening rewarded the hard work that went into the preparation. John Martin, then a new dance reviewer at the *New York Times*, referred to it as "a good show" and recognized the importance of the performance: "That it is basically something far more significant does not in any way interfere with its sprightly and vivacious surface values." He continued, "She has actually isolated the element of a folk art upon which more consciously creative and sophisticated forms can be built as time goes on. This is cultural pioneering of a unique sort." He was intrigued by the anthropological basis of the works: "Miss Dunham has composed a primitive ritual in a somewhat mythological vein and has graduated her material from this point through rituals that are for the release of personal tensions in primitive and semi-primitive societies down to the jazz and swing variants of those same impulses that are current in sophisticated communities. This sounds tremendously anthropological and 'important,' and it is; but it is also debonair and delightful, not to say daring and erotic." Martin singled out Archie Savage for praise: "He can not only dance like a house afire but he is a good actor and a genuine stage personality." John Pratt's costumes were described as "beautifully effective and ingenious," and the program "well staged." Martin applauded the fact that a series of further performances was to be given.[71]

Martin judged the dance group as "handsome and competent," but he criticized Talley Beatty for introducing ballet technique into the ethnic materials. In his generally positive critique of the Dunham Company, he continued to object when he believed the balletic element was too intrusive, especially when the company returned to New York after tours in Europe. It was if he had decided to categorize black dance as "ethnic" and to rule out any overt European influence.[72] This way of thinking was common in American criticism of African American artists; it was less pronounced in Europe, where perhaps audiences and critics were more cosmopolitan and did not share the cultural psyche that spawned the minstrel show.

Talley Beatty, who became a noted choreographer in his own right, recognized the impact of the Dunham Company on New York theater: "Dance changed on Broadway when Dunham came." But he felt that she was not given sufficient recognition, then or later.[73] No further contracts were awarded after the performance.

When *Pins and Needles* closed, Dunham took the group back to Chicago to join the dancers who had remained there. Lucille Ellis recalled that she "came back with a few of her New York group with her . . . Carmencita, and of course Roberta, Talley, and, yes, Lavinia [Williams] was from New York. Tommy and I entered into the true training then. We worked in Chicago for awhile . . . we had the Auditorium building, which was part of the University. Then we opened the night club at the Sherman Hotel."[74] Dunham persuaded the Sherman management to present her dancers in the company of Duke Ellington and other more traditional nightclub shows. The unconventional nature of this engagement was revealed by the management's reluctance to allow them to dance barefoot. Ever the pragmatist when it came to the survival of her troupe, Dunham solved the problem by offering to paint sandals on their feet. These were the first of many night club appearances, which extended the reputation of the Dunham Company far beyond that enjoyed by most dance groups and allowed it to continue as a dance company in a society that did not generally support dance.

After the excitement and triumph of New York performances, the return to Chicago was experienced as something of an anticlimax. Although "L'Ag'Ya" and other presentations had been critical successes, Dunham was disappointed by the Chicago cultural establishment's general lack of support. Nevertheless, she saw the early period in Chicago as "impressionable years"; anthropology receded into the background of her life, "diminished by the stirrings of a desire to create something new and wonderful, to include myself in it, and to make of it something permanent."[75] During those years, much of the company repertoire was created: "Rara Tonga," with Polynesian themes and movements that reflected the influence of Margaret Mead; "Barrelhouse"; and Dunham as the "Woman with a Cigar" (later included in *Tropical Excursions*), along with other dances, were presented at the College Room at the Sherman Hotel. Archie Savage's "New York street savvy" was influential in the creation of "Barrelhouse," based on a Florida shimmy. Such Americana as "Bre'r

Rabbit an' the Tah Baby," recalling stories her father had told her, "Cake-walk," and plantation squares—with a bow to Noble Sissle, who had taken her to Harlem to learn the dances from "old Tom Fletcher" in 1939—were presented at the Goodman Theatre, along with "Rara Tonga" and *Le Jazz Hot*, in which "Barrelhouse" appeared. When Dunham's parents attended a performance, Annette Dunham was shocked by "Barrelhouse" and tried to persuade Dunham not to perform it.

Papa Augustine, a Haitian drummer and consultant who also occasionally danced, became an important member of the company during this period. He believed that the sacred drums Dunham brought back from Haiti had been played by too many people from other places with different religions. Since Damballa was known to be a jealous god, he sacrificed a white rooster to Damballa before a performance at the Goodman. He was one of many Haitians with whom Dunham maintained a long-lasting creative collaboration.

Mary Hunter, who was the director of the Cube Theatre and a niece of the anthropologist Mary Austin, was acquainted with George Balanchine and suggested he attend one of Dunham's Chicago performances. Dunham recalled, "He and Vernon Duke came and saw us at the . . . Goodman Theatre. . . . They didn't waste any time getting us signed up. Louis Schaefer was slightly hurt: I would be going into a typical Broadway show instead of putting the [entire] Company into *Pins and Needles* or something new for the Labor stage."[76] They signed onto *Cabin in the Sky*.

Cabin in the Sky, originally entitled *Little Joe*, was, according to Lucille Ellis, the vehicle for integrating the Chicago and New York dancers into one group: "With *Cabin in the Sky*, we all became a full company." *Cabin* opened in 1940 on Broadway with an all-black cast, including Ethel Waters as Petunia, the virtuous wife; Dooley Wilson as her wandering husband; Katherine Dunham as Georgia Brown, the temptress; and Rex Ingram as Lucifer Jr. According to a biographer of Balanchine, "Balanchine put more of himself into *Cabin in the Sky* than any other [Broadway] show he did."[77] He put his own savings into it and staged the entire production. According to the same source, he choreographed the show; however, in an interview, Balanchine revealed an ambiguity in the artistic credit: "What is the use of inventing a series of movements which are a white man's idea of a Negro's walk or stance or slouch? I only needed to indicate a disposition of dancers on the stage. The rest almost improvised itself."[78] His statement reflects the common view of African American movement as "natural" to black dancers, as well as a situation that was not uncommon in Broadway shows at the time: black dancers choreographed numbers for which either white choreographers were credited or else no one was listed as choreographer.[79] As Dunham remembered it, Balanchine gave her artistic freedom in the dance sequences and identified her as joint choreographer. Also, she staged most of the show, although she was not given credit for this. Tommy Gomez recalled, "He [Balanchine] had never worked with black dancers before . . . he was from the Bolshoi. . . . He couldn't quite get into the mood of the show. It ended up with Miss D helping him. And finally he bowed out and Miss Dunham did the choreography for the show. I think she got the credit, too."[80] In his memoirs, Sol Hurok, who became the group's impresario following the tour of *Cabin*, referred to Dunham's "enormous success as actress, singer, dancer *and dance director*" in *Cabin*.[81]

Another Balanchine biographer, the dancer Don McDonagh, noted that in *Cabin* Balanchine had a cast of "trained black dancers" so that he approached his task differently than in the opera *Aida*, for which he "had created a sensual ballet based on black dance movement that he recast for his white dancers' abilities." Appraising Balanchine's strategy in *Cabin*, McDonagh reported, "The approach succeeded, as the company was praised for its lack of self-consciousness and its intense projection. The leaping smoothness of the men was singled out, as were the fluent arms of the women. Dunham, in particular, as the wicked Georgia Brown drew praise for her brilliant 'somewhat orgiastic' dancing."[82]

Describing the significance of *Cabin*, McDonagh seemed, in a rather backhanded way, to confirm Beatty's assessment of Dunham's impact on Broadway: "Balanchine's direction [of *Cabin*] was praised and the door was opened for the professional director-choreographer. In the next three decades, Jerome Robbins, Agnes De Mille, Michael Kidd, Michael Bennett, Bob Fosse, and Gower Champion would use the position brilliantly."[83] Years later, at the premier showing of *Divine Drumbeats*, the PBS *Great Performances* documentary of Dunham's career, Balanchine sent a congratulatory telegram. However, neither he nor other director-choreographers, with the exception of Agnes de Mille, publicly credited her role in the integration of dance into the Broadway musical. Throughout her professional career, Dunham experienced the lack of recognition with which many black artists have had to struggle.

Despite the success of *Cabin in the Sky*, Dunham and Pratt had originally reacted negatively to the script, which was superficial in its treatment of racial matters and contained negative stereotypes of African American life. But Al Smart of *Esquire*, their friend and colleague, asked, "Who are we to criticize success?" Although the company had previously experienced artistic success, now, for the first time, it was beginning to enter into the business of commercial entertainment, and Dunham had to become an entrepreneur so it could survive.

With popular success came requests for help from many people and for many causes. Al Smart warned her, "There are so many sycophants in the world who want to flatter and attach themselves to anyone who's moving forward, that it takes a pretty stable person with a background of tough sledding to combat it."[84] Many of the solicitations, such as for benefits for the Rosenwald Foundation, the Actors' Fund, a Harlem children's fresh air fund, and a foundling home, were worthwhile, while others were merely demands for money or favors by individuals.

It was when Dunham decided to perform in *Cabin in the Sky* that she fully realized she would have to give up the idea of becoming an academic anthropologist.[85] In asking her to review a study of dance for the *American Anthropologist,* Adeline (Mrs. Ralph) Linton inquired if she was abandoning her academic interest, which Linton felt brought authenticity to her work.[86] Although Dunham felt some conflict and even guilt about the decision not to complete her graduate work, she learned subsequently that most of her mentors approved of her dance career as it developed and appreciated her way of doing anthropology. Continuing professional recognition included an invitation from Yale for a lecture-demonstration; and Franziska Boas, Franz Boas's daughter who was also a dance instructor, invited her to serve as a discussant for a seminar in which Geoffrey Gorer, Harold Courlander, Franz Boas, and Cora Du Bois, among other distinguished scholars, presented papers on "The Function of Dance in Human Societies." She remarked that Dunham would likely bring up points these anthropologists would overlook.[87] Erich Fromm, who was establishing the Department of Psychiatry at Columbia University, introduced her to his circle of intellectual friends, which provided another intellectual outlet for her.[88]

Working with Balanchine in *Cabin in the Sky* resulted in career boosts for other company members as well. He offered Beatty, Gomez, and Arthur Mitchell, who studied at the Dunham School, scholarships to the American Ballet School. They were the only black dancers enrolled. Gomez recalled, "It was the finest school in America and the classes were always packed. It was so crowded, the students would come in and put a towel on the barre and claim that particular space. . . . Everybody was in the classroom on time, waiting before the class started for the teacher." Their ballet teacher was Russian and spoke nothing but Russian and French. "We hadn't been anywhere and didn't know anything," Gomez continued. "But that was a great thing for us, to have Balanchine get us a start at the American School."[89]

The company went on the road with *Cabin*, taking it to the West Coast. Gomez described the theatrical rituals of the times: "All the shows, when they closed on Broadway, they'd go to the Coast. And they had special show trains for the cast, who would occupy the whole train. The company had our own car and we'd meet in the dining car and there'd be drinking and parties—great, great fun!"[90] At the end of the tour, the company stayed in California and performed at clubs and in a series of movies. In Dunham's words, "We did these things to hold it together."[91]

Dunham's association with film, both from the production and the performance standpoints, had remained strong since she had filmed "L'Ag'Ya," the beguine, the calenda, and other dances during her first field trip to the Caribbean. A film scholar and critic described these first attempts:

> I am impressed with Dunham's eye for broad dance movements as well as for individual phrasing and nuance. Long shots of recurring theme statements and transitions of a line of male dancers precede close-ups of foot, arm, and hand movements. And even though the drums are inaudible, the beat is clearly depicted as heads, torsos, and shoulders counterpoint the rhythms of the feet and legs. Frames explode with percussive movement, whirls, leaps. The pans show indispensable complements of people, architecture and place. . . . Throughout these films Dunham communicated to us a sense of time and space uniquely Haitian, Jamaican, Trinidadian.[92]

The films were valuable in developing her choreography, as well as in teaching students. She continued to film religious rituals, bullfights, and dances in Brazil, Sicily, Barcelona, and Colombia.

Dunham's relationship with the commercial film industry began in 1941, when Warner Brothers Studio made a film of the company performing her choreography. *Carnival of Rhythm* was a twenty-minute film of Brazilian music and dance, in which she had considerable control over the production. In *Stormy Weather* (Twentieth Century–Fox), which starred Lena Horne and Bill Robinson, she appeared with members of her company; she executed a dramatic and sensual ballet while descending a ramp. Elaborate scenes of descending stars and choruses were common in Hollywood musicals of the time, but Dunham's projection of emotion and sexuality electrified the scene, introducing a new spirit into the routine. Her stage persona, expressing inner-focused and poised sensuality, was fully developed, and the spirits of DéGrasse and Téoline seem to hover nearby.

Other Dunham dancers who appeared in *Stormy Weather* were Talley Beatty, Janet Collins, Lenwood Morris, Tommy Gomez, Lucille Ellis, Lavinia Williams, and Syvilla Fort.[93] Dunham appeared in the film revue *Star Spangled Rhythm* (Paramount), along with Eddie ("Rochester") Anderson, Bing Crosby, Bob Hope, Dorothy Lamour, Veronica Lake, Alan Ladd, Paulette Goddard, and many other Hollywood stars. This was one of the patriotic movies produced during World War II. She also choreographed dance interludes in *Pardon My Sarong* (Universal), starring Bud Abbott and Lou Costello with Dorothy Lamour. Her anthropological background was again called upon, since, like "Rara Tonga," it was set in the South Pacific. She choreographed or played minor roles in *Casbah; Green Mansions*, with Audrey Hepburn and Anthony Perkins; and *The Bible*, starring Peter O'Toole, Ava Gardner, and Charles Heston and directed by John Huston. She choreographed *Mambo* for Sylvano Mangano, who, Dunham said, "had no rhythm," and *Botta e riposta*, a Franco-Italian film starring Fernandel, as well as at least one film in Mexico (see appendix B).[94]

Dunham was also a trailblazer in television. The Dunham Company was the first dance group to air an hour-long broadcast, on NBC in 1940. It also performed on Australian, Canadian, and European national broadcasts.

The film scholar Roy Thomas maintained that while Dunham's involvement with commercial film was limited, the totality of her impact on the world of film places her in the vanguard of dance filmmaking. He believed that her anthropological background caused her to involve more of herself in the act of filming: "This involvement, I contend, enhances rather than diminishes the value and use of film because the film-maker responds affectively to those projections emanating from the people being filmed. . . . Here is a way of seeing with a heightened sense of expectancy, even epiphany. . . . Such looking almost always leads to the discovery of new worlds, new truths about the human condition and physical universe. It is at this point that I locate Dunham with her camera transporting us to the interiors of dance in the human experience."[95]

While the company was on the West Coast, it appeared with Pierre Monteux and the San Francisco Symphony Orchestra. Paquita Anderson, the company's pianist, transcribed the music and rehearsed it with the orchestra, a task that was not completed until shortly before the performance.[96] The company also appeared with the Los Angeles Symphony. Dunham always worked with top-flight musicians and composers and carried symphony arrangements on tour, for times when orchestras were available. She has a worksheet on a tango with music composed by

Stravinsky that was never produced. Balanchine introduced her to the composer during one of his Chicago visits prior to the *Cabin in the Sky* production. This was only the first of many collaborations with musicians; others included Heitor Villa-Lobos, the Brazilian composer; Mario Castelnuovo-Tedesco, the Italian composer; and the jazz guitarist Django Reinhardt.

Lucille Ellis remembered that it was in San Francisco that Lenwood Morris, who became ballet master, joined them, sent by Archie Savage, with whom he was working in Los Angeles. The company remained in San Francisco for several months: "We were working in little clubs there in the Bay Area. She [Dunham] was choreographing and sustaining us; we were not working, and so she was writing and selling articles, and that is how we lived. We stayed together, all in one house." People were generous: "they would get something from just watching us, and they would want to help out. So then we would meet friends and have dinner parties, and that helped a lot."[97]

From Dunham's perspective, their stay in San Francisco was an exhilarating time, during which she associated with many prominent people. The United Nations held its first meeting while they were there, taking over the San Francisco Opera House, where the company was appearing. They had to move across the Bay to a movie house, which had a smaller capacity; Walter Winchell complained that he had to sit in a chair with the orchestra. The Russian ambassador Georgy Malenkov invited her to a party and insisted that she come.

The Dunham Company appeared in nearby Carmel, where Langston Hughes was staying. Hughes and James P. Johnson had asked Dunham to choreograph a Negro folk opera and had sent her a libretto the previous year. This was the first of several proposed joint projects with the poet that never materialized, most likely because there were no producers interested in dramatic works by black artists. Hughes, in a letter to Arna Bontemps dated July 4, 1941, wrote that he was "rushing off to San Francisco to see Katherine Dunham about some movie shorts."[98] In October of the same year, Bontemps informed Hughes that he had seen *Carnival of Rhythm*, calling it a "beautiful picture," and he asked Hughes to pass on his compliments to "Katherine et al."[99] It was presumably around this time that Hughes arranged for the company to appear in Carmel, since by the following January, he was in New York.

Ruth Beckford joined the company while it was performing in California. She recalled meeting Dunham at a performance of *Cabin* in San Francisco, as a high school student. She was asked to demonstrate her talent before the entire company, and, after three weeks of intensive practice, she was invited to join the group on a tour through the Northwest to Canada.[100] The tour was arranged and managed by the impresario Sol Hurok. The company, now seasoned and with a reputation for lighting up the stage and energizing audiences, was an attractive proposition for the impresario, who handled artists of many genres, including the singers Blanche Thebom, Marian Anderson, and Jan Peerce; the guitarist Andres Segovia; the violinist Isaac Stern; the Gypsy dancer Carmen Amaya; and the Russian Ballet Theatre. Hurok wrote that when Dunham came under his management, she had a company of dancers "superbly trained by herself" and a production repertoire "with ingeniously economical sets and costumes designed by her artist husband, John Pratt." He noted that the company performed under such contrasting venues as nightclubs and opera houses: "Such is the ambivalence of her art, that she performed 'Barrelhouse' number both in San Francisco's Art Museum and in Chicago's Chez Paree, to the rousing applause of both audiences."[101] He recognized her struggle to keep the company afloat: "She had shuttled between concert and night club with her troupe in the effort to keep the company together, for she held herself responsible for their livelihood whether she had work for them or not." He saw them perform in New York and, impressed by their professionalism and versatility, he determined to "routine her repertoire, which was still for the most part new to New York, into a revue which would be acceptable both on Broadway and the road as a theatrical production, and which could be toured in the concert halls as well."[102]

During the first year the company toured with Hurok, he supported a band of musicians and John Pratt's elaborate costumes and stage settings. During the second season, they had a full orchestra, but then Hurok began to pare down on expenses. After a season of lavish productions, Dunham realized that, in her words, "he'd send us out with half an orchestra the second year and the third year, a piano and two curtains." She told him he would be deceiving the public if he presented the company under scaled-down conditions. "We have a certain reputation I have to keep up," she declared. The company was respected and admired by other professional dance companies he would be bringing in, she informed him, so that such economies would in the long run be harmful to his image.[103] Rather than compromise the integrity of performances, she persuaded him to let her buy out her contract. It was the first time he had done this; they haggled over the price and finally settled on $25,000. It took her two years to pay it off, but she felt it was worth it. She believed in herself and what she was attempting to do: to maintain a dance group with the highest professional standing, not to be an "exotic" seven-day wonder. Later she told an interviewer that Hurok stressed sex in their performances, which no doubt contributed to the popularity of the group in the United States but was unsatisfactory from Dunham's perspective. The narrow focus on sexuality was incompatible with her artistic aims, which incorporated the erotic in larger themes of life and death.[104]

The program for *Tropical Revue*—the outcome of Hurok's "routinization" in 1943–44—was the model for later Dunham Company shows. They opened with the lively Latin American and Caribbean dances for which the group was noted. In the second part, dramatic ballets telling a story, such as "Rites de Passage" or "L'Ag'Ya," were presented in the *chauve souris* tradition. The finale would usually consist of Americana, such as plantation dances, spirituals, and American popular or social dances.

Tropical Revue was on Broadway for three months; it began as a two-week engagement, then was extended, but was finally forced off Broadway by a theater shortage. The critical response in New York and on tour was overwhelmingly positive. After a "layover," during which the company appeared in clubs and small theaters, it opened in *Carib Song* in Broadway's Adelphi Theater for a two-month run. According to Eartha Kitt, "It was a love story with music. Dunham sang, danced, and acted."[105] The program was not the standard Broadway fare and did not enjoy the same success as *Tropical Revue*; the company went back to the revue format with *Bal Nègre*, which opened at the New York Belasco Theatre in late 1946. The ballet "Shango," which was introduced in *Carib Song*, was retained in *Bal Nègre* and became an audience favorite.

While on tour with Hurok, John Pratt was drafted into the army, and Dunham assumed charge of the costumes and sets, in addition to directing the company. She had members take on the responsibility for costumes, each in charge of a set of items, such as shoes, jewelry, and hats. Pratt was discharged in 1946, in time to join the company for the *Bal Nègre* production.

Between Broadway productions, the company appeared in such clubs as Chez Paree in Chicago, where Joe ("Ziggy") Johnson worked with them on jazz dance; El Rancho Hotel and the Trocadero in Las Vegas; and Ciro's in Hollywood, where it appeared frequently through the years.

Dunham choreographed *Windy City*, which was presented at the Shubert Theatre in Chicago in 1947. The producer asked her to translate into choreography "the people of State street" in Chicago: "Its racetrack following burlesque stars, cheap cabaret entertainers and petty grifters—have the same easy-going cat-like vitality as the back-country Cuban Billys and Haitians whose dances Katherine Dunham studies and brought back to American theatre-goers for their amazement."[106] The ballet was not a popular success, a fact that contributed to the negative view Dunham sometimes expresses about her birth city. Apparently Chicago audiences were not attuned to its social insights and preferred more exotic settings. Many years later, Jerome Robbins reportedly remarked that his choreography for *West Side Story* owed much to *Windy City*.[107]

In the meantime, Dunham choreographed *Bal Nègre*, described by Eartha Kitt as "one of Dunham's spectacular revues," following the same three-part pattern as in *Tropical Revue*. It opened with an overture by Gilberto Valdes, based on Afro-Cuban themes; performers listed were Kitt, Jean Leon Destine, Mariam Burton, and the Sans-Souci Singers. The second part of the overture was the Haitian "Congo Paillette," performed by Katherine Dunham, Lenwood Morris, and the Dunham Company. After a group of Caribbean dances, the company performed "L'Ag'Ya" as the dramatic part of the performance and then concluded with Americana, with Lucille Ellis dancing "Kansas City Woman," and some vignettes showing intercultural encounters ("Two Lady Tourists") and historical settings ("Havana—1910"). After a nine-month tour, *Bal Nègre* was presented at the Belasco Theatre in New York. It was this production that attracted European producers, leading to the first European tour; it also resulted in an invitation by Doris Duke, the tobacco heiress, to appear in Mexico, under contract with Teatro Americano.

Fighting Prejudice

North American audiences and critics were intrigued and entranced by the Dunham Company's artistic and skillful portrayal of what were viewed as "exotic" materials. But despite the company's success, its members constantly encountered the closed social system that existed throughout the country before the civil rights movement. The problems with discrimination that had plagued Dunham in Chicago continued throughout the tours, with the added problem of having to find suitable living quarters. In New York, Erich Fromm had arranged for Dunham to stay in an apartment leased by Harry Stack Sullivan, who was out of town. However, there was no heat during the freezing New York winter. She built a fire in the fireplace, but since she knew nothing about drafts, the apartment filled with smoke.

Throughout the country—from New York to Hollywood, as well as in the southern states—Dunham and her company found hotels and rehearsal halls closed to them. "You think it will be better the farther north you go . . . or that an art colony [such as Carmel], will be more liberal. But it is not true," she commented.[108] In some hotels, the company was housed on a certain floor that was set aside for "colored people." Some hotels that would accept them were substandard: Dunham complained to her agent about rats in the beds of two of her male dancers in a Toronto accommodation.[109] When she protested that she could not go to first-class hotels and demand reservations, he replied that she should "get influential friends to get accommodations or write personally without revealing her race."[110] He continuously pointed out how difficult the arrangements were to make and felt that he was very conscientious in finding suitable living quarters, such as the rooming house in St. Louis, where hotels would not accept Negroes.

Tommy Gomez recalled "the problems of trying to house the company in whatever city we were," noting that the "advance man would go to the black area or to one of the black churches and ask the minister to ask members of the congregation to house us. So we went through the problems of racial prejudice all the time, from the very beginning of the company."[111]

Their treatment sometimes led to dissension in the group. Talley Beatty remembered problems in finding lodging in the West—in Sacramento and Portland. They would rent rooms from landlords who would "throw dirty mattresses on the floor" for the members. When he angrily complained to Hurok, blaming Dunham for the humiliation, he was challenged about questioning her integrity. His bitter accusation led to his departure from the company, according to Beatty, at her request.[112]

Eartha Kitt wrote that in Las Vegas, the company had to stay outside of town, although Dunham was given accommodations in a hotel. That she was sometimes—though not always—given "special" star treatment not granted to other members of the company was for some a source of resentment. To be sure, "headliners" were always given more privileges, but the greater disparity in living arrangements because of the color line exacerbated the jealousy. They were all acquainted with segregation; segregation was the rule at the time, and the kind of respectful recognition that the company sometimes received was the exception. The difference was, as a member stated, "[In the theater] we were treated like any other group, not as second-class citizens."[113] It was the contrast between their recognition as artists and their social rejection that was especially galling.

Lucille Ellis recalled staying in "whorehouses" in the Midwest. She acknowledged that conditions were bad at times: "but it wasn't *that* difficult . . . it wasn't strange to me because I had always been around theatrical people. I knew the things that were going to happen, I'd heard about them because I was always in that kind of atmosphere." She would call acquaintances and ask, "Who did you live with when last on tour? We're going to that city." They would send her names, and she would see if they could stay there.[114]

In Cincinnati, Dunham was asked to leave the Netherlands Plaza Hotel when the members of the American Federation of Labor Union of Culinary Workers threatened to pull out unless she moved. She refused to do so—threatening to jump out a window when hotel representatives came to eject her—and called on her acquaintance Harry Bridges, president of the International Longshoremen's and Warehousemen's Union (ILWU), for help. She had raised his consciousness by comparing the plight of her people with that of the Jews and by pointing out that black Americans were fighting and dying in a war against the foes of his fellow Jews. A powerful union leader who controlled cooks and waiters as well as dock workers, he responded to her plea by threatening a boycott of deliveries and other services to the hotel management. She was allowed to stay. Before she left, she made a reservation for Paul Robeson, who was to appear in the city, and thereafter visiting black artists were given accommodations.

Only in San Francisco did they find pleasant accommodations without any trouble. Dunham had a three-room suite at the Mark Hopkins Hotel and rented an apartment on Telegraph Hill, where she stayed while she taught classes and performed with the company. It was here she had met Harry Bridges, who came to one of the parties she threw at her apartment. In San Francisco and in New York, where she had worked with the ILGWU, she had influential union allies who helped her. She displayed a temerity despite her youth and race that led her to believe that she could initiate whatever changes were necessary, and she attracted and garnered the support of others.

She was especially angry about the segregation during wartime, when black and white soldiers and civilians were united in the war effort: "If we don't win the war, your people and mine will be in the same fix," she said to the hotel manager in Cincinnati.[115] After a performance before a segregated audience in Louisville, she announced that this would be the company's last appearance in that city: "There comes a time when every human being must protest in order to retain human dignity. I must protest because I have discovered that your management will not allow people like you to sit next to people like us. I hope that time and . . . this war for tolerance and democracy, which I am sure we will win, will change some of these things—perhaps then we can return."[116] At the American Theater in St. Louis, some of the workers threatened to strike because of the presence of a white woman in the company. Dorothy Gray, Charlie Chaplin's niece, had been a child star and was at loose ends when she reached adolescence. She attached herself to the company and traveled back and forth between Hollywood and the cities in which the Dunham Company was appearing. She was only one of many talented white artists and assistants who were at various times associated with the group. But bigoted people in St. Louis could not tolerate her presence in a predominantly black company. When the theater manager offered Gray a job to put right the "offensive" situation, she refused, content in her work with the Dunham Company. She joined it on the tour to Mexico but ultimately remained there, marrying a prominent Mexican.

Albert and Annette Dunham traveled to St. Louis to the American Theater performance. They had adjusted to the fact that their daughter was a theater personality and had proudly attended performances in Chicago and Joliet. The audience was segregated, but she got them tickets for box seats so they would not be subjected to Jim Crow status.

Everywhere they performed, the company was a force for change, whether quiet or confrontational. Sometimes when restaurants were reluctant to give company members service, there would be whispered consultations in which the management was informed that they were performing in a nearby theater, and then they would be served. In some cities, Dunham worked with the National Association for the Advancement of Colored People and the Urban League to open public accommodations to black citizens; in others, her husband or a white assistant would obtain rooms for the company or for her. She would use any means she could to ensure that engagements were met, choosing the most effective times and places to take stands. During a Latin American tour, she was asked to leave a hotel in São Paulo that was owned by a Texas entrepreneur. She knew some politicians in Rio who took up her cause. Their action and the publicity that came out of the incident led to the first public accommodations law in Brazil.

Because of the success and visibility of the Dunham Company, other black Americans would sometimes ask Dunham to assist them in gaining entrée to her performances in segregated settings. Thurgood Marshall came to her dressing room at the Eden Rock Hotel in Miami asking her to reserve a table for him and his friends for a dinner performance. She recollected, "I thought I'd be put out." She got similar requests from Paul Robeson in Chicago, from Josephine Baker at the Stork Club, and from Sammy Davis Jr. in Las Vegas. "You like to do it when it's furthering a cause," she remarked, adding wryly, "*I* never wanted to eat in those places because I thought they'd spit in the soup."[117]

The discrimination that the company encountered was the malignant underside of the acclaim it received from audiences and critics. Discrimination affected members in different ways: for Talley Beatty, it was a factor in his departure from the company; for Lucille Ellis, "the main issue was that we were together and doing what we all liked to do, that was the great thing. So the things we liked to do outweighed what we were going through. The prejudices that were there, they were there all along and they still are. We were strong enough in our own beliefs to continue to stay because that was what we loved, doing what we were doing."[118]

Some of the company members also challenged segregation in their own ways. Dunham recalled that during a tour Carmencita Romero (then Lily Butler) went to the Pullman car for breakfast, even though Negroes were not welcome. She made a scene, sending back her eggs three times and asking for only the whites of eggs, scrambled. "[John Pratt] just sat there, he wasn't embarrassed, he just watched," Dunham recounted.[119]

Faced with the responsibility of directing and supporting the group and making and filling engagements, Dunham could not devote full time to challenging social barriers. Nevertheless, Dunham and her company were breaking new ground, and wherever they went, the impact of their presence reverberated in the community.

Years later, Lucille Ellis expressed pride in their legacy: "we have left a lot of good feelings so that people are accepted where they would not have been accepted if it had not been for us. We paved the way, we pioneered all that time; that's what we were supposed to do, and that's what she was supposed to do, to take a band of people and change some of these things that have been going on for years."[120]

Sharing the Vision: The Dunham Schools

Throughout her career, Katherine Dunham continued to respect and exemplify the teachings of her intellectual mentors. Whenever she stayed in one city for extended periods, she opened a school dedicated to the humanities in addition to dance training. Talley Beatty was with her when she opened her first school in New York in 1945: "She opened a school with two students, out in [Greenwich] village. It was just a little studio place. And then we went to the Franziska Boas studio." Boas was teaching children "a very free kind of jazz dance," and they tended to invade the studio. As the number of her students grew, Dunham opened a school in Caravan Hall (Isadora Duncan's former studio) on Fifty-ninth Street, which included dance, speech, drama, and allied theater techniques. Later, it was moved to West Forty-third Street into a building owned by Lee Shubert. "It was upstairs . . . a rehearsal hall . . . suspended over a theater. It kind of swayed because it was suspended," Beatty remembered. Courses in the social sciences and humanities were added to impart the social and cultural background of dance and the arts. Beatty has pleasant memories about teaching at the school: "That was a great period. The Strasbergs taught there and Marlon Brando—everybody—went. It was just the thing to do. I taught there whenever I wasn't touring."[121]

A certificate from the Dunham School of Culture and the Arts, as it was then called, lists, in addition to dance, courses on dance theory and history, drama, theater, history, stage management and makeup, and cultural studies, including anthropology, psychology, philosophy, language, and music appreciation classes. Lucille Ellis reminisced about her years with the school: "It was right after the war and everyone was looking for some place to go; it was just the right time for the school to be there, and so they came and it was wonderful."[122]

Because of Dunham's heavy schedule, John Pratt was acting director of the school. At various times, the faculty included Papa Augustin, Syvilla Fort, Tommy Gomez, Lavinia Williams, Archie Savage, Talley Beatty, Dorathi Bock Pierre, José Limon, and Todd Bolender, among other dance instructors. Lee and Susan Strasberg, Herbert Berghof, and other distinguished directors and actors taught drama; and graduates of Columbia, Cambridge, and Fordham universities taught social sciences. Margaret Mead and Anthony Tudor were guest lecturers. Most of the academic instructors had master's and doctor's degrees, and all had widely varied cultural experiences. Columbia University accepted credits from the Dunham School, and classes at the school were accepted for the G.I. bill. Many subsequently famous people attended: in addition to Brando, Geoffrey Holder, Shelley Winters, Ava Gardner, James Dean, Doris Duke, Butterfly McQueen, Jennifer Jones, Arthur Mitchell, Louis Johnson, Eartha Kitt, Chita Rivera, José Ferrer, and Peter Gennaro, among many others, were trained at the Dunham School.

The school included a library, but, according to Lucille Ellis, neither the dancers nor acting students fully realized the literary opportunities they were given: "They didn't take advantage of that particular aspect of the school, which was unfortunate, because they didn't allow themselves to grow . . . the thesis [Dunham's] was in the school and they never even took the time [to read it]." Ellis felt the company was fortunate in being able to learn Dunham's philosophy and approach during rehearsals, through her choreography and her thought processes in determining what she wanted them to do: "Sometimes rehearsals would go on until two or three o'clock in the morning. If dancers did not listen to her message, they would be lost when they started to perform, since she had explained in depth what she wanted them to project."[123]

It is hard to assess how the nondancers were influenced by their work at the school. Marlon Brando was fascinated by the drums and, in Dunham's words, "fancied himself a drummer."[124] His cosmopolitan interests, as well as his actor's sense of timing, were at least reinforced by his work at the Dunham School. The subtle presence and beat of the bongo drums in the film *The Last Tango in Paris* hint at the enduring effect of his initiation into Dunham technique. The charisma and screen presence of James Dean, who always gave credit to the Dunham School, were likely enhanced by working with the outstanding artists on the faculty.

Dunham did not run an exclusive school. The aim was to communicate and disseminate a new way of doing art, of looking at peoples and cultures. Many young dancers were granted scholarships, including Eartha Kitt; others (including Peter Gennaro) were on the G.I. bill. Some became company members, and many developed strong careers in dance. Popular attractions at the school were the "Boule Blanche" parties, monthly celebrations of Martinique culture. These were attended by members of the New York cultural set, including Claude Lévi-Strauss, who was then (in 1946–47) a cultural attaché at the French consulate. Cuban Mongo Santa Maria, Tito Puente, and other Latin drummers and performers who were playing at the Palladium, which was two blocks from the school, came to jam with the other musicians at the parties. Through these parties, money was raised for the school.

Dunham wrote in an article for *Esquire* magazine that in Martinique, the beguine danced at a Boule Blanche was performed out of the "pure love for dancing," even though visitors often saw only lascivious movements: "They dance the beg[u]ine as a ritual of fecundity. The consummation is in the dance itself. . . . Now her hips are moving and they describe a double circle at opposite ends of a loop . . . a figure eight . . . the movement is no longer side to side, but under and up, hips looping on rigid torso, knees bent, heads lowered as they look into each other's eyes, moving a half inch to the right with each under and up movement, each revolution of the abdomen. Strong feet and arches keep the rhythm smooth. They find a pleasure in the artistry of the dance."[125] Uninitiated observers may expect the dance partners to leave the floor together to meet in private, but instead they return to their seats on opposite sides of the room and wait for their next partner. "They are satisfied in the accomplishment of an artistic feat—in matching techniques."[126]

While Dunham was touring, Syvilla Fort was dance director of the Dunham School. She was assisted by Walter Nicks, and John Pratt would drop in now and then to check on its operation. The school was subsidized primarily through Dunham Company performances. Dunham was

forced to close the school in 1955, partially because of unfavorable exchange rates during a European tour. Another factor was Fort's departure
to establish her own school, taking the children she taught with her.
Dunham felt betrayed.

Years later, Talley Beatty remarked on Dunham's generosity in allowing other dancers and choreographers to use her studio: "A number of
people used the studio to work their own material. . . . [Martha] Graham
doesn't do it, [Paul] Taylor doesn't do it, but she was quite generous in
that way."[127] This generosity contributed to education and contacts acquired by the Dunham dancers, as they became acquainted with other
dancers and their art.

The Dunham School of Culture and the Arts in New York was merely
one of several ambitious, all-encompassing educational programs Dunham would undertake. She opened schools while on tour, in European,
Latin American, and African countries and on the West Coast. She held
classes in the Chelsea Hotel in New York for a time in 1962, but because
of complaints about the drums she had to move. She opened a smaller
school in 1963 on Forty-second Street, but it was short-lived. Later in the
decade, Dunham turned her attention to the Midwest, where she hoped
to build a cultural center like those on the East Coast and West Coast.
Most notable was the Performing Arts Training Center in East St. Louis,
established in the 1960s and 1970s as part of Southern Illinois University's Experiment in Higher Education. Her first school set the standard;
thereafter she never would be satisfied with a mere dance school.

Touring Mexico

After a six-month tour in the United States in 1947, Dunham took *Bal
Nègre* to Mexico City. The company gave its first performances without
costumes and scenery because their luggage was held up. Audiences were
exhilarated by the dancers' verve and audacity, and when the costumes
arrived, people flocked to the performances. Afterward the company traveled to Acapulco, Guadalupe, and Veracruz. "Veracruzana," which Dunham choreographed while in Mexico, became a part of the company's
repertoire. Dunham returned to New York for a time to dance in a Broadway production for Billy Rose, leaving Lenwood Morris in charge of rehearsals. The company remained in Mexico for several months, performing at clubs, including Ciro's in Mexico City. Taking advantage of the
lower living costs there, the dancers rehearsed for a Hollywood film.

In this first extended professional tour outside the United States,
Dunham, "La Katerina," as she was affectionately called, used her cultur-

al awareness to advantage: "I was invited, with members of my company, to call on President Miguel Aleman who was most gracious in his praise of our performance. He was particularly pleased that we spoke to him in Spanish, such as it was, an effrontery in view of his good English, but one that broke the contretemps and established a friendly feeling at once."[128]

Her kinship with art and artists of various media and the vitality of Dunham performances continued to attract other artists, including the Mexican artist Miguel Covarrubias, who brought his students to the theater to sketch company members. The Italian composer Mario Castelnuovo-Tedesco, who resided in Mexico City, wrote music for "Octoroon Ball," a Dunham work in progress. Company members were entertained with parties and received dinner invitations from artists and intellectuals—Diego Rivera, José Orozco, and Carlos Chavez, as well as members of the diplomatic corps. The Mexican tour prepared the company for further forays outside the United States, and the opportunity to tour Europe soon presented itself.

In New York, Dale Wasserman, who was stage manager on and off through the years, began to prepare the company for a European tour. Ellis described Dunham, Pratt, and Wasserman as very close: "They were meant to be together."[129] Dunham's relationship with Wasserman was sometimes stormy, but all three were perfectionists and artistically in tune.

Before the European tour, Wasserman met with Ellis and other lead dancers to see if they would be comfortable with a white dancer, the only student at the Dunham School who Dunham felt was ready to join the company. They replied there was no problem, as long as she could dance.[130] So Julie Robinson, who later married Harry Belafonte, took a departing member's place. European audiences were probably more receptive to such an arrangement than were Americans. The dancers were all weary of the racial barriers in U.S. cities while other black artists had been received with acclaim in European cultural centers, where there was eager appreciation for the vitality of African American art. Tommy Gomez expressed relief in escaping American prejudices: "We didn't get away from [prejudice] until we finally left this country and went to London. And we had such a fantastic reception in London."[131]

8   *Taking It Abroad*

Without Europe we couldn't have survived.
—Katherine Dunham, 1978 conversation with author

IN 1948, PEOPLE in postwar England were tired of shortages and struggles, and they hungered for the energy and brilliance in Dunham Company performances. Eartha Kitt elaborated, "For six months, the Prince of Wales Theatre was the centre and the joy of the London theatre district. Ours was the most exciting show that had hit London since the war. London still grieved from that horror. I could see and feel her wounds."[1] Pearl Reynolds recalled the scream of recognition from the audience during the performance of "Shango," which projects feelings associated with the god of thunder and war in Caribbean cultures.

A writer in the *London Observer* described the impact of the Dunham Company on English audiences: "Certainly one cannot readily classify Katherine Dunham's 'Caribbean Rhapsody'—the Negro show which has been filling the Prince of Wales Theatre and causing intense interest amongst professional dance producers. . . . Chiefly it is ballet, but of a quite unusual kind . . . her bare-footed company made classical dancers seem like waxwork figures . . . the impact of her company's visit [is comparable] to the arrival in Paris of Diaghileff's ballet in the year 1908."[2]

In *Katherine Dunham, Her Dancers, Singers, Musicians*, Richard Buckle, a London dance critic, referred to Dunham's many-sided nature as "explorer, thinker, inventor, organizer and dancer," as well as a "young woman with charm, wit and purpose, and with the thoroughness, grasp of detail, and determination of a great soldier or explorer." He lauded her "creative genius" and "the passionate artistry of her dancers," expressing surprise at the fact that she ran the "largest unsubsidised company of dancers in the United States."[3] His book includes pictures and stories of the ballets performed by Dunham, Lucille Ellis, Vanoye Aikens, Tommy Gomez, Lenwood Morris, Julie Robinson, Eartha Kitt, and others, as well as of the dancer and drummer La Rosa Estrada and the Sans-Souci Singers, who sang for a ragtime sequence. The work is a treasure trove documenting the artistry and skills of the Dunham dancers and portraying the beauty and grace of the young Katherine Dunham and the early company members at the height of their youthful vitality.

Their programs were patronized by the royal family, whose members appeared in the royal box from time to time. Like many Americans, the dancers were attracted to and intrigued by the "royals." Royal members, too, were superb performers and understood the importance of costume and drama, especially in wartime and postwar England. According to Tommy Gomez, the dancers just missed meeting one of the royal family: "Dickie Buckle published a little periodical monthly on opera and ballet. Someone important on his staff was related to the Queen Mother." He arranged a meeting with her, "but we left before it came into being, and we were so sorry about it." But Gomez did catch a glimpse of the Queen Mother on a narrow London street: "I saw a Rolls-Royce and I was wondering who was in this car, it was the largest Rolls-Royce I'd ever seen . . . and there was the Queen Mother, with the turban she wore so often, with a little flounce with egrets . . . she had gotten past before I realized it was the Queen."[4]

Company members became acquainted with the dancers in the Sadler's Wells Ballet, the top dancers in London. Alicia Markova, the prima ballerina of the Ballet Russe de Monte Carlo, introduced them to Margot Fonteyn and Frederick Ashton. They had met Markova and other ballet members in New York. In London, Fonteyn, Ashton, and Moira Shearer started coming to Dunham classes. Margot Fonteyn's brother, a noted photographer, took the pictures of the company. Fonteyn and her brother asked them to tea almost every Sunday. Gomez voiced the elation experienced by the Dunham dancers in being accepted in London cultural and social circles: "And it was so wonderful, just to sit across a table in polite British society with someone like Margot Fonteyn." He remarked that there was more class consciousness than race consciousness in Europe; the people they encountered were sure of their status and did not feel the need to assert their superiority. "It was such a wonderful relief, being able to relax, and knowing we could go anywhere we wanted to as long as we had the money," he exclaimed.[5]

After a tour of "the provinces"—Liverpool, Manchester, and Birmingham—the Dunham Company departed for Paris, perhaps the greatest success of their first European tour. Parisians anticipated their arrival. "We had such fantastic press and word of mouth that people began to come over from the continent to see our performances," Gomez reported. "Finally we took a boat-train and we opened in Paris."[6]

If London was a smashing success, Paris was a triumph for the company. It opened at the Theatre de Paris in Mont Martre. Gomez described the theater: "It was one of those precious theaters, all red velvet and gold leaf. . . . And they imported part of the jungle, they covered the walls—all this red velvet plush—with foliage . . . because we were considered exotic. And we weren't from Africa, like many of the companies they imported."[7] In the midst of this exotica, the company members worked tirelessly to achieve the perfection for which they were celebrated. Marjorie Scott, Dunham's secretary at the time, recalled that the dancers were at the theater at least an hour before the performance to warm up. "And after every act she used to get everybody up on stage to tell them what she thought had gone wrong," she recalled.[8] Gomez retained a vivid image of Dunham as taskmistress, remembering that she wore a red plaid dressing gown over her costume when she was chilly: "She was always there in the wings making notes and we could see this red plaid robe."[9] She got them onstage for coaching between acts, and they continued with classes every morning while touring.

Josephine Baker offered to introduce Katherine Dunham to Paris, but, coming from the London success, Dunham felt that she did not need an introduction and communicated this to Baker. Gomez was concerned that Baker would be insulted, but on opening night she came backstage with Maurice Chevalier, Jules Cocteau, Jean Marais, and Mistinguette. Gomez recalled, "Miss D came on the stage with her red plaid robe around her costume and went right on to her dressing room and we were flabbergasted! She expected them to come to her dressing room and they did!" While Baker was backstage, she personally congratulated the entire company, especially the "little people," as she called them, who were not "stars" but without whom no production could go forward. Gomez recounted, "And then the next day, when we came for the first class in the morning, in our letter boxes there was a big white envelope . . . from Josephine Baker. And she thanked every member of the company in her own handwriting, and she was saying how wonderful the show was and how beautiful we all were."[10]

In the 1920s and 1930s, jazz musicians had demonstrated to Parisians the creativity of African Americans. Josephine Baker's inspired and uninhibited theatricality whetted the French appetite for more intensive exposure to African American expression. But Parisians responded to the cultural and intellectual content as well as to the aesthetic appeal of the Dunham Company presentations. A program note expressed a complex response: "The ability to go from emotion to orderly movement in which emotion is echoed and amplified is not, it seems, an ability that is equally held by all human beings . . . it is born of the transformation of the capacity for feeling, which everyone has, into the privilege of making others feel, to which only a few have access. . . . It was the vocation of Katherine Dunham to conceive and undertake the venture; it is her glory to lead it well in terms of a surprising alchemy which unites knowledge and instinct in a marvelous manner."[11]

The French celebrated the Dunham phenomenon in their inimitable style: French designers developed fashion lines inspired by her persona and John Pratt's costumes. The artist Andre Quellier made sketches of Dunham and company members, which were exhibited during a later tour, and a sculptor modeled and had her feet cast in bronze for display in the Museé L'homme. She and Pratt attended parties with Jules Cocteau, Maurice Chevalier, Mistinguette, Josephine Baker, Orson Welles, and other international stars.

To escape the stresses of public life, Dunham began to paint while she was living in Paris. She exhibited her paintings in Paris, Milan, London, Sydney, Lima, and Buenos Aires, and some are now on display at the Dunham Museum in East St. Louis.

During the first and later Paris appearances, Dunham and Pratt visited and ultimately grew attached to an infant girl who was in a Catholic convent nursery. They adopted Marie-Christine in 1952, when she was deemed old enough to travel with the company. When she was of school age, she returned to the convent for schooling and later resumed her education in Swiss boarding schools, joining her parents during holidays and school breaks. Company members became her "extended family" and helped introduce her to the ways of theater.[12]

While in Paris, company members worked long hours, but they also took time to enjoy its beauties and pleasures. One of the high points for Tommy Gomez was his own meeting with Josephine Baker, who had taken Paris by storm twenty years earlier. According to Gomez, "She was Paris and she owned Paris." He was surprised that she was continuing to perform, since very little was heard about her in the States. Baker invited Gomez and Lenwood Morris to lunch; she wanted them to dance in her Follies, which they were not permitted to do because they were under contract. But they were glad for the opportunity to gain her acquaintance. "We noticed," Gomez related, "that she just had a satin scarf tied around her hair and there were big dark 'satchels,' [as] we called it in the theater—circles—under her eyes; she said she'd be just a moment, dahlings; and when she finally came back these big, dark circles were gone . . . her skin was flawless, and tight, you know, no wrinkles—cosmetics in Paris are so far ahead of us. And she was the one who produced this preparation that was made especially for her when she straightened her hair and it had that patent-leather look." Baker spoke French to her maid and German to her chauffeur, and while they were enjoying their lunch and thinking about the right silver utensil to use among the many beside their plates, Gomez reminisced, "all of a sudden a little tiny brown hand came up over the side of the table and I jumped . . . and it was her pet monkey. He screamed when I jumped and [he] ran under the table, then up the drapes." The monkey, Mika, would accompany her at times, dressed in the same outfit she was wearing.[13]

Many people gave Dunham and members of the company gifts, some of them very costly. According to Gomez, one of the first of Dunham's many European admirers was Porfirio Rubirosa, the famous European playboy, who, as he recalled, gave her the largest black diamond in the world. When she wore it in Paris, she had security guards who followed her around and watched from the wings when she wore the jewelry onstage; when she came off, they would escort her to the dressing room. Queried about this in 1994, Dunham laughed and said there were a lot of rumors, many of them started by Lenwood Morris, who had actually said it was Aly Khan, not Rubirosa, who gave her the diamond. In reality, she said, she bought it herself, and that piece and her other jewelry and expensive personal items were pawned at various times to move the company or pay expenses. Gomez confirmed her point: "Many times she had the most fantastic collection of jewels but she had to pawn them to get a particular set of costumes for a ballet or to get the company from one place to another. Her fur coats—you know, no sacrifice was too big for her, to keep that Company going."[14] Now, Dunham laments, she has no jewelry. Once she pawned jewelry for expenses, and when she went back to reclaim it, the dealer said it had been taken in a robbery. Although he was obviously running a scam, there was nothing she could do about it.

Marjorie Scott commented on the expenses while on tour: "In rehearsal, we couldn't do anything without getting the whole of the [stage] crew out. . . . In England, because of union laws they were not allowed to use their own pianist; three pianists who could not play the music were sitting in the pit at all times. It became a quite costly business, keeping all those people. . . . There were about forty people all together, year in, year out, whether they were or not working. It's amazing that she managed to survive without getting any subsidy at all." Besides the dancers, the company included the manager, wardrobe mistress, an English corrector, the musical director, and musicians; Dunham insisted on having a harpist, a live musician, who played only two arpeggios. Otherwise, she felt, the music would not be authentic. Regardless of cost, Dunham would not perform a number unless she felt everything was right. They had musical scores transcribed for a symphony orchestra, as well as for an ordinary orchestra. Scott asserted, "She will not do anything unless she can do it as she wants to do it. She's right, there's never been anything like the Dunham technique."[15]

European artists and managers were eager to associate with members of the Dunham Company and to incorporate their artistry into their own productions. The ballet master of the Paris Opera asked Gomez to appear as a guest artist in the role of the Polivitsian chief in *Prince Igor.* "I wanted to do that so badly, but Miss D said 'No.' I thought it would be good publicity for the Company." But Dunham was concerned to keep the Dunham Company together. Laverne French, one of the original members, left to teach Dunham technique in the Paris Ballet. He taught there for more than twenty-five years, with breaks to appear in such New York productions as a revival of *Showboat,* which also employed former Dunham dancers Talley Beatty and Claude Marchant. Others were tempted to leave to take advantage of some of these opportunities, but financial arrangements discouraged this. Gomez reported that part of a member's salary would be sent home and that the balance was paid in the currency of the country in which they were appearing. He was married and was just about to have his first child, so he felt he could not afford to take any chances. "But Kitty [Eartha Kitt] made the break," he recounted.[16] Eartha Kitt appeared in Paris night clubs and was discovered by Orson Welles and other impresarios. They found her work exciting and interesting and helped her attain opportunities outside the company.

In her memoir, Kitt described her decision to leave the company when it returned to Paris after a tour of Europe. Her departure was partly in reaction to a company agent's attempts to keep her from appearing in nightclubs and to persuade her to remain with the company for the South American tour. Dunham, she noted, quietly informed her that the prestige of the company would be affected by outside performances and referred her to her agents, who expanded on company policies. The relationship between the two women was not permanently affected by the break, but Dunham felt increasingly challenged by the attempts to lure members away, threatening the artistic future she envisioned for the company. A black dance group directed by a black woman was a monumental departure in the artistic world, and she continuously had to fight to maintain the artistic and physical integrity of the company.

During the company's first Continental trip, it toured France, Italy, Germany, and Sweden. Excerpts from a Milano program entitled *La Quinta Caterina* reflects the prestige that Katherine Dunham's name carried throughout Europe:

> A century and a half . . . had to pass after the disappearance of Catherine the Great from the European scene before another Katherine, herself great . . . would enter onto the stages of the entire world . . . let us welcome Katherine and her magnificent actors and companions in art and accomplishments, the "Dunham Company" . . . [a] mobile house of artists, the "Company of Players of Black Art" and intending the word "players" as meaning the quintessence of any interpretive dramatic art, with all its music, its mime, its gesture, its rite, its superstition: art when it speaks a language universal.[17]

The Dunham Company returned to Europe on many occasions after that first tour, later adding North Africa—Algeria and Morocco—and the Middle East to the schedule. In addition, it toured South American, African, and Asian countries, sixty-nine countries in all. Marjorie Scott recounted, "And we used to go every year to Europe, every year to the States. And [to] South America, every country in South America except for Paraguay."[18]

Vanoye Aikens recalled that in every country "Miss D" would collect "something": a cultural expression, a movement, a local musician, or a dancer.[19] Scott confirmed this: "She used to take dancers from everywhere, just amazing, and put them on the stage. We had a Zulu, I think, Japanese, Australian, Cubans, and Mexicans, Haitians, Argentineans, all different nationalities. She'd put anybody on the stage; I think there were about 17 different nationalities in the company."[20] Madeline Preston, who was with the company in the 1950s, echoed these remarks: "She always picked up people. When we were in Australia we had an aborigine tenor who traveled with us for awhile."[21] According to Scott, "We took drummers from Haiti and they had never seen bathrooms or taps; they used to turn on the showers and flood the hotel. And then people got far too grand, and would walk around with furled umbrellas and bowler hats."[22]

Scott was one of the outstanding assistants/secretaries who were attracted by the opportunity to work with Katherine Dunham. Maya (Eleanora) Deren, who had asked to collaborate with her on a children's book on dance, was one of the first, and Jeanelle Stovall, who is still with her, is the most recent. The position has changed through the years, as Dunham began to focus more directly on the role of art in community, but the commonalities are broad cultural interests and language skills. Scott, who was with her from 1949 to 1960, was formerly employed by British intelligence. Dunham was planning to tour Italy and wanted someone who could speak Italian. Scott, then in London, spoke Italian and joined the company in Paris as Dunham's personal secretary. "It involved everything, if something happened, you would either do the lights, or help her dress, or look after the music [or] answer the correspondence," she recalled.[23] While they were in Paris, another "acquisition," Django Reinhardt, joined the company and toured with it in several European countries. Dunham's father had played the guitar—her favorite instrument— and she claims to have known almost every great guitar player of her time. When she and the company returned for a later tour, Reinhardt was not available, but his son, who also played guitar, appeared with them.

While on tour in South America in the early 1950s, the company stayed in Argentina for six months. It was during the Perón regime, and Marjorie Scott described the attention lavished on them by the "royal" couple: "[Eva Perón] took us all around to see her 'good works.' She took all the prostitutes off the streets and put them in houses and made them do embroidery, the poor things." Scott was amazed by the fact that Eva remembered the names of all the company members. The Peróns invited them to a party in the winter palace and one in the summer palace and served Argentinean steaks.[24]

In *Island Possessed,* Dunham, who had friends among the aristocracy Evita Perón hated, revealed her personal animosity toward the Peróns: "After a benefit for the 'Benefactress,' a command performance at the Colón Opera, I was literally ordered the following morning to review the orphanage, various nurses' training schools established in the confiscated homes of some of my friends, the refuge for prostitutes or mothers without husbands where one or two complained bitterly to me as though I could waive their, literally, prison sentence." She noted that prostitution "is practiced with great dignity in most Latin countries . . . the result of her cleaning up was a scourge of male prostitutes."[25]

The "Tango," Dunham's interpretation of the traditional Argentinean dance that the company performed in Buenos Aires, expressed nostalgia, a hearkening back to pre-Perón days, as well as defiance and protest against the state's repression. The audiences sensed and responded to her message, although many were afraid to show their approval openly.[26]

The company also stayed for an prolonged time in Brazil, in Belem and Rio, and performed in Bogotá, Colombia, and in Chile, among other places. Dunham collected movements and rhythms and choreographed many numbers from these South American tours, which became an important part of the Dunham Company repertoire. In the "Cumbia," she captured women of the Colombian seacoast doing a stately circle dance while smoking cigars. From this dance, "The Woman with a Cigar" became identified with Dunham performances. In the "Batucada," she presented rope weavers of Bahia joining with a Batuke tribal girl to do the samba, the carnival dance of Brazil.[27] The elaborate, intricately designed and fashioned costumes Dunham wore in these and other dances, all the work of John Pratt, are displayed in the Katherine Dunham Museum in East St. Louis, Illinois.

Giovannella Zannoni, currently a film producer in Rome, traveled with the company as stage manager in the South American tour. She commented, "The impact of the show for me and most of my generation was tremendous. We had never been exposed to anything so culturally different from us and yet with such a power of total involvement. It was much more than the enthusiastic reaction to a brilliant theatrical experience. It was an exposure to a different civilization, to a sense of magic and of beauty we knew nothing about. I think that for many of us this was an authentic cultural initiation."[28]

Political and Personal Trials

In Santiago, Chile, in 1951, the Dunham Company presented *Southland*, portraying a lynching. Although it was not based on an actual lynching, Dunham described it as "the story of every one of them because behind each one lies the violence of the mob against the defenseless."[29] Forty-three lynchings of blacks in the United States had been reported from 1936 to 1946.[30] Pearl Primus's solo dance to the poem "Strange Fruit" in 1943 and Talley Beatty's *Southern Landscape* in 1947 had dramatized white brutality, yet the assaults continued. In 1949–51, eight black youth were, under doubtful circumstances, convicted and executed for the purported rape of a white woman. All of these events assaulted Dunham's sense of justice. The American legal system's failure to prosecute crimes against blacks led black Americans to believe with justification that there was no fairness in the judiciary system. Emmett Till, a distant relative of company member Glory Van Scott, was lynched in Mississippi in 1955. Speaking onstage, Dunham vowed to continue presenting the ballet until the lynching of black males in the United States ceased. In the prologue to this powerful ballet, Dunham stated, "Though I have not smelled the smell of burning flesh and have never seen a black body swaying from a southern tree, I have felt these things in spirit, and finally through the creative artist comes the need of the person to show this thing to the world, hoping that by so exposing the ill the conscience of the many will protest and save further destruction and humiliation."[31] Julie Robinson played a starring role in *Southland* as a white woman who colluded in the lynching of a black man, played by Ricardo Avalos, who had tried to assist her when she was attacked by her white lover, danced by Lenwood Morris. Dino DiStefano, a Jesuit priest, composed the orchestral arrangement of spirituals, blues, and popular songs, including "Strange Fruit"— sung by Claudia McNeil—which had been popularized by Billie Holiday.

The ballet revealed a side of U.S. society that the government did not wish to have exposed abroad—especially in a country with communist and anti-American activity. The anticommunist fervor of the 1950s was directed toward human rights and civil rights activities, which were censured as anti-American. Representatives of the U.S. State Department were sent in vain to try to stop the performance. All reviews were suppressed, and visas were canceled, forcing the company to leave Chile. Thereafter, the State Department sponsored other events at the same time as Dunham performances in South American and European capitals, which they ordered diplomatic personnel to attend. The local elite, following the lead of the diplomats, also attended the competing productions. Later Dunham Company appearances in Paris consequently did not have the success they had had earlier.

During a 1956–57 tour of Australia and the Far East, Dunham was invited to travel with the company to the People's Republic of China. The State Department's refusal to allow her to accept the invitation reflected the continuing distrust of both Dunham and China on the part of the U.S. government. In the meantime, the State Department had sponsored other dance companies touring Latin American and other countries, and all support was denied the Dunham Company. Although Dunham and her dancers were unofficially described as "cultural ambassadors," they were never accorded the support given to officially sponsored groups.[32]

According to one writer, "Although *Southland* instigated the [eventual] dissolution of Dunham's company, it laid the moral groundwork for subsequent expressions of affirmation and dissent."[33] But because of their vulnerable situation, the company members felt insecure about performing the ballet. Dunham understood their dilemma: "Their idea in leaving America was to lose any feelings of racial difference, to try to forget what the whole thing was about. . . . [*Southland*] took them down to the very bottom, to a reality they felt they had never known."[34] Lucille Ellis expanded on this view: "*Southland* took our security blanket away. . . . If we were run out of the country, where would we be? We were in limbo."[35]

This was only one of many instances when Dunham's artistic integrity affected her career. The performance of *Southland*, as well as Dunham's refusal to cooperate in identifying Nation of Islam members, gained her the enmity of FBI director J. Edgar Hoover, who apparently began a campaign to undermine her career. Walter Winchell had always given her positive mention in his columns until Hoover intervened. When Winchell stopped writing about her, she asked him why; he replied that at a party Hoover had remarked on his favorable comments about her and made a vicious slur.[36] Winchell, whose column and broadcasts carried considerable influence, was himself open to intimidation by this other powerful, destructive agent.

In addition to the mental stress resulting from such political harassment, a strenuous schedule, the food in public establishments, and changes in diet and water caused Dunham to suffer bouts of illness during tours. On one occasion, in Milan, she was hospitalized with a high fever; the diagnosis was septicemia. She sent word to Dr. Max Jacobson, in whom she had great faith, to send a drug "cocktail" that had helped her in the past. The Italian Medical Association confiscated the first shipment, so she requested that it be sent through Switzerland. She spoke of "heavy ankle and foot swelling," the incision from her knee surgery separating, and her skin peeling. She felt she was on the point of death, and when the medicine finally came, she wrote him that she felt better.[37] The doctors prescribed a long rest, but she insisted on performing after two weeks; she knew she did not have the luxury of a long convalescence.

Dr. Jacobson treated many famous people, including Jackie Onassis. According to Dunham, he helped pull Onassis through the terrible period after President Kennedy's death. He believed in getting people to feel well, as well as to function, and would help them become self-aware and conscious of why they have pain. But the medical establishment did not approve of his methods and some of his means of relieving pain. His license was revoked by the American Medical Association, and he was dismissed from the Pasteur Institute for providing treatment that was not legitimate, specifically, medications that were unacceptable to the medical profession. Dunham, as well as others he treated, testified in his defense at the hearing. The examiners were trying to get her to admit she had become dependent on the amphetamines he prescribed, which she denied.

Dr. Jacobson kept her functioning physically through more than twenty very stressful years. He also put her on hormones, which alleviated her arthritis and other conditions, so that she did not start menopause until she was sixty-seven. Marjorie Scott knew Dr. Jacobson and talked to his secretary frequently: "He used to do quite a lot for the people in Haiti, too. She used to get medicines to take out to Haiti. She would

have people lining up in the morning; they used to come for various in-
jections. I used to keep a list of their names and what they'd have."[38]

Dr. Jacobson died soon after they took his license and removed him
from the Pasteur Institute; Dunham believes he committed suicide.
Within the same year, Erich Fromm and Rosita, Dunham's Cuban
santera, or healer, also died. Although she did not believe she could survive these bereavements, she found the resources within herself to continue. She gives these advisers much of the credit for her longevity and
successes, and she shares many of their teachings and techniques with
her followers.

Friends and Admirers

Despite a grueling schedule, Dunham developed a number of deep friendships through the years. During the European tours, she came to know
Bernard Berenson, with whom she corresponded during the last decade
of his life. She visited him at I Tatti, his residence near Florence on a
number of occasions. She was sometimes accompanied by Marjorie Scott,
who was impressed: "It was an amazing place! . . . He had a fabulous
collection of Sienese paintings. Nikki Mariano was his secretary and
hostess when his wife died."[39]

Dunham recalled with pride that Berenson included her in his collection of beautiful ladies. In his memoirs, he wrote, "Katherine Dunham
talked with . . . a cultivated accent and vocabulary and revealed an un-
usually subtle but rational personality, completely free of mannerisms
of any kind. . . . She thought the best ideas come while daydreaming,
ruminating, and not when searching as for a bull's eye in the dark. Much
else that was deeply sincere."[40] He recognized her abilities and asked her
to be his eyes and ears during her travels. He rather condescendingly
described himself as the mind analyzing her observations. He was, of
course, a brilliant and talented man, another of the distinguished intellectuals attracted by her unique combination of artistry, intelligence, and
beauty, and she was proud to regard him as a friend. Their long relationship took on the characteristics of a courtship: the elder man appreciat-
ing the beauty and passion of the artist and she attracted by his intellect,
worldly knowledge, and personal power. He was opposed to *Southland*,
taking a politically conservative view, and she replied to his criticism
with a spirited support of the freedom of speech.[41]

Another admirer was Serge Tolstoy, the novelist's grandson, who
was one of her escorts while she was in Paris. He was a physician, who,
because he was recommended by Max Jacobson, was the only other

doctor she would allow to treat her. They conceived a "grand passion," which, however, was ephemeral. She attracted the admiration of many men of wealth and power, but her marriage with John Pratt, based on artistic collaboration as well as personal feelings, survived all of these "affaires de coeur."

Dunham also made close women friends. She met the novelist Han Suyin in Zurich, Switzerland. The two felt a kinship, she remarked, because there were attempts in the entertainment world to make both of them second-class citizens. "She and I would go shopping for materials for *cheongsams*. I had twenty made. They were like military uniforms, there were no variations except the materials."[42] She maintained a long-term friendship with Doris Duke, who studied at the New York school, although they had lost touch by the time of her death. Doris Duke had wanted to join the company, but Dunham did not feel that she "fit in," in contrast to Julie Robinson and Raimonda Orselli, both white. Robinson had a "feeling" for African American culture, and Orselli danced classical ballet and Dunham technique beautifully. Duke's philanthropy may well have benefited the company, as well as Dunham's later activities, but artistic values came first.

Madeline Preston has remained a stalwart friend and supporter through the years. She joined the company for the tour to Australia and the Far East in 1956. She was in California singing with the Hall Johnson Choir when she went to see the Dunham Company program at the Greek Theater. She was enthralled, returning for two more performances. When four of the Hall Johnson singers vocalized for "Miss D," Dunham asked Johnson, "Who was that with the high voice?"; he used to call her a "piccolo soprano," Preston recalled many years later. Dunham asked her if she wanted to audition: "I didn't know left foot from right foot. I joined as an apprentice; Lenwood [Morris] taught me. . . . Lenwood was the sweetest and most generous [person] . . . he was like a brother." As with most of those who joined the company, she became Dunham's lifelong friend. "I came to class with a 'cello—I had just come from school. I think that was why we're friends to this day; her brother, Albert, played the 'cello," Preston commented.[43]

Dunham had a show in Ciro's in which Preston had a singing part. She was one of the five singers for "Dark-Town Strutter's Ball" and "Cakewalk." When the group went on the Far East tour, she went with them. "I left my car and Hall Johnson in LA when I went crazy about the Dunham group. I was madly in love with the music and dancing," she declared.[44] The company left San Francisco on a trip by ship to Hawaii, Australia, and the Far East.

Australia and the Far East

The company landed at Melbourne on May 30, 1956. "Here were all these black people just off the boat; people surrounded us, staring at us. Where did all these people come from?" But the Dunham Company received a warm reception: "The Australians loved Miss D and the Company. I loved the Australians," Preston recalled.[45]

The company appeared in Melbourne for two or three months, then stopped in Sydney for several months, where Dunham and Pratt rented an apartment, which Pratt decorated. Preston stayed with them. "I wasn't being paid; they took me as part of the family," Preston remarked. Touring was different then: "They were not one-night stands; people got apartments and shared."[46]

The reviews in Australia and in New Zealand—their next stop—were generally positive. An Auckland reviewer wrote that Lenwood Morris "wanted to dance: hitch-hiked halfway across America, joined the company as a student at 11 dollars a week. Now, as star and ballet-master, he commands the respect of European critics. [He] has been ballet master and leading dancer for 13 years, despite offers from virtually every major ballet company in the world.[47]

When they left New Zealand, they went on to Asia: Singapore, Korea, and Japan. Marjorie Scott recalled one of her responsibilities during a performance in Tokyo: "She said, 'No photographs, go down to the stalls and stop the people taking photographs.' Have you ever tried stopping Japanese from taking photographs? And she stopped on the stage there and waited [for them to stop taking photos]—not many people could do that."[48] After their Far East tour, they returned to Australia. The Australian promoters wanted the company back because it was so popular. At that time, Glory Van Scott, Ural Wilson, Lenwood Morris, Vanoye Aikens, Lucille Ellis, Pearl Reynolds, Julie Belafonte, and Camille Yarbrough were dancing with the company.

Pratt left the company in Australia to oversee building projects at Habitation Leclerc. The Australian press played up problems between the couple and with other company members, allegedly arising from Dunham's "temperament." It was, undoubtedly, a trying time, after decades of touring and keeping the company together, of illness and pain. Dunham was approaching her fiftieth birthday, and the arthritis that has plagued her throughout her life increasingly limited her movement. She suggested in her memoirs that Pratt could be caustic and unkind in an intimate relationship, even though he had a reputation of being gentle and sweet-tempered—especially among female members of the company—and their daughter, Marie-Christine, worshiped him. Like Dunham, he was a complex individual; he was highly sophisticated and impatient with pretensions of any kind. A friend at Southern Illinois University, who worked with him on costumes as a volunteer, described him as a generous, even selfless, man; she said he would often exclaim, with genuine feeling, of Dunham, "She is the queen!"[49] Despite their marital troubles, Dunham and Pratt were dependent on each other. When Dunham heard about her mother's final illness, she wrote and asked him to be by Annette's side in her stead, since she still had obligations abroad.

At the end of the tour, Dunham temporarily disbanded the company. Because the members had performed for the military troops in Korea, the U.S. Air Force covered their airfare to return to the United States after their last appearances in the Far East and Australia.

Dunham was tired of tours and wanted to settle down for a time and write. Scott commented on the stress of constant touring: "Really, the time you were most relaxed was when you were traveling." In Dunham's letters to Bernard Berenson, she complained that the company was becoming increasingly burdensome. He encouraged her to write to become independent of the company.[50] She originally planned to portray the years of touring, but she could not get publishers interested. Years earlier, Erich Fromm had counseled her that the best thing to do when she was depressed was to read biography and autobiography.[51] The next logical step— writing her own memoir—arose out of her own need and genius. With the encouragement of Berenson, she began an account of her early years and stayed for a year in Japan, working on the manuscript. She dedicated the published work to him.

A Touch of Innocence is a remarkable narrative recalling the childhood of a woman at the height of her dance career, whose spectacular success had attracted the attention and admiration of members of powerful elites throughout the world. Memoirs by celebrities at the time tended to be ghost-written and generally pro forma accounts of successes, sprinkled with a few disappointments and struggles to overcome obstacles, and perhaps a hurried gloss over an uncomfortable childhood. Instead, in the often riveting account of many painful and often disturbing experiences, the reader is apprised of some hard lessons for a young child described by a mature woman.

There are parallels between events in the child's life and the woman's experiences that may help explain the timing and the nature of the narrative. When she wrote the memoir, she had lost her brother, her father, and, soon after, her stepmother. She had disbanded the dance company she had led and nurtured for twenty years. The company would come together again for a time, but the end was anticipated. In 1978, she reflected on this time in her life: "What has been hard has been a personal adjustment to a lack of the audience, and I missed the company terribly at first. When I went to Japan and wrote a book of the first eighteen years of my life, I wept for the first two weeks."[52] In *A Touch of Innocence*, Dunham recounts how she had lost her birth mother and was anxious about being too immature and too weak to fulfill the needs and expectations of those around her. She placed a high value on loyalty to those who had been kind, especially her brother, whom she imbued with virtues of wisdom, integrity, and near-omniscience. In reverting to those times, Dunham may have hoped to renew the strength that had brought her so far. The adult reaffirmed the childhood imperative to be loyal and resourceful, perhaps gaining courage through the faith and eventual triumph of the child. In future years, after she had disbanded the company, Dunham would call its former members back time and again to renew the dream.

Marjorie Scott stayed on to type the manuscript for *A Touch of Innocence*, the better part of which Dunham wrote during that year in Japan. Madeline Preston and Joan Storely, the company's Australian stage manager, also remained for a time in Tokyo. Preston recall that Dunham "lived in a nice place . . . it overlooked Mt. Fuji."[53] It was a large room with a roof terrace, and the owners lived downstairs. The social pattern of Dunham's life had changed radically from that of the lonely child portrayed in *A Touch of Innocence;* even when the company was not touring, she surrounded herself with surrogate family members.

Dunham had felt an attraction to Zen Buddhism since she was a young girl, and she and Pratt shared a deep appreciation for Japanese art and culture. Pratt designed a "very elegant, charming Japanese room" for her dressing room in Tokyo.[54] Years later, he used Japanese themes and artifacts in designing her office at the Katherine Dunham Museum.

Following her year in Tokyo, Dunham returned to Hollywood in 1958 to choreograph the dance sequences for the film *Green Mansions*, with Audrey Hepburn and Anthony Perkins. After a brief stay in Hollywood, she joined Pratt and Marie-Christine in Port-au-Prince. Having received a book contract from Harcourt Brace, she completed *A Touch of Innocence* and signed and dated her manuscript in Haiti, she later acknowledged, to give some recognition to her adopted country.

Not only were the critical reviews of the book outstanding, but also she received personal letters expressing deep sentiments and approval. A friend wrote, "I am proud to know you. It has everything and is all yours."[55] Berenson had died before the book he inspired came out, but his companion, Nikki Mariano, wrote, "Your letter arrived just before Mr. Berenson died and I was still able to tell him about the dedication and it pleased him. I wish I could read them [memoirs] to Mr. Berenson. He admired the few chapters he had read in the manuscript very much."[56]

The Final Tours

In 1959, Dunham brought the company together for one last European tour, adding Greece, Lebanon, and Austria to the itinerary. Some of the critical comments from the tour show that the Dunham Company magic still held European audiences in thrall. A Danish reviewer spoke of her "queenly sureness, lightning temperament and a spirit that explains her leader ability," concluding, "She is alone in her field."[57] Another wrote, "Even the smallest detail shows Katherine Dunham's style, her nerve, her ability to dramatize the material with the help of fine, small nuances . . . her living feeling for the dramatic effect, both serious and light, her bubbling fantasy. . . . There is a life content in all this that fascinates."[58]

As reflected in many reviews, Dunham's stage presence was that of an artist of movement rather than a dancer in the usual sense of the term. The distinction is crucial, because it explains how someone suffering throughout her career from arthritis could continue to perform as lead dancer. She commented in a 1977 interview that her sense of "dynamic energy," that is, her confidence in movement, stemmed partly from her arthritis; it guided her into developing an orientation that was noncompetitive, avoiding the sudden bursts of energy required for high leaps and other feats.[59] The effect was that of subtlety and control, in which every movement counted. "And she manages," Doris Hering wrote in *Dance* magazine, "with an indolent bump or a leggy extension, to rivet the audience's attention despite the feverish and far more intricate dancing of the young swains encircling her. . . . She is always her own cool and languid self, moving deliberately, making each gesture count in her composite picture of the eternal Lilith."[60] Her style, having none of the "mindless exhibitionism" she abhorred, appealed to European audiences. An English reviewer commented, "Every moment she is on the stage, her gestures, expressions and movements are alive and pertinent to the situation. How few artists have the power to hold an audience by the simple gesture of a beautiful hand or a tensely held head with the eyes alone giving a clue to the terrifying situation!"[61] Her dancing was described as a true welding of mind and body: "One finds in her productions the thought, the culture, and the accuracy of a real mind—dance and culture are wonderfully mated."[62]

While some critics in the 1950s noted a certain familiarity in the Dunham materials and were critical because they did not have quite the same impact as in the early years, others indicated that they were far from bored and perceived a honing of talent: "Some same sets, some freshness . . . the same wise humanity and unbelievably sure taste and sense for style. But an even greater mastery has developed; often they are satisfied with only the suggestion, an art that is served with a sureness that takes ones breath—whether it concerns deep seriousness, crazymad humor or accurately aimed satire."[63] In the article "Ballet on Bare Toes," the reviewer wrote that Lucille Ellis still had "fine rhythmic sense and plenty of humor."[64] The interpretation of the lovers in "Rites de Passage" by Ellis and Clifford Fears was described in terms of the current views about the "primitive," as projecting "something anonymous, making them a part of the original tribe," and the writer noted that the love episodes were very different from European expressions of love. John Pratt's artistry was still recognized: "Finely styled equipment—imaginative lighting effects."[65]

Financial problems, exacerbated by the promotion of other performing groups by the U.S. State Department, and ongoing and increasing conflicts within the group resulted in a second breakup of the company while it was in Austria. Because of a heavy tax debt, Dunham had formed a new corporation, Corporation Leclerc, in Panama. She waged, as she put it, "serious battles with the American government," arguing it was unjust to have to pay social security and taxes while touring because if company members were out of work, they could only make a claim at the place of earnings. She was unable to keep up the property at Leclerc, and her insurance lapsed. The company no longer buoyed her: "I am fatigued unto death with Company complaints and nagging. . . . I have come to the decision that I would prefer to abandon my business than to further compromise with dissatisfied elements." She admitted, however, "The crisis is more within myself than in the company."[66]

Dunham and Pratt were again having problems. Emotionally, their turbulent relationship seemed to combine the stormy quality of her relationship with her father and her closeness to her brother. She wrote to her lawyer in New York, "I cannot either physically, morally or financially go through what I went through in Haiti." She expressed distrust of Pratt, believing that he may have sold some of her gold coins and perhaps other things. Although her lawyer reported that he was working, designing labels, and that he had talked to Harry Belafonte about doing a play or movie about Marie Laveau, starring Dunham, she was not reassured. She was afraid he was running up bad debts at the Algonquin in New York and speculated that he was possibly living on an inheritance from his mother but had not offered to help her out. She even considered hiring a private investigator to follow his movements, while insisting she was "emotionally quite free."[67] She wrote to Edith Bel Geddes, who was then staying at her home in Port-au-Prince, "Things are pretty near the breaking point with us. I have had no word from him. . . . He wants nothing more to do with Leclerc, with me," and she stated that she was trying to separate the property.[68]

Aware of the central role of their partnership in the company, friends worked to bring the two of them back together. Bel Geddes wrote to her that Pratt always had good things to say about her, and her lawyer informed her, "John will drop everything if you want him in Italy."[69] In March 1960, she wrote Bel Geddes, "No news of John; Marie-Christine asks after him constantly."[70] He joined them in Vienna but soon left to stay with a friend. Dunham wrote to her lawyer that she was concerned about him, worried that he was drinking himself to death. She again mentioned putting all property in her name or otherwise nullifying the marriage.[71] As it turned out, they remained married and partners until Pratt's death in 1986.

Vienna in 1960 was disastrous for the company. The local impresario died, and his son, who replaced him, did very little advance publicity for the group. Reviews were good, but attendance was light. One or two of the dancers were unable to pay their hotel bills, and a local newspaper picked this up, publishing a highly defamatory article about their attempts to cheat the hotel, the imminent break up of the company, and a threat by the police to take Dunham's jewelry if the bill was not paid.[72] A planned tour of Iron Curtain countries—Yugoslavia, Hungary, Czechoslovakia, and even the Soviet Union—did not materialize, and the group was stranded in Vienna.

Ever resourceful, Dunham signed a contract to do a television show to air in Cologne, then one in Milan, followed by a lecture-theatre in Club Rome; by these means she raised enough for fares home. Some of the company returned to the United States, while others formed a "club unit" and played in night clubs in Madrid and Rome. Dunham borrowed six thousand dollars from a wealthy Swedish family and traveled through the south of France and Majorca in a "middle-aged Jaguar" with Serge Tolstoy. In a letter to Preston, she referred to Vienna as a "fatal grotesquerie" and admitted she was "seeking relief, running away," since she did not want to return to Haiti without money.[73] She did eventually go back, however, accompanied by Dick Frisell, the son of the well-to-do Swedish family, who was attracted by the Dunham mystique and the romance of the artistic life. He was enchanted by Haiti and invested in property improvements at Leclerc.[74]

Bel Geddes, who had worked on costumes for such Dunham productions as *Bal Nègre*, had been inviting "rich friends" and "important people" to Leclerc while Dunham was on tour, trying to get them interested in developing a resort. The aim was to "make the property a historical showplace" for tourists so that it would be self-sustaining.[75] In a letter to her lawyer, Dunham complained about "Edith's [Bel Geddes] attitude," as though "only when she was there was anything done. . . . I'm like a mother bobcat about Leclerc."[76] When she returned, she threw herself into developing Habitation Leclerc, applying her usual vision and scope. Attractions included ceremonial *voudun* dancing and a zoological exhibit, under Frisell's direction. Advertisements in the travel section of the *New York Times* touted the unique qualities of the resort: "An evening at Katherine Dunham's famous Habitation Leclerc cost $11.50 complete. This covered drinks, dinner and the show, which included a voodoo ritual at an outdoor amphitheatre and Mme. Dunham's own dancing."[77] However, the Duvalier regime was not sympathetic to tourism, and the reputation of the Ton-ton Macoute, as well as the open poverty of Haitians, discouraged tourists.

Forced to relinquish her plans for Habitation Leclerc, at least for the time being, Dunham turned her attention back to dance, attempting to reassemble the company. She wrote to Ricardo Avalos in New York, "One of the problems with the last Company was that we were too long without roots, and a school."[78] She was approached by the producer Stephen Papich to do another Broadway production. During a previous visit to Morocco, she had met the crown prince, the late King Hassan II, and was impressed by the dancers at his court, especially the Ouled Nail, or "blue women." She returned to Africa and collected materials and dancers for *Bamboche*, which, after a brief tour, opened in New York. Following the opening section of Moroccan dancing, the program continued in the established pattern: a dance drama, "The Diamond Thief," set in South Africa, and American gospel and jazz numbers. It was an innovative and stunning production, according to most critics, although Allen Hughes in the *New York Times* found the Moroccan sequence "diffuse and confused," preferring the dance drama and American sections.[79] Dunham still regards it as the company's finest production: "It was a beautiful show! The best dancers: King Hassan's favorite, a tall female dancer. Bedouins from Marrakech, tall black men, whirling; a male belly dancer."[80]

A number of conditions forced the production to close after a short run. The Bay of Pigs crisis focused public attention elsewhere, and a newspaper strike prevented the advertising necessary to support a large New York production. As a result, audience attendance was unsatisfactory. In addition, Dunham remarked, Jewish women's organizations that regularly bought up the seats to the Wednesday matinee performances at the Fifty-fourth Street Theatre did not attend *Bamboche*. The Moroccan venture had received considerable publicity, and the Jewish clubs looked upon the presentation of Islamic culture with disfavor. The lack of their usual support hurt ticket sales.

To add to Dunham's problems, the company had to provide for the return of the dancers to Morocco. They came to the lobby of her hotel every day, dressed in native costume, reminding her of their need for passage home. To pay for the fares, she booked the company for a performance at the Apollo Theater in Harlem, which was having problems signing artists because of a fear of violence associated with the growing civil rights movement. The performance was the final one for the intact Dunham Company, although some members came together for later celebratory performances.

After *Bamboche* closed, Dunham was asked to choreograph *Aida* for Metropolitan Opera Theater performances in 1964 and 1966. Coming from an African involvement in producing *Bamboche*, Dunham embraced the view, not widely accepted at the time, that the Egypt of the Pharaohs was African rather than Middle Eastern. The program notes described the triumphal scene: "Miss Dunham's conception includes: a) Bedouin girls swathed voluminously in shades of pale and indigo blue . . . antecedents perhaps [of] the Blue Women of Gulimin in southern Morocco"; b) a "band of four high-leaping Somalis from south of Ethiopia," a composite type recreated "in the absence of clear records of pre-historic black Africa"; c) a band of Nubian warriors who perform the "striking, punching, kicking and springing movements of traditional *karate*."[81]

Dunham hired a karate expert to train company members for the triumphal scene, since her research had indicated that the martial arts had been practiced by Egyptian warriors. She wrote, "The Triumphal March of *Aida* has always been a production challenge. Until the last decade, however, authenticity counted for less than random extravaganza. Today with television, motion picture spectaculars and distant lands readily accessible to the general public, the production staffs of operas of exotic themes are obliged to restudy scores and original notes and research in ethnic and archeological backgrounds in order to satisfy a more demanding audience and give a new authority to material."[82] Opening night was a grand occasion, with President Lyndon Johnson in the audience. The audience was enthralled, but some of the critics were unhappy, preferring the more traditional dances for the Verdi classic.

Since there were no black dancers in the Met company other than

Janet Collins, dancers, including children, were brought in from the Dunham School on Forty-second Street. Mary Vivian, Dana McBroom, and Marcia McBroom played town children. They auditioned before Dame Alicia Markova. She was looking for two sets of twins to appear with the group of Moors accompanying Amneris, and Dana, Marcia, and later Mary were chosen. The children were very mischievous: Dana McBroom recalled carrying large fans and hitting some of the musicians on the head as they processed down onto the stage.[83]

Leontyne Price played Aida. "She was such a wonderful human being, very nice to work with; she took care of us like we were babies. When we were getting ready to go on, she'd stop to see how we were," Dana McBroom remembered.[84] Rudolph Bing was the director of the Met at the time and was also very solicitous of them. Zubin Mehta conducted, and Richard Tucker, Brigitte Nilsson, and Martine Arroyo sang in the production, with Arroyo replacing Leontyne Price on one occasion. Dunham had the entire Met dance company take classes at the Dunham School, working with her, Vanoye Aikens, Ural Wilson, and Lucille Ellis. Arthur Mitchell came to teach ballet.

Dunham was painstaking with the costumes and makeup. Black wool was used in the young girls' hair to extend their braids for the "Egyptian look"; this was before braid extensions were a common practice among women. Eye makeup was carefully applied. "We had sparkles on our eyes, all the way out to the hairline; it was very authentic, you could look at Egyptian photos and look at us and it was exactly the same. I learned a lot about makeup," Dana McBroom related.[85] They were told that often people would fall asleep during Met performances, but they never slept during the Dunham dances because they were so exciting. The other Dunham dancers left after one or two seasons, but Dana McBroom stayed for five years. Afterward, all the black dancers were replaced by the regular company members.

Aida was Dunham's farewell to New York and served as a passage back to her philosophical roots and to the Midwest. A delegation from a midwestern university came to New York to attend a performance of *Aida*, with the aim of persuading her to accept a residency to choreograph the opera *Faust*. Accepting the proposal, she subsequently moved further from show business and back to a concentration on the social functions of art, which she had never really relinquished.

9 Katherine Dunham and Her Dancers

> We were all together, a family, growing and developing and [it was] her nurturing which was teaching us and developing us . . . building those individual personalities as well . . . a Hell of a job, you know? It was incredible!
>
> —Lucille Ellis, 1991 interview by author

KATHERINE DUNHAM HAS COMPARED her relationship with the company while on tour with that of a lioness protecting her young. In a public lecture, she told an audience that she was everything to the company, including anchor as well as choreographer. Lucille Ellis appreciated the difficulties of Dunham's role: "We were young and she was also a very young woman, and she had all this to take care of—to be responsible for all this group of people. We were like teenagers growing up." Dunham would tell them, "Now we're going to go out and see what we can do in this great big world, but we're going to do it together."[1]

In her memoir, Dunham wrote that she "picked up clothes, ironed ruffles," and scolded members, combining roles of prima ballerina and company mother. She tried to get company members to wash their lingerie regularly; she even washed them herself one time to embarrass them into doing it, but it didn't work, she said ruefully. She tried to get them not to leave the white clothes for "Shango" around backstage. Once she washed a pair of pants and a skirt in the bathtub and hung them up to dry; the clothes were still damp at performance.[2]

John Pratt pointed out that Dunham never actually lived with the company, however, but kept herself apart; this was how she was able to manage things and hold it together.[3] According to Eartha Kitt, Lucille Ellis was actually the "head of the family," the cook, and overseer, and all the company members took turns in cleaning up or shopping.[4] Tommy Gomez referred to Ellis as "Miss Dunham's sergeant."[5]

Years later, Ellis remembered the relationships within the company with great nostalgia: "That was the beautiful part of being in the company because it taught us so much about how to live with each other, also to have respect for each other . . . by learning from each other we'd have respect, and that gave us a lot of bonding." The older members would help the younger ones and those joining the company.[6] Dunham has acknowledged that the troupe replaced family for the dancers, often causing their families to be "mad at me."[7]

Ellis testified to unity in spite of differences: "[There were] all [kinds] of personalities . . . [we] move[d] as ONE, one group of people: I used to call it a neighborhood, a whole neighborhood, just constantly moving. But we were stronger because we were together." Dunham's leadership style was autocratic, yet in some ways democratic: "She would ask us what we thought about certain things and we would reply, but she would ASK . . . and that's why it was like family." At other times rather than asking them, she would say: "'I'm not too thrilled about it, but we'll have to do this.'" Ellis also spoke about the conflicts, but she tended to downplay them in the interests of harmony: "There are always problems when you have people, but nothing that wasn't solved or resolved: it wasn't always solved, but it was resolved to where we could get on with what we were doing. And what was the most important thing, with . . . great respect."[8]

In the 1990s, Ellis and Gomez reminisced about when they joined the company as the youngest members. Gomez's parents did not want him to join the group and travel to New York to perform at the Windsor Theater. His mother talked to Dunham and gained her promise to look after him. Dunham put him in Archie Savage's care; Savage's sister had an apartment in New York and Gomez was to stay with them.[9] While the company was in New York for *Cabin in the Sky,* Gomez's mother wrote, enlisting Dunham's cooperation in helping to "bring my son Tommy to his senses." Savage had written her and reported that he had moved out and was "throwing money away on drinking and night life." He had sent her no money, and she asked Dunham to hold back half of his salary.[10]

On the bus from Chicago to New York, during that first trip, Gomez and Ellis carried box lunches provided by their parents. No one else had any food, so everyone helped themselves to theirs, and they were too awed and intimidated to object. Savage intervened and told the others to leave them alone. When told of this incident years later, Dunham remarked,

"I wish I had known." She remembered that she had to protect the young Ricardo Avalos from the others as well: "There is nothing like dancers for making you miserable."[11]

Years later, she asked the former company members if they felt that she was a different person now. Gomez maintained that she had become much more approachable. In earlier years, he was often afraid to approach her, fearing it would be an intrusion. "The magnetic circle," Dunham once explained, referring to the protective psychic space around oneself that she advises students to observe.[12] Her listeners glimpsed an image from the past: the defenses of a glamorous star, under great pressure from the adulation of fans, the demands of artists in her entourage, and the responsibilities of running a company with no external support. The company was the most important thing in her life, and she paid the price. A reviewer noted, "Money, security, family—all these have been sacrificed as occasion demanded."[13]

Eartha Kitt provided an insightful perspective on her mentor in her autobiography, *Thursday's Child:* "She was not the kind of person one walks right up to and buttonholes. I couldn't really reach her—but I got sensitivity from her. A spiritual kind of feeling, like a wave being received, but uneven. . . . When I got a warm word from her, it was a rare one."[14] As a senior matriarch—or "earth mother," as she half-seriously refers to herself—with a record of successes for herself and her protégés, Dunham has even greater authority, if less formal power, in her later years, but she is more relaxed. With greater wisdom comes a willingness to let others come close, and with more psychic detachment comes, paradoxically, less need for privacy.

In the early days of the company, she began to insist on being addressed as "Miss Dunham" when, during the production of *Cabin in the Sky,*" she heard stage hands and everyone else calling the great Ethel Waters, "Ethel," as though she were the cleaning lady. In turn, she refers to everyone but students—even to friends, in public—by their title, "Dr.," "Miss," "Mr.," or "Mrs."

Because of her intense involvement in the company, Dunham was particularly wounded by what she perceived as betrayal by its members. Lavinia Williams, one of the outstanding lead dancers, left the company abruptly, taking along her meticulous notes of Dunham technique. She subsequently used them when founding a dance studio in Haiti. A former company member remarked that this was particularly hurtful, since Dunham had long wanted to open a school in Haiti but was too involved in touring and in keeping the company solvent to do so.[15]

Williams had joined the company when she was nineteen. A former member of Eugene Von Grona's Black Dance Company, she was enlisted in 1940 to perform in *Cabin in the Sky*.[16] After the show closed, she joined the Dunham Company. In 1993, Williams's prospective biographer asked Dunham during a public lecture about Williams's contribution to knowledge of the *voudun*. She replied that Williams had known nothing about the *voudun*. She could not imagine Williams's undergoing what she would have to, what she herself underwent, to know what it was about. She felt that Williams developed Haitian dance as theater and technique, which lent it respectability, but she understood little about it as sacred theater.[17]

Gloria Thornburg observed that Williams was very confrontational with Dunham and that she had "absconded" with her choreography. She felt that it was the *way* Williams acted rather than her action itself that was galling. If she had acknowledged Dunham's authority on the *voudun* and her role as a mentor to whom she owed much of her knowledge and opportunity, she could have established herself in Haiti with Dunham's blessing and assistance.[18] Whatever their difficulties in the past, Dunham was at Williams's bedside before she died in 1990, and all was forgiven, if not forgotten. Williams, she stated at a 1993 lecture, was a great performer and a fine teacher.[19] According to Penny Godboldo, who studied with Williams, she frequently expressed her indebtedness to Dunham.[20]

A similar situation developed when Maya Deren, who had acted as Dunham's secretary/assistant, wrote about Haitian religion without acknowledging her debt to her former employer or even citing Dunham's publications. She had been privy to Dunham's notes and films and had edited some of her writings. Deren had also met many of those who assisted her in her career through her work with Dunham, including her own husband. Deren collaborated with such former Dunham Company members as Rita Christiane, Janet Collins, and Talley Beatty on dance films.[21] She wrote *The Divine Horseman*, which, despite her sense of Deren's disloyalty, Dunham acknowledged as the best work on the Haitian *voudun*.[22]

These instances suggesting a lack of faith on the part of close associates hurt deeply. In a time when African American artists and cultures generally—and Dunham technique in particular—were being imitated without credit or acknowledgment, courtesies of recognition assumed special importance. Even now, Dunham has protested, people who have been associated with her in various capacities are writing about her life and work without informing her or providing her with outlines or preliminary manuscripts.

The Dunham Company produced stars, many of whom went on to

develop independently as artists, but there was one primary star in the company: Katherine Dunham. This caused inevitable jealousy; at one point, two members left the company, ostensibly because of problems with racism while touring, but, Dunham acknowledged, such problems would not have caused them to leave if things were all right in the group. She averred that they left when she bought a fur coat for herself, tacitly recognizing that they were jealous of her special status. The two—Janet Collins and Talley Beatty—both went on to develop outstanding dance careers.

Archie Savage left the company in Los Angeles at the close of *Cabin in the Sky*. He was dissatisfied because he could not get his name "outside the theater" on the marquee: "I was what they called 'and Company.'"[23] He talked to Beatty and Roger Ohardieno about it, and they knew he was leaving. "It was all a little messy," Beatty remarked.[24] In 1941, Mary Hunter, Dunham's manager, wrote, "Archie is really a mess," and she was critical of his "self-seeking" traits, deploring the fact that ego satisfaction was more important to him than professional opportunity.[25]

Having worked with Asadata Dafora in Orson Welles's production of *Macbeth* and in Oscar Hammerstein's Broadway version of the opera *Carmen*, Savage was an older, more established artist than other company members. He went on to dance in other Broadway productions, including *Finian's Rainbow* in 1947, and in films. Beatty and other company members intimated that there was more involved than Savage's ego in the 1941 episode: Ethel Waters tried to lure him away from the company. Beatty stated, "Ethel was—Dunham probably won't say anything about this because she's above this sort of thing—Ethel was really beyond believability. . . . Archie went with the company [but] the company split in half, almost, because of Ethel Waters."[26]

While Waters was the star of *Cabin in the Sky*, Katherine Dunham was also singled out in reviews for special praise. This inevitably caused problems, and Waters, unlike Dunham, was not diplomatic in her professional relations. There were problems over dressing room assignments. Waters objected to being placed next to the bathroom, though it was intended as a convenience: "'I told them they better not put me next to these shit houses.'" According to Dunham, Waters was a "great, great woman" who had "black anger" against whites: "I was in trouble when John Pratt appeared." Waters brushed off Dunham's background with "'I don't know nothin' about no anthropology, but I do know about wigglin' your behind.'" She was suspicious of Dunham's support of unions, because the crews she had toured with were nonunion. Moreover, she refused to join the fight for hotel rooms, since she preferred to stay with acquaintances in black neighborhoods.[27] It was a classic conflict of class and regional backgrounds, Waters having grown up in the South.

The contretemps with Waters was the first of a number of conflicts Dunham would have with other stars, although she was always careful to maintain a civil exchange. Her handling of sensitive areas in her relationship with Waters is instructive. In a letter to her manager during the touring of *Cabin in the Sky,* she expressed a desire to have the publicity reflect the Katherine Dunham group as an entity and not be submerged, while she recognized Ethel Waters as a "stellar attraction" and had no desire to detract from her press.[28] From the earliest days, she fought for the integrity of her dance group. She recognized that her own artistic achievement was inevitably linked to the realization of her creations by a well-trained group of dancers.

Although Savage remained with the company throughout the tour of *Cabin in the Sky,* he departed shortly afterward. Beatty and Ohardieno left soon after as well. But Beatty, like Savage and many others, never left the Dunham group in spirit. Lucille Ellis attested to the continuing magnetic pull of the Dunham Company: "even members of the Company who left us . . . they'll call me, you know, 'How's everything going, is Miss Dunham all right? Does she need anything? Let me know if I can do anything.'" It was important to Dunham to "hold onto" people she had not heard from for a long time: "They were still a part of this movement. . . . Their contribution was just as important."[29]

Gloria Thornburg, who had previously performed with Denishawn,[30] downplayed complaints by company members. She commented that most of them did not fully recognize that Katherine Dunham was the creative genius, that the materials and responsibility for the company were hers, and that for audiences she was the primary attraction, the performer with the greatest charisma, if not the most accomplished dancer.[31] In contrast, Eartha Kitt painted a convincing picture of the awe in which the dancers held Dunham: "Her choreography was unquestionable. Each of us longed for her to choreograph a dance featuring us." They would wonder: "Is she watching me? Does she think I am good? . . . Every time she reprimanded a member of the class for not doing good work, the others were relieved not to be the one, with a false feeling of being her favorite."[32]

Still, they complained about working conditions and their relative prominence in performances, and they occasionally left the company without warning (Dunham learned to train everyone to fill different roles so that she was not at the mercy of discontented members). Even in retrospect, Kitt recalled how demanding and dissatisfied the Dunham Company dancers were. She candidly observed in her memoirs that "we were all pretty dependent on our leader. We would talk about her unmercifully. Anything to downgrade her in our own eyes because she held a power over us that we could not understand and that we resented. At the same time, we idolized her, for the courage and strength to accomplish what she had, for her leadership and protection." They were ambivalent, wanting to develop independent careers but not having the courage to leave. Kitt reported that Dunham told them that "the outside world was cruel and hard, that we didn't know how well off we were to be getting this training and experience."[33]

Predictably, the dancers reacted negatively to this counsel and felt she was holding them back. Kitt herself sometimes wondered why she did not give them a better chance to show off their talents: "At times I thought Miss Dunham was unfair, but I knew too that she had to fight hard in order to survive. . . . It wasn't until years later that I learned for myself just how true most of her words were about the outside world being difficult and about that long, narrow, rocky path to success and what the word 'success' really meant."[34]

Kitt described company members as living "in a bed of tension and intrigue" and undecided as to whether they loved or hated themselves and one another: "the constant pressure of insecurity kept us from liking others or ourselves. . . . We hated what we were but we loved it too, for the Dunham Company meant something in many ways." They understood that Katherine Dunham had created a better world for many of them, "at the same time making the path easier for those who had guts enough to follow."[35] Her tough-minded assessment indicates the knowledge and wisdom that Kitt gained later from her own hard-won successes.

Dunham has affirmed that "Kitty" always gives recognition to her experiences at the Dunham School and with the Dunham Company in public appearances, a courtesy that is not extended by all former students.[36] Kitt received a scholarship to the Dunham School when she was very young and has kept in touch, in spite of her break for independence during a European tour. She visited Dunham's class in East St. Louis one year during a St. Louis production of *Timbuktoo* in which she starred, and she called on her in 1995 during a tour in a one-woman show.

Penny Godboldo, a dancer and student of the Dunham technique, commented that Dunham's philosophy and leadership style allowed her members to develop their own creative powers and therefore encouraged independent artists, such as Eartha Kitt, as well as excellent teachers, such as Lavinia Williams and Syvilla Fort.[37] As a reviewer once wrote, "To a large extent, the company creates its own stars. [Lenwood] Morris, for example, had never danced a step until he joined Dunham, after running away from dental college. . . . Vanoye Aikens was plucked off a New York street—he had the physique wanted for a particular role; the personality of Eartha Kitt, today's fabulous Hollywood star, was mould-ed largely in Dunham's classes."[38]

Roger Ohardieno—often described as more talented as a singer than a dancer—preceded Aikens as Dunham's partner. According to Gloria Thornburg, Dunham was wholly responsible for Ohardieno's success as a dancer: she developed parts especially for him, to display his good points.[39] Beatty agreed: "She could bring people off the street and make them dance, who couldn't dance, really. 'Cause Roger got a sensational career out of her and Roger couldn't dance . . . but he looked so good, you know, in Archie's [Savage's] part."[40] Ohardieno became Dunham's prima-ry partner and was with the company for a long time. Lucille Ellis com-mented, "He was there to do the things that were required in that male quality of projection on the stage, which gave it a stronger element . . . along with the drummers."[41]

When Ohardieno left, Dunham soon had a replacement in Aikens, who was a student in her school in New York. He had appeared with the company from time to time, but now he became her main partner, con-tinuing until the company disbanded. She felt he was everything she desired in a leading man: handsome, with a strongly masculine aura.[42] As recently as 1980, he danced a lead role in "Rites de Passage" in Nash-ville, which was filmed for public television. She has been able to count on Aikens to rally to her assistance many times over the years.

Katherine Dunham's practice of utilizing and developing talents and idiosyncrasies is a hallmark of her career. However, she also left her own artistic mark on the dancers. Marjorie Scott commented, "She made anyone a dancer. You could see peoples' bodies changing from the [Dun-ham] technique, lengthen, strengthen." She observed that the company was highly disciplined and that there was much respect for Dunham.[43] She tended to be authoritarian, but, as Ellis pointed out, she did not de-mand conformity.[44] She remained true to Hutchins's ideals of education in producing a diversity of well-rounded, accomplished artists and in-fluencing others who remain outside her "entourage," or clan, as she refers to the faithful who continue to keep in touch with her and sup-port her work. She frequently refers to herself as primarily a catalyst. But as Marjorie Scott wryly commented, "Others have taken from it [Dun-ham technique] . . . that's the trouble if you are a catalyst."[45]

According to Gloria Thornburg's recollection, there were only two other dance companies with any credibility when the Dunham Compa-ny was formed: Martha Graham's and the Ballet Russe.[46] A comparison of Dunham's pedagogy with that of other dance directors highlights the distinctive character of her technique. Graham, of course, is recognized as a dominant force in modern dance. The policy of "growing" dancers, which some attribute to Dunham, contrasts sharply with that portrayed by a former student of Graham: "Martha just took our insides out and inhabited the body. She ate out the inner shell. . . . And she said 'I have to break this one and that one and then rebuild them.' And of course you can't rebuild anybody you break. . . . She felt that each one of us would be glad to be used as a Johnny-one-note, and she developed each of our particular notes very beautifully. But in developing them, she did not develop that note in anyone else, so *we* couldn't grow as rounded artists. But I felt it an honor to be part of it."[47] Apparently, Graham commanded total control and loyalty.

Dunham's approach stemmed from an alternative view of art, and her praxis reflected a radically different philosophy: art for life's sake, not art for art's sake. This did not mean that art is subordinate to life; it meant that art influences people's ways of viewing themselves and others. Her humanism and her functional viewpoint, inherited from her intellectual mentors, were equally strong forces in her life, as was dance: indeed, they were all conjoined. She informed students that she asked them to repeat a movement because "we want to work it into your muscle so you know what you're doing, not so much that you become bored." She wanted not "zombie-like" dancers, who were merely observers of their own movements, but dancers fully engaged with their actions, who are socially involved.[48]

Talley Beatty said that he felt secure with Dunham technique; he worked with Graham, Balanchine, and others but felt most comfortable with Dunham technique because it "comes from within": "We learned about a society while learning a dance, so we knew it!" This knowledge was visceral and resulted in a "richness" of the performance. "We did a lot of interior work; what was on stage was a result of what you were spiritually. . . . I love Dunham technique; it's what I always teach. It's logical/creative."[49]

The Dunham adventure, for everyone involved, including more recent followers, wrought a fundamental transformation, and it welded them into a social group in which, despite separations and differences, they live with and through one another. Until his death in 1999, Gomez phoned "Miss D" every week, and Madeline Preston calls every week while Dunham is in East St. Louis. Surrounded by friends and enlivened by their children, Katherine Dunham has re-created the family environment that her company once provided.

As a senior matriarch, Dunham has carried her concern for a broad education for dancers into the public arena. Along with other artists, she testified before a Senate committee in 1963 about the importance of dancers and other artists, who were seldom given credit for their role in educating the public, and the need for a comprehensive education for dancers themselves. The National Endowment for the Arts and the National Endowment for the Humanities grew out of this commission. At the hearing, she recalled stating, "When I was in Brazil, working with the ballet company, they were educated; most black dancers [in the United States] had little education."[50] The testimony reflected her agenda for the following decades: retiring as a star performer, she brought to the fore her identity as social anthropologist, teacher, and humanitarian, translating her role as leader and visionary into a new sphere.

10 Arts and the Community

> In comprehending Miss Dunham . . . one has to think
> not just of dance, not just of drums, not just of primitive
> rhythms, but of a totem-woman of African spirituality
> and cultural wealth. . . . She took up residence at North
> Tenth Street in East St. Louis, amidst crumbling build-
> ings, night-piercing sirens, and on the turf of the Imperi-
> al War Lords.
> —Eugene Redmond, 1976 interview in *Kaiso!*

IN THE LATE 1960s, Katherine Dunham was still at the height of her creative powers, but she lacked a medium to communicate her spirit and vision. She found a context for her mission of "culturization," as she termed it, in the ravaged city of East St. Louis, Illinois, by joining with the black social and political movements of the time.[1] As the East St. Louis poet Eugene Redmond phrased it, she appeared in the community like a falling meteorite.[2] Coming from the dizzying heights of international stardom, she encountered a tightly knit but economically devastated community in turmoil.

Dunham was a veteran of the civil rights battles in the 1940s and believed that much had been achieved. The lynchings portrayed in *Southland* had receded in memory, if not in the psyches of African Americans. During the civil rights movement in the 1950s and early 1960s, Dunham was directing her attention outside the country, expanding her vista to embrace Asian and African cultures. In Haiti, popular discontent was being contained by Papa Doc Duvalier and by the peasants' absorption in religious ceremonies. So like many of her generation, she was shocked by the open expression of anger and frustration by the young people in

East St. Louis and other urban centers. She realized that, unlike Haitians, they knew little about their African heritage, and she thought that part of the key to their survival and growth lay in that knowledge.

Her experience in the Caribbean had prepared her for the dense social world of East St. Louis; she remarked years later that it was the family orientation of East St. Louis that had attracted her. Because of its village-like qualities, she likened the city to Port-au-Prince and Dakar rather than to the more cosmopolitan Harlem or Chicago. She encountered folk expressions similar to those she had studied in Africa and the Caribbean. She was challenged to educate the community about its cultural origins.

Dunham was reoriented into midwestern life as artist-in-residence at Southern Illinois University (SIU) at Carbondale, where she choreographed the opera *Faust* for regional audiences. Continuing her penchant for linking up with kindred spirits, she was recruited by Delyte Morris, the first chancellor of the Southern Illinois University system, who saw *Aida* in New York and was impressed by her unorthodox approach. His aspiration was to establish a cultural center in the southern part of the state that would match that of Chicago and its satellites in the north. He sought like-minded faculty, bringing together imaginative, creative artists and humanists, such as Buckminster Fuller, Katherine Dunham, and Marjorie Lawrence, the Metropolitan Opera's prima donna, to help realize his dream. John Pratt's brother Davis, who taught in the School of Art and Design at the university, functioned as a link between Dunham and Morris.

For *Faust*, Edith Lutyens (Mrs. Norman Bel Geddes) was invited to assist with costumes, and Marjorie Lawrence functioned as producer. The opera was performed not only on the Carbondale campus but also at Monticello College, near Alton, Illinois, Annette Dunham's hometown.

Dunham was invited to develop a dance and cultural arts program at the northern campus of Southern Illinois University, which was then located in Alton. From there, she submitted a proposal in 1965 to the Office of Economic Opportunity (OEO) for a cultural center at East St. Louis; in the meantime, she held classes at the Alton campus. She dedicated the program to Annette Poindexter Dunham.

Establishing a program in southern Illinois was very different from directing a company on tour. Josephine Beckwith, then Josephine Wilson, who worked in the administrative offices, helped her with logistics and "showed her the ropes." She recalled that Dunham's revolutionary approach to art faced considerable opposition, from both the community and the university. Despite its controversial nature, her vision was compelling, and her magnetism continued to attract and enlist those who shared her ideals. Beckwith and some faculty members championed her enterprise; serving as Dunham's secretary, Beckwith used her own contacts at the university and in the community to assist in getting the program started. She spent her vacation time for two years working for the program. Her son Everett Wilson recruited friends to take classes.

Dunham and Pratt were staying at the house of a faculty member who was on leave; when the family returned, they had difficulty finding another suitable domicile. Even though it was 1965, a mixed-race marriage was not socially acceptable in Alton. Some friends of Beckwith helped them find a house on the campus—Beckwith's current residence. Butterfly McQueen stayed with Dunham and Pratt when she came to teach in the program and attend classes at the university. McQueen was at a low point in her career since playing the role of a slave in *Gone with the Wind.* Dunham was known to remember people who were forgotten and to give them opportunities.

While working at SIU, Dunham continued to be involved in international dance. In 1965, after the production of *Faust,* she choreographed a film and a stage production in Rome, as well as a show in Paris, and she reassembled the company for a New York performance at the American Ballet Theatre's twenty-fifth anniversary gala.

Dunham was invited to train the National Ballet of Senegal by President Léopold Senghor, whom she had met while in Paris. He appointed her adviser for the First World Festival of Negro Arts, held in Dakar in 1966. The poet-president and Dunham became fast friends. For the first time, the State Department gave Dunham official status: she was named U.S. representative to the festival in Dakar. In Senegal, she met Mor Thiam, a master drummer, whom she invited to teach in East St. Louis.

Life in Senegal—like Haiti, a former French colony—felt compatible to Dunham and Pratt, and they leased a house in Dakar. There she found time to write *Island Possessed*, published in 1967. She also wrote a fantasy for young people with a Senegalese setting, *Kasamance.*[3]

While they were in Senegal, Dunham learned that Edmond Rothschild, owner of the Club Méditerranée (Club Med), was purchasing rights to build a club on the Isle of Goré, the island on which captured Africans had awaited transport to the New World. The negotiating process between Rothschild and the government was underway when Dunham heard about it. She learned that Rothschild intended to deny membership in the club to Senegalese and other Africans. She approached President Senghor, who was shocked but told her it would be difficult to influence the process at that point. Determined to challenge the scheme, she decided to approach the marabouts—religious leaders—in the villages, who held very traditional Islamic beliefs. She took an interpreter, since they spoke no French. The marabouts wore starched, spotless white attire, she recalled, and their compounds were immaculately kept. They were appalled by her communication, and three of those she talked to were interested in pursuing the matter. They apparently exerted serious pressure on the government, for the Club Med was never built on the Isle of Goré. It is now a historical monument and a symbol of the enslavement of millions of Africans.

On her return to SIU in 1967, Dunham continued promoting Morris's dream of a cultural mecca. She collaborated with Buckminster Fuller on a visionary proposal for a cultural arts center in East St. Louis, which included plans for the arts, housing, food, and all basic human needs. They saw East St. Louis as the future hub of economic and cultural development on the east side of the Mississippi. Fuller's world-famous energy-conserving geodesic dome was projected as part of a riverfront development. Some people in the community supported these proposals, but many of the townspeople were threatened by the idea of being "contained" by such a dome. While east side riverfront development proposals have been revived periodically, none include Fuller's geodesic dome. The only local reminders of his vision are a small but beautiful dome over the Religious Center on the Edwardsville campus of SIU and the Climatron at the Missouri Botanical Garden in St. Louis.

Dunham was successful in her OEO proposal and approached East St. Louis administrators with a $400,000 grant in hand for a cultural center. Politicians initially resisted the proposal because they had applied for federal money for such projects as parks, streets, and support for the school board, and they did not see the need for the proposed cultural program. Disappointed, she left to work on overseas projects, determined not to return to East St. Louis. While she was abroad, however, she began seeing that the city "needed assistance as much as, or more than, areas in the so-called underdeveloped countries."[4] When she returned, she was again encouraged to develop a cultural center. The Equal Opportunity Commission funded her proposed educational program, and it was established in 1967 as part of the SIU Experiment in Higher Education.

Dunham continued her program at the Alton campus and started classes in 1967 at Rock Junior High School in East St. Louis. At the outset, there were only two other teachers at the East St. Louis center: Marcia McBroom and Ricardo Avalos, former members of the Dunham Company. Dunham and Pratt moved to East St. Louis in 1968.

Three years after her initial disappointment, Dunham was presented with the key to the city, but that occurred only after considerable opposition and criticism. In 1967, on her first night after returning from Dakar, she was jailed in East St. Louis while protesting the arrest of a student.

The SIU administration and city officials had hoped that Katherine Dunham could work her magic to calm the political unrest among the youth in the troubled city. They became alarmed as she succeeded in reaching the young people through identifying with their causes. At one point, the authorities asked her to leave East St. Louis, claiming that her life might be in jeopardy because of her association with black activists. "That's the wrong thing to say to me," she told the president of the university. "Now I'll never leave."[5]

East St. Louis has been a problematic city from its inception. Historically, it functioned for St. Louis, as Las Vegas and Reno did for California cities: it was "wide open," with gambling, prostitution, and other vices. St. Louisans crossed the Mississippi River to be entertained in the clubs that flourished along the river. With all the money coming in from illegal activities, it is not surprising that the city government was notoriously corrupt. The then white mayor was replaced by a succession of black mayors who were no more corrupt—in some instances, markedly less so—although the negative reputation of the city continued and, unfairly, even increased, after the political changeover.

During the two world wars, black southerners had migrated to the area in search of jobs because of economic decline and increasing Jim Crow laws in the South. Packinghouses, stockyards, and metal industries provided a large number of jobs, and white workers—representing Polish, Italian, and other ethnic groups—were threatened by economic competition from black workers. During World War I, rumors of attempts by companies to break nascent unions by importing large numbers of black workers led to hostilities, and interracial conflict was increased by false newspaper accounts claiming that Republicans planned to pack ballot boxes by bringing in blacks to vote illegally. These reports were circulated by interested parties: the companies themselves spread rumors about black workers to deflect white workers' anger, and the Democratic party accused the Republicans of "colonizing" black voters. In this volatile situation, a spark provided by a shooting incident involving police officers set off the explosive race riots of 1917, in which "about" thirty-nine African Americans and nine whites were killed; it was one of the worst race riots, in terms of bloodshed, in U.S. history, and it was initiated by whites.[6] It left feelings of anger and frustration that extend to the present day, along with persistent negative views of the city.

Industries began pulling out of the area after World War II because of labor troubles and race relations; at the same time, white residents moved away in great numbers, many to nearby Belleville, Illinois. Bitter about leaving their homes, they blamed the black residents, claiming that the crime rate was higher—a false view that continues to the present day. In the 1980s, a bridge across the Mississippi was blocked to prevent pedestrians from East St. Louis from attending the Veiled Prophet Fair in St. Louis.[7] In the meantime, financial institutions, businesses, and entertainment also fled the city. The remaining social institutions—churches and sororal and fraternal organizations—served the older generation, but unemployment and a lack of cultural and social amenities demoralized the younger citizens of East St. Louis.

In designing her community program, Dunham directed her attention to the "unchallenged youth" of the community, using art as a method of, in her words, "arousing awareness . . . of surpassing alienation, and of serving as a rational alternative to violence and genocide."[8] This was during the period when black leaders, such as Stokely Carmichael, H. Rap Brown, Malcolm X, and James Foreman, were advocating various forms of resistance. In East St. Louis, there were such campus groups as the Student Nonviolent Coordinating Committee and the Congress of Racial Equality; the local fraternities and sororities were also taking political stances. The college students favored a nonviolent approach, conducting sit-ins and protests. Those who were not attending college joined such organizations as the Black Panthers and Black Culture, Inc.—founded by the Reverend Charles Koen of Cairo, Illinois—emphasizing black pride, as well as such gangs as the Disciples, Gangster Disciples, and Imperial War Lords. Occasionally, representatives of the P-Stone Rangers would come down from Chicago and recruit from neighborhood groups.

John Brooks, a former student, stated that while most of the students in the SIU at Edwardsville Experiment in Higher Education knew all the members of the hard-core gangs, they were not members but on the periphery. Until he was about sixteen years old, he belonged to a neighborhood group, a standard teenage gang in which the members united against outsiders who harmed someone in the community. They formed football and baseball teams: "If we weren't [playing sports], then we were standing on the street corners, under the lights, doing what they call 'do-wap' songs," he reminisced. During the late sixties, some members of these groups were recruited into the various political action groups. Others became members of the Disciples or other gangs, although it was sometimes hard to draw a line between the gangs and the political action groups. When he returned to East St. Louis after military service, he found "everybody was armed." The police department was predominantly white; all the officials were white, including the man who had been mayor for more than twenty years. They were all seen as a part of the Chicago political machine. According to Brooks, "[T]heir reaction to all the militant groups was to shoot and beat the hell out of them first and ask questions later. So it was like both sides were entrenched in this standoff."[9]

This tense situation lasted for several years. With the heightened state of awareness, incidents would happen, such as Malcolm X's murder or H. Rap Brown's arrest, and there would be an escalation of violence. On the night that Martin Luther King was assassinated, all the windows that were not already broken on State Street were shattered. "Because of that," Brooks reported, "the police were on a heightened alert, so you would be stopped for just about anything—they were looking for weapons. And guys with their back up didn't respond too well—that was the situation in which she [Dunham] came." The first time he saw Dunham was the day that H. Rap Brown and Stokely Carmichael had come to East St. Louis and had spoken at Lincoln High School. "After they had spoken, all the people in the building poured out into the streets—Bond Avenue was full, from the sidewalk on one side of the street across to the other sidewalk for blocks was just full of people milling around." On Fifteenth and Broadway—in the central part of town—Darryl Braddix, who had attended classes at Dunham's Performing Arts Training Center, turned over a barrel and jumped up on it. "He really didn't have to say anything because mob psychology was already there. . . . The next thing you know, somebody had picked up a brick and [the trouble started] from there," Brooks recounted.[10]

Sometime before this event, Dunham had begun to contact some of the younger gang members of East St. Louis, through such intermediaries as Everett Wilson—Josephine Beckwith's son—who worked with the Office of Economic Opportunity. Since Wilson's mother had graduated from an East St. Louis High School, he knew the community. He could talk to the young men because he was only slightly older than they were. He accompanied Dunham on the streets, talking to those who were prone to violent behavior, and she was struck by the needs of the young people for some kind of hope and social identity. When she had gained their confidence, Braddix set up a meeting for her in a tavern on Fifteenth and Broadway with some of his peers.

When Braddix was arrested on suspicion of breaking windows, stemming from the earlier melee, Dunham went to the police station to support him. Brooks, who was in the bar when Dunham came in asking for directions downtown, recalled, "And Miss Dunham came in, just about everybody knew she didn't come from here . . . and there were a lot of guys who were paranoid and they're asking, who's that broad who's asking how do you get to the police station? Nobody is really rushing forward to volunteer any information." Brooks was standing closest to the door so she came over to him and asked him to direct her to the police station. He got into the car with Dunham; her daughter, Marie-Christine; and Jeanelle Stovall.[11] Dunham and Stovall had met at the First World Festival of Negro Arts, and Stovall, who had served as Dunham's interpreter in Senegal, had taken a month's leave from her job at the United Nations.

At the station, Dunham demanded to see the chief of police and to know the charges against Braddix. The police became irritated with her when she would not back down and arrested her as well as Stovall, who tried to assist her when a policeman jostled her. They spent part of the night there, but when the officials discovered who Dunham was, they freed them, and an official apology was forthcoming. As reported in *Muhammad Speaks*, the Nation of Islam publication, "Miss Dunham kept her identity secret so she could see how unknown Negroes are treated."[12]

The clash with authorities was a daunting if opportune introduction to the troubled city, shaping Dunham's future in two important ways. First, it fashioned an inseparable bond between Dunham and Stovall—whose month's leave stretched into years—that proved to be a productive association. Second, it convinced the young people that Dunham was an ally. Eugene Redmond corroborated this point: "At that time, I still had only seen Miss Dunham, had heard her speak or had seen elements of her troupe perform around the area, but I hadn't met Miss Dunham personally. . . . It was right after that I sought her out."[13]

An East St. Louis native, Redmond had participated in the Experiment in Higher Education (EHE) program, "Tenth Street Tech," as they called it. Redmond graduated from SIU at Edwardsville and attended graduate school in St. Louis. He was teaching at EHE when Dunham established the Performing Arts Training Center (PATC) as part of the program.

Redmond was one of the few people in his peer group who realized who Dunham was when she first arrived in the community. He had read about her in newspapers and magazines and had seen movie shorts in which she appeared: "[In school] they'd put clippings and notices on the current events board, most of those things would be geared toward achievements and advancements: out of the *Chicago Defender, Pittsburgh Courier . . . Baltimore Afro-American, Amsterdam News*, as well as the local papers . . . and *Jet* magazine. At the theaters that were designated for Negroes, they gave you news from the black world . . . the black troops in Europe. And there'd be fan clubs of Cab Calloway, Katherine Dunham, Joe Louis."[14] He knew that Dunham was a scholar as well as a performer, and when she arrived, his knowledge elevated him among his peers.

Like other young men in the community, Redmond was attracted by the drums, which acted like a "magnet": "I'd played drums as a kid, bongo drums. So I started sitting in, I'd just be around, catch productions, catch classes, and many of my students at EHE were also dancing."[15] Warrenton Hudlin and Reginald Hudlin[16]—now film directors—and Jackie Joyner-Kersey signed up for classes, as well as many other currently successful individuals with less national name recognition, including Sylvester ("Sunshine") Lee and Keith Williams, who currently have their own dance companies; Anne Walker, an advertising executive; Doris Bennett-Glasper, a Girl Scout director; and Darryl Braddix, Ed Brown, and Theodore Jamison, who teach classes and workshops at local schools and universities. At first, many of the young men refused to dance, so classes in martial arts and drumming were offered.

Dunham attracted others as well. A young woman with a minor physical handicap, Ruby Streate, loved dance lessons but felt she could not perform in the touring company that was made up of the more dedicated students. Dunham encouraged her to participate fully, and she became one of the star performers. She currently teaches Dunham technique to children.

Dunham came to identify Redmond as someone who was often on the sidelines during classes, and he offered her his services and considerable knowledge of the East St. Louis community. He became a teacher-counselor at PATC, or, as Dunham termed the position, a senior consultant, receiving a daily stipend that was supported by the federal grant. For the second time in her career, cultural programs funded by the federal government helped her attain some of her goals. According to Redmond, "Miss Dunham's thinking and the thinking of the sixties was very consistent with a history of that kind of thing, from the Federal Theatre, the WPA in Chicago, *Pins and Needles* in New York, ILGWU, the New Deal, it peaked in the New Frontier, the War on Poverty, [which was] the actualization of the New Frontier. . . . We had so many different projects and programs at the time, with acronyms like WIN and DAP and SIP, and STEP."[17]

The War on Poverty, growing out of the civil rights movement in the fifties and the rebellion of black youth in the sixties, included a cultural component and was aimed at building communities. The social climate supported innovative teaching, Redmond pointed out: "It was consistent with what a lot of people were proclaiming at the time, not just Miss Dunham alone, that everybody was part of an educational process, the total community was the classroom."[18] Dunham's program dovetailed with this policy, and she was able to obtain funding for many community educational activities by demonstrating the relationship between art and community development: "The Center aims to seed the locality with residents of the area who, having benefitted from the program themselves,

will then become participants . . . in community service projects. Through
such programs, the Center hopes to exert an influence for growth and
adaptation upon the leaders and educators of the area."[19]

The overall objective of PATC was to employ a creative and adapt-
able educational methodology "in pursuit of the fullest possible human-
ization and socialization of the individual and the community," emphasizing the performing and cultural arts.[20] Redmond was an enthusiastic
participant: "There wasn't a day that I didn't pop by. I found out two
things, one is that there would always be some good conversation, there
would be interesting people here, and that you didn't have to call."[21]

Redmond's role in the program was complex. He characterized himself as something of a ambassador and "translator." Dunham enjoyed the
nightlife in East St. Louis, whose clubs had hosted many superb performers—in their younger days, Miles Davis, Josephine Baker, Chuck Berry,
and Ike and Tina Turner, for example—and were still offering good entertainment. Redmond acted as her driver and at the same time introduced her to the language of the streets: "I think 'The Education of
Katherine Dunham' might be the title of one essay in a book somebody
might do about her time here, the things Miss D picked up: it was
definitely a two-way street," Redmond commented.[22] She was again fully engaged in fieldwork.

Through her work with gang members and politically active young
people, she became identified with the most radical element in the community. "Miss Dunham was at the center of everything . . . of the revolution in this region, of the avant-garde, the advanced activity and thinking of the revolution. Her house was like a salon, the equivalent of those
cafés in France," Redmond reported. He felt she had not intended to get
as involved in politics as she did but was led into it through her concern
for and identification with the young people. "It was exciting to her, but
it was also dangerous. Miss Dunham I think enjoyed living on the edge . . .
that was one of the things that drew us two together because I lived that
way myself," he mused. When Redmond and his friends advised her about
the danger from certain people in the movement, she listened: "We knew
what the cops knew; [sometimes] we needed to get away for a day or
two. . . . When she looked out and saw certain people around the house
counseling, she knew it was a concern."[23]

According to Redmond, some of the young men would leave their
weapons at Dunham's house when they crossed the bridge near her residence to go to St. Louis. They were afraid of the police in St. Louis, which
was the only major city in the country that had not experienced a black
rebellion: "The police were very, very terrifying, and we knew that it was

a different state, you know, Missouri was a slave state, it was a whole different ambiance . . . they had a way of keeping folks in check. The thing that all of us dreaded the most was going into a Missouri jail, for any reason. 'Cause you would not have an immediate future outside . . . they just held you, forget any kind of laws or rights."[24] They didn't want to be caught in St. Louis with weapons, but they didn't want to be in East St. Louis without them; they would leave them by her door and would pick them up as soon as they got off the bridge on the way back. In 1986, at the time of the Haitian coup, Dunham wrote to Redmond that she recognized some of the weapons she saw and heard in Haiti because of her experiences in East St. Louis.[25]

According to Redmond, Dunham was the first to identify the pathology in the black movement. Some of the members would notice that things were not going just right, orders would not be followed, and something unplanned would happen. "Miss Dunham would say, 'If everybody is armed, and you're in a room together, if that person is tricky, they'll kill you. They're going to kill anybody of this skin, or anybody of this gender.' . . . She was sensitive—sometimes she'd be wrong, but she was right in many instances."[26]

The FBI again tried to gain Dunham's assistance through betrayal of her friends: they called and left a message asking for information about one of the activists. She did not return the call and heard no more from them.[27] Because she had gained the trust of the young rebels, she could influence some of their actions and policies, and she was not about to threaten that trust.

Dunham took a group of young men to consult with Erich Fromm in New York as a part of her effort to encourage constructive behavior. She called Redmond at 2 A.M. and told him they were leaving on an 8 A.M. plane to see Erich Fromm. "It was quite an exciting, very profound experience," Redmond recalled. "I'm not sure all those people understood it." Fromm talked about mob mentality and the psychology of violence in the individual as well as in groups. He warned them about the violence that was prevalent in the country, pointing out that they needed to control their troops, "paramilitary units," as they referred to the groups of activists that made up the movement. "He outlined certain steps we needed to take when we were massed up in public places like parks . . . he was talking about how a peaceful group could be sabotaged and how people who are headed in the same direction could be turned against each other," Redmond recollected.[28]

Redmond observed that Fromm was a very pleasant person and a gracious host. They stayed at a hotel but were at his house in constant exchange for two days. Redmond was fascinated by the urbane lifestyle of the Fromms; there he met Suzanne Ndiop, a member of the Senegalese Supreme Court who, in Redmond's words, was "a very penetrating intellect." He was surprised that there was a woman on the Supreme Court of Senegal, predating by many years the first woman appointee to the U.S. Supreme Court. Redmond described the group that visited Fromm as including people who joined Ché Guevara and were with him when he was killed: "The sixties was a very fascinating time, because there were [African American] people in South Africa and West Africa as well as in South America and Canada who were working, so it was truly international."[29]

Although Dunham and her programs were popular with youth, many of the older residents were suspicious of her because she was an "outsider" and because of her identification with young radicals. She has remarked that because she did not join the social groups—churches and sororities—that shape the social life of the city, she was not accepted. In addition, her husband was white; he was mugged twice, walking to the store. Redmond and his friends protected him, but they sustained a great deal of criticism for befriending a white man.

The support she received from some of the older leaders was lukewarm, and parents were ambivalent as well: "I don't think she really cared how the older people reacted to her," Redmond opined. "She communicated to them and to the community at large through the instructors—myself, Ural [Wilson], Tommy [Gomez], Lenwood [Morris]. And whenever she showed up, people would flock to see her." The children and the young people were the real connection: "That was the strength. That was what made the bourgeois and everybody participate. The kids were the ones that came. The parents and the groups could be stand-offish, but she was offering so much that [young] people were saying to friends, 'I don't care how you go about it, but I'm going, I want to dance.'"[30]

There was much offered besides dance: photography, theater, martial arts. "We got a lot of male kids who never would have touched dance because of the stigma associated with it," Redmond pointed out, adding, "But we also had karate, that was masculine enough to get them on the scene." A young man would come in for the karate and at first might just watch the dance classes. "Then a little bit later you'd see him in there actually trying to dance."[31] In 1978, Eusebio Da Silva from Bahia, Brazil, taught *capoeira*, a martial arts thought to have originated in Angola and been brought over by slaves. The Brazilian government had outlawed it, and it had been disguised as an intricate dance form, accompanied by music and performed during celebrations, until the 1940s, when it was legalized. "Brazilians now understand that capoeira's most important cultural legacy is the lesson of survival by the use of creativity, cunning and imagination. . . . Basically, capoeira is a philosophy of life, a way *not* to fight. . . . A true capoeirista is always ready to improvise and has a great ability to deal with the unexpected. He studies nature and learns well from it [the movements imitate those of the cat, the scorpion, the monkey and the snake]. He desires, above all, freedom, and he is ready to guard that gift," wrote Alina Rivero in a 1979 article in the *St. Louis Post-Dispatch.*[32] Little wonder that the young East St. Louisans were attracted to *capoeira.* Reginald Hudlin became especially proficient in its skills.

In talking about those early years in East St. Louis, Dunham spoke of survival as the heart of the belief system of the young East St. Louisans: "[The meaning of] religion is that you have to have belief and confidence in yourself . . . it doesn't matter what you call it. It's survival. Survival means something different to different people. Working with young militants—it's practical survival to them, to eat, stay alive."[33] It was her ability to understand the young people and to start from where they were that helped her build a successful program in the city. She was concerned about the drug use among youth and proposed a program of getting heavy drug users together to find out why they take drugs and to offer them alternatives, based on Fromm's ideas. "We were putting up bail day and night; I was at my wits' end . . . [and I thought] we need to find out what satisfaction they need," Dunham reflected.[34] The university blocked the effort in another example of its rocky relationship with Dunham that prevailed beyond her retirement in 1982.

From the outset, Dunham's aim was to lessen social isolation and disunity in her adopted city. During her 1992 fast for Haitian refugees, she placed East St. Louis in the center of a national movement, with people in other parts of the country joining in and others making a pilgrimage to East St. Louis to support her. Dick Gregory came to join the movement and advised Dunham on her fast. President Jean-Bertrande Aristide and Jesse Jackson visited her in the blighted East St. Louis neighborhood in which she resided to publicize her effort. She again convinced her supporters in East St. Louis—now both young and old—and elsewhere that in her eighties she was still a fighter for human rights.

The Glory Days of PATC

Katherine Dunham had expanded her views on education in the years between the closing of her New York school and the founding of PATC. The program was the ultimate fulfillment of her view of "art for life's sake," and while PATC did not have the glamour associated with the artistic celebrities in New York City, it had its own romance lent by the legend of Katherine Dunham herself, as well as by the young political activists, visiting African and Caribbean artists, governmental representatives, and distinguished African Americans, and, most important, by the talent and enthusiasm of children and youth who were her hope for the future. She brought in exceptional artists and scholars from around the world to enrich the lives of East St. Louisans. The instructors at EHE—some permanent, others on a visiting basis—included the artist Oliver Jackson, the sociologist Joyce Ladner, and the writer Henry Dumas; for PATC, Dunham brought in Giovannella Zannoni from Rome, Ural Wilson, Lenwood Morris, Tommy Gomez, Clifford Fears, Lucille Ellis, and Camille Yarbrough, all former Dunham Company members; Mor Thiam, René Calvin of Haiti, Christiane de Rougement from Paris, Suzanne Ndiop, the dancer Glen Standifer, the jazz musicians Oscar Brown Jr. and Julius Hemphill, the artist Charles White, the tap dancer and animal mime Archie Savage, the origami instructor Haru Kuraii, the Nigerian artist Paul Osifo, and the poet Eugene Redmond. Dunham submitted a proposal for an associate arts' degree, with plans for an eventual four-year program. Out of these activities grew an Equal Opportunity Commission grant for two neighborhood centers for PATC, which ultimately moved to the Broadview, a renovated hotel. Dunham envisioned PATC as the focal point for a cultural center and developed a proposal for an international house to expand the cultural activities. These plans, as well as the associate arts' degree, were not funded, as institutional support for the program weakened. However, the years from 1968 to 1974 were the high point of PATC activities. During this time, Lenwood Morris (1971), Archie Savage, Tommy Gomez, and Clifford Fears (all in 1972) came to teach in the program.

For a time the Experiment in Higher Education, including PATC, was located at the old high school and the junior high school, across the street from Dunham's house on Tenth Street. Tenth Street was bustling with dignitaries and artists who were walking up and down the street, moving around, going to the stores, being a part of the scene. Redmond remarked, "We've never before and never since had so many performers, being seen out and among the people . . . in the churches, in the markets, in the bars."[35]

Dunham worked with the materials she found in the community and adapted her choreography to local themes. "A 'hip' walk contained *yonvalou*; Damballa became the cool cat at Fifteenth and Broadway. She was able to work those kinds of fusions and merges, so that she was teaching a lot of elements at the same time and transmitting a lot of images: depth charge images," Redmond recalled. She used the language of the children and youth as a vehicle, to be translated into theatrical form. "[She] took those words, she took the movements and she reconstructed those with her own choreography, her own vision of a new America based on this encyclopedic understanding of culture and people and ideology and what she felt were the most pressing needs of America at the time," Redmond related.[36]

Examples of community celebration included the *Ode to Taylor Jones*, in honor of a local civil rights worker who had died in an accident, with poetry by Redmond and choreography by Dunham. Redmond's lyrics were influenced by the Greek chorus, Scottish rites, and the ritual traditions and ceremonies of West African and West Indian cultures. Dunham dancers, including Dunham herself, often celebrated community events, funerals, and even business openings. "I remember," Redmond reminisced, "that a fast food place opened up and Miss Dunham bless[ed it], performing a ritual dance at the opening. . . . I don't think America had ever seen anything like that before. She would actually bless and consecrate or ritually anoint all over town."[37]

PATC members, including Mor Thiam, the Senegalese drummer, performed at the funeral of one of Redmond's friends. In the 1990s, Sunshine Lee, a former PATC student, and his dancers observed the funeral of the daughter of state representative Wyvetter Younge; and Jeanelle Stovall read a tribute written by Dunham. Younge, a longtime friend and supporter of Dunham, takes classes at the Dunham Technique Seminar every year, and her deceased daughter had also studied Dunham technique.

The tradition of community service continues to the present: public building dedications, social events, and fund-raisers are occasions of performance, formerly by PATC, more recently by Katherine Dunham Children's Workshop dancers and drummers.

In 1997, the children danced at a celebration of nearly thirty years of service by Leman ("Chico") Davis, who had returned to work with youth at the Salvation Army in Olivette Park—the neighborhood in which the Katherine Dunham Museum is located—after receiving a degree from the University of Illinois. As a teenager, he had taken classes at PATC. "It was a fantastic program . . . we learned black history, how to get along with people of all races; we were taught how to communicate with each other," Davis related.[38] A speaker at the celebratory dinner for Davis remarked that she never had a thought of fear when her children were at the Salvation Army; as far as she knew, Davis never carried a gun, but because of his good reputation in the neighborhood, troublemakers never intruded into center activities. Davis proudly described the achievements of his former wards, who include an engineer, sound technician, players of professional sports, a musician, teachers, a police officer, a social worker, and a small business owner. It would be difficult to assess the total cascading effect of Dunham programs on people in East St. Louis.

When Dunham began to organize PATC, she asked Archie Savage, who was teaching and performing in Italy, to help her set it up. Savage later sent for Norman Davis, who was also in Italy, to be his assistant. Davis was a powerful dancer; he had studied with Bob Cole and was good in both jazz and Dunham technique. According to Ronnie Marshall, who studied and performed with the PATC dancers, the ensemble achieved its highest level under Savage and Davis. Dunham asked Lenwood Morris, a perfectionist with a memory for detail, to be the ballet master.

Lenwood Morris taught the balletic element of Dunham technique: placement, how to turn, focus. Morris had been not only a ballet master but also a character actor in the Dunham Company. In later years, he lost a leg; wielding his cane with a flourish, he suggested a benevolent version of Baron Samedi, a role he had played with devilish glee in company performances. Always smartly dressed, with panache, he was especially dapper in a bright yellow suit. He was informative, funny, and warm and handled serious matters with a light touch; he would openly joke with "Miss D" about his status as a "queen." She recalled that he had been a favorite of the German kaiser's son, who presented him with a ring formerly belonging to the kaiser. Openly gay at a time when the lifestyle often led to ridicule, he responded to rudeness and bigotry with grace.

Morris recognized Marshall's acting ability and gave him such character parts as the possessed boy in "Rites de Passage" and Julot, the villain in "L'Ag'Ya," both played by Tommy Gomez—whose acting ability was identified by Dunham—on company tours.

Tommy Gomez was also one of the primary instructors, although he left in 1976. He worked Marshall very hard in Dunham technique. "He wanted them to see the Dunham in my body," Marshall commented.[39] Ural Wilson, originally from South Florida, had a "straight lineage" to Caribbean and African cultures; in the Dunham progressions across the stage, his movements were authentically African. A fierce taskmaster, according to Marshall, he insisted the male dancers perform as many jumps as they could. They would compete with one another, and East St. Louis students Ed Brown and Michael Green always topped the class. Wilson worked with Dunham until 1974, when he was killed during an argument stemming from a fight in a local bar.

Ruby Streate had Ural Wilson as her first teacher. She was recruited from a Catholic school. The Catholic schools readily accepted what Dunham was offering, although the public schools became open to it only later, when they allowed dance lessons through the physical education department. Streate was attracted by the instructors' personalities: "[They] were very compassionate and loving, and that kind of touched me, and then the things that they were doing were so exciting to me." She liked the contrast with what she was learning at school. "The feeling of the square dances that I learned from Miss Dunham's technique nowhere near has the feel [of] those dull square dances that I did in the gym class. First of all because the music was European, the rhythmic structure was not the same. When African Americans dance they have a whole different feeling about the music even though they were copied from the European dances." She liked the musicians' improvisation, the room for expressing feelings. She felt the same contrast between Dunham technique and ballet, although she also enjoyed ballet: "The ballet is so architectural, whereas Dunham technique is more earthy, more moving . . . nonarchitectural . . . differently structured." She feels good about Dunham technique because "it's not just a physical technique"; it teaches relaxation and to be "conscious of all the things around you . . . when you become more spiritually attuned, then you certainly have a higher level of understanding."[40]

Streate learned that the instructors had good minds as well as bodies: "They were tuned to everything, they had a conscious understanding about many things." Her love for dance got her involved, but later on she was rewarded by doing better in school as well: "I was learning about life. . . . I was learning academically [what] I didn't want to sit in the classroom and learn. When the teachers asked me questions I was able to respond."[41] She concluded that it is possible to learn while having fun, knowledge she was able to put to use years later, as principal instructor of the Children's Workshop. Through this experience, she came to appreciate Dunham as an educator as much as a performer.

Streate knew that Ural Wilson was a good teacher: "He would not let you get by just arbitrarily making a movement happen, he wanted you to understand where it came from, the dynamics of the movement." Lenwood Morris was precise about ballet and Dunham technique as well: "Mr. Morris said, 'Ruby, they said for years that our bodies weren't designed for ballet, and it's not the truth.' Because he mastered it; he had the most gorgeous body."[42]

Another instructor, Clifford Fears, was extremely energetic in motion and incorporated ballet movement into his instruction. He had been recommended to Dunham by Ziggy Johnson, a famous Chicago tap dancer who helped her with stage productions. Fears knew how to train bodies, and he worked on stamina and power. He was close to Alvin Ailey and danced with his company. Fears later developed a dance company in Detroit. Streate described him as "phenomenal, he was like the wind . . . [he] was like an eagle, he could soar through the air like an airplane."[43]

Streate described the high energy when the instructors came together: "They fed on each other." They had a sense of humor and could laugh in the face of adversity; even though she knew they had faced many obstacles in their careers, they were not bitter: "They laughed and said we will not be defeated; otherwise we wouldn't have a legacy that we all are a part of." She was, and still is, in awe of Dunham and is sometimes at a loss for words when she is with her. She identifies with her because she also has a "marvelous sense of humor, and I like to laugh." All of the instructors "would sit around and laugh and have you laughing and they gave you that motivation to learn."[44]

Some of this spirit comes through at the annual Dunham Technique Seminar, but few of the original instructors are still living. John Brooks believed he saw the last real application of Dunham technique when Morris, Wilson, Savage, and Gomez were at PATC: "Lenwood had a photographic memory, Ural and Archie and Tommy—when you put all four of them together, between them and Miss Dunham, they could reconstruct most of the acts, and it was precise, like the original."[45]

Archie Savage, who was famous for his mimicry of serpents and other creatures—employing the muscles of his arms, legs, and torso independently—was a knowledgeable and articulate exponent of dance as well. He created dances, including tap solos, for the PATC company. Vanoye Aikens, too, occasionally visited and taught jazz dance.

Lucille Ellis, who was heading a dance school in Chicago, sometimes taught and performed at PATC bringing in students, including Ronnie Marshall, whom she had instructed in Dunham technique. Ruth Beckford and Pearl Reynolds came through East St. Louis on occasion and taught workshops. But other than Dunham, the regular instructors were men. Streate stated, "When I went to New York to do the performance at Carnegie Hall, they were saying that we were stronger or more masculine than the average female dancer . . . it was [because] all of [our] instructors had been male instructors."[46]

Ronnie Marshall, Ricardo Avalos, and Eusebio Da Silva, a Brazilian dancer who studied and later taught at PATC, shared the "corner house," currently owned by Dunham but at that time by Southern Illinois University. Avalos worked with Marshall to "put a little flavor" into his dancing; he was "very Latin, very macho," a "great character actor," and he groomed both Marshall and Da Silva, Marshall recalled.[47] He coached Marshall in the role of the entertainer, in a dance to Scott Joplin's rag of that name, as well as in the Senegalese rhythms of Julio Mendez and La Rosa Estrada, drummers in the original company. Marshall studied Senegalese drumming with Mor Thiam, whom he met during summer rehearsals for the Mississippi River Festival, performed on the SIU Edwardsville campus. In the festival performance, Marshall danced the cakewalk in "Flaming Youth"; Thiam played the policeman who broke up a fight between Ruby Streate—then a student—and Lucille Ellis.

Redmond pointed out that Dunham has always attracted people of different backgrounds: "Miss Dunham advanced the idea of a global village without preaching, on a personal level." She refused to take white people out of the cast, for example, just because they were performing in a particular city. "I remember," Redmond continued, "we got a cool response from Coretta King because Christiane de Rougement was part of the cast and it hadn't been anticipated. . . . It might be a white female dancer and a black male dancer had to move her around some. So in the whole arena of culture, gender, race, class and language, ethnicity, she just blew that wide open . . . that's one legacy, one contribution that endured."[48] She also encouraged white students to participate in classes.

John Pratt designed costumes and scenery for PATC. John Brooks, who served for a time as stage manager, admired his mastery over his craft: "He designed all of the costumes, most of the stage, most of the lighting for Dunham and traveled all over the world with them." Pratt was often playful in relating to the young amateurs. After the portable stage they had built for a summer festival in the park collapsed, Brooks approached him for help. Pratt hedged, modestly admitting that he had *some* experience with portable stages while touring. When the younger man insisted that Pratt tell him his secrets, he finally explained that they needed to use thicker plywood and have separate legs for each section. "He would never just outright tell you anything; you had to learn for yourself," Brooks remarked.[49]

In addition to designing costumes, Pratt taught batik and tie-dye. Like Brooks, Ruby Streate was in awe of his abilities: "He was so well organized, and he knew what he was going to do. I'd ask him, 'Mr. Pratt, what do you need this for?' and he'd say, 'Ruby, I don't know what I need it for right now, but I'm going to need it, believe me'; and when we'd get to a certain point he'd say, 'Ruby, remember those beads that I bought? Bring them here, they'll fit now.' It was just amazing how he put things together! He could look at a dancer and size each one up, saying 'You need this for your costume and you need this to enhance yours.'"[50]

In the late 1960s, the Performing Arts Training Center spawned a semiprofessional dance group, made up of the more experienced students. The group performed a number of dance programs, including the *Ode to Taylor Jones*. Dunham collaborated with other PATC staff members to stage and choreograph Langston Hughes's "A Dream Deferred." Scott Joplin's *Treemonisha* premiered at Morehouse College in Atlanta and was also presented at Wolftrap Park in Vienna, Virginia, and at Kiel Opera House in St. Louis. In Atlanta and at Wolftrap Park, *Treemonisha* was conducted by Robert Shaw, and in St. Louis, by Kenneth B. Billups, a prominent black composer and choral director. *Some Rags and Such*, including "Cakewalk" and "The Entertainer"—in a brilliant interpretation by Ricardo Avalos—was danced to Joplin's music at Wolftrap and elsewhere.

The PATC company toured midwestern, southern, and eastern United States with *Missa Luba*, based on the 1968–70 Congolese version of the Catholic mass, taught to Congolese choirboys by missionaries. *Missa* was performed with the Saint Louis Symphony in 1972. It was conducted by Billups and choreographed by Dunham, and the cast included the Metropolitan Opera singers Carmen Balthrop and Robert McFerrin (singer-conductor Bobby McFerrin's father).

Choreographing choral music was not a new experience to Dunham. As a child, she had spent many otherwise irksome hours in church services visualizing dance movements to hymns and chorales. In 1969, the choral director Hall Johnson gave a three-day workshop for PATC and other students.

Other programs on tour included an African suite, a South American suite ("Carnival," "Damballa," and "Los Indios"),[51] and North American "Poems of Militancy" and "Afro-Jazz," with Julius Hemphill and Mor Thiam. In 1973, Glory Van Scott and Darryl Braddix danced "Floyd's Guitar Blues" in Winston-Salem, North Carolina, as a part of a prebicentennial festival staged by Agnes de Mille. Most of the performances were in the college circuit and at politically oriented activities—in Streate's words, "things associated with civil rights, black power movements. A lot of issues were confronted: artists are the ones who motivate people . . . to [have] ideas."[52] Their power derived from the ability to express ideas and feelings in ways that have more impact than that of speech.

Dunham choreographed "Shaka Zulu" in honor of the great African king. Later when Streate saw Turner Broadcasting's production about Shaka, she realized she had learned that and much else from her years at PATC: "Miss Dunham had taught us who Shaka was, she never thrust us into choreography without giving us a background, historical perspective on what we were doing or why we were doing this." Streate was learning a lot through "osmosis": "I was so young, I didn't realize the impact of what I was doing. . . . I was caught up in the fact that I was loving what I was doing, just engrossed in the fact that here I am involved in dance, something I've loved passionately since I could stand up."[53]

Streate described the grueling schedule kept by the performers: "We'd be in a little bus or van and we'd go from this spot, do a show, go to that spot, do a show, go to that spot, and come back and rehearse." No one felt like saying, "I don't want to rehearse tonight because I've worked too hard."[54]

The Performing Arts Training Center included three active programs: the dance company, the children's auxiliary company, and the educational center. The administration of the center was in itself an arduous task. Dunham was the director, and those who were responsible for the day-to-day administering of the programs understood and implemented her philosophy of art, life, and education. She recruited people just as she had while the Dunham Company was on the road: wherever she found them. She was adept in seeing people's potentialities and adapting them to her ends.

A number of talented women worked as secretaries at PATC, including Henrietta Knight and Claudia McClinton. In actuality, they served as administrative aides to Dunham, emulating Marjorie Scott and others who had worked in the company. Knight, who was working in logistical operations at Scott Air Force Base, took a leave of absence and came to work for Dunham after the assassination of Martin Luther King Jr. and stayed eighteen months. She picked up Dunham's concept of administration: "I watched how she dealt with people and how she structured things—she gave the parameters."[55]

Robert Lee, who was stationed at Scott Air Force Base, retired from the air force to join the program, first as an audio-visual technician and later as company manager. He stayed with Dunham, despite relatively low pay, and currently coordinates and manages the East St. Louis programs.

Brooks used the phrase "recruited me to go to war" in describing his first contacts with Dunham. A week after his initial encounter with her on the night she was arrested, he and a friend were walking in a deserted hall at school after taking an exam, making plans for the evening. A door opened: "There was Miss Dunham again." She had a script in her hand: "She came storming out and looked up and down this hall, and there wasn't anybody in this hall except this guy and [me], and she looked at me and asked if I can read, I told her I could. She said, 'Well, come on' and she thrust this script into my hand." He followed her into a room full of people, and it turned out to be a rehearsal for *Ode to Taylor Jones*." He was told to read the script. "And that's basically how I got involved in theater with her," Brooks mused. She "commandeered" him from the beginning: "I don't even know her and she's telling me 'I want you to do this, I want you to do that, I want you to go over there and get this.'"[56]

When Brooks was stage manager, he would check out the nature of the facilities at performance sites and found that conditions were not always the best: "We've changed clothes in churches, in taverns, in bathrooms, and some of them weren't that great—water all over the floor and you hope it's water."[57] Redmond managed the dance group on occasion and spent a lot of time backstage overseeing dressing. "At first I thought 'WOW,'" he said, "but after awhile, it was like snap! three minutes to get these costumes on. . . . It doesn't matter you're looking at a sweaty body, you've got to get this stuff on or someone's gonna pay."[58]

Redmond's perspective on the human body changed radically during his time with Dunham: "There's something about dance, something about the body, something about freedom, about relaxation, and at the same time exhibitionism." He came to appreciate "the beauty of the body, the sanctity of the body, the potential, the resourcefulness of the body." He learned that Dunham works on the mind through the body: he saw people in classes who came with perhaps an incredible torso but with undeveloped minds; they moved "light years" toward greater understanding. "It doesn't take her long to [to get] under your skin," he exclaimed. Some people could not take the intensity of her temperament and demands: "I saw people who couldn't take it, cause there's a crush, a psychological pressure that you can't identify at the time, when you're working under Miss Dunham. And I saw people wandering out on the street, like, 'What hit me?', you know, staggering; and we lost a lot of people."[59]

Redmond observed her working her magic on Brock Peters, who was collaborating with her on a television production: "You know that kind of domination she does? She sits a person over there and she asks questions around the room, boomerang questions; and she says, now I think we ought to hear from Mr. Peters—and she's looking over at me or somebody—about his belief or allegiance." Peters handled it well, but he said he was drained afterward when Redmond took him to a bar for a drink.[60]

Such incidents gained her the title of "The Witch of Tenth Street,"[61] and rumors about her fearful effects on people flew around PATC and, to some extent, the East St. Louis community. While Redmond was privy to these claims, he could not confirm any of them; but he did experience the psychological "vice" that terrorized those who were not prepared to give their all. Redmond realized it was a chance he had to take to learn as much as possible from one he recognized as superior in knowledge. He is writing a biographical poem on Dunham and is trying to convey this aspect of her character. "She transmits and creates on so many levels and reaches people on so many levels," he asserts.[62]

Redmond spent two years with Dunham, seeing her almost daily, before leaving for California. She advised him to leave so that he could accomplish what he needed to. Then, he related, "The minute I left, Miss Dunham called me every other week for years, asking me about my allegiance to East St. Louis, when was I coming back? Someone would say, 'Hold for Katherine Dunham,' and she would come on and say, 'Eugene, where is your commitment to East St. Louis? What are you going to do?'" He regards Dunham as a mentor and a friend, and although their relationship has "gone through changes," their mutual accomplishments cannot be gainsaid. In 1990, Redmond went back to teach at SIU at Edwardsville and to mentor and nurture young local artists, and he was named the poet laureate of East St. Louis. He publishes a series of African American literary criticism entitled *Drumvoices Revue,* an appellation he would not have considered before his work with Dunham.[63]

Dunham's concept of education through the arts, involving both mind and body, broadened the concepts of art and education alike, Redmond believes. PATC prepared graduates for more than performance or "stardom," although these were certainly goals. Dunham's vision and practice allow her to reach those not interested in further academic work to attain their potential. She also instructs on a different level those with advanced degrees: Redmond, William Strickland from the University of Massachusetts, who came as a consultant from the Institute of the Black World in Atlanta, Glory Van Scott, Jeanelle Stovall, Albirda Rose, and the author of this biography, among others.

As "an intellectual artist," "a well-educated woman of African extraction" who did not fit into the usual categories of schoolteacher, nurse, cosmetologist, lawyer, or other traditional roles for educated black women, Dunham opened up new possibilities for women and men alike, Redmond contended: "She stood in and outside of art, in and outside of social structure, in and outside of [academics], in and outside of gender."[64] She made room for talented young people who might not have found an outlet without her programs. Former students have pursued careers in sports, film, dance instruction, teaching, school cultural programs, and social services, among other areas. While some have combined performance with teaching, not one of them has become a full-time professional dancer. Because of the lack of support for the arts, in general, and dance, in particular, few such opportunities exist. And, despite the leadership of Dunham and others, few black dancers are employed in professional companies.

Because of her work in East St. Louis, extending far beyond dance training, Dunham has received numerous humanitarian awards. In 1979, she won the Albert Schweitzer Music Award "for her contributions to the performing arts and her dedication to humanitarian work." In conjunction with the award, "A Katherine Dunham Gala" was presented at Carnegie Hall on Martin Luther King Day. It was produced by Glory Van Scott, and some of the original Dunham Company members performed in their former roles. PATC and former PATC instructors and students joined them, representing three generations of dancers.[65] Lenwood Morris was the ballet master, and John Pratt was the costume designer. Other Dunham Company members served as honorary hosts and hostesses. The program listed 231 Dunham performers—dancers and percussionists—past and present. It was a nostalgic evening for former company members and an exciting one for PATC members, who had the chance to appear with many of their idols on the famous old New York stage. Many of the older generation have died since 1979, and others are now unable to perform, so it was a once-in-a-lifetime experience.

Nineteen seventy-nine was an eventful year for both Dunham and her youthful dancers. Besides the Carnegie Hall gala, the PATC company performed in *Treemonisha* in St. Louis. The international opening of the Katherine Dunham Museum was held. Dunham won honorary doctorates from Brown, Westfield State College, and Dartmouth; achievement awards from the National Association of Negro Musicians and the Midwest Black Theatre Alliance; the State of Illinois Governor's Award; and a Citizen of the Year Award from the Omega Psi Phi Fraternity. Visitors to the community included Brock Peters, Geoffrey Holder, Eartha Kitt (who was appearing in *Timbuktoo* in St. Louis), Butterfly McQueen, Barbara Ann Teer—an East St. Louis native who was producing stage drama in New York—and the Oakland Ballet Company.[66]

Dunham continued to receive numerous awards from many sources throughout the eighties and nineties—including the Kennedy Center Honors Award in 1983—and walls and shelves in her museum office and her home are covered with plaques, statuettes, and honorary degrees. International visitors continue to come to East St. Louis, and Dunham-trained dancers remain in demand for regional events.

Establishing an Independent Program

With the funding cuts for arts and inner-city programs in the 1980s, PATC became a shadow of its former self. When Dunham retired in 1982, her assistants and most of the instructors were given pink slips by the university. While continuing to use her name, SIU at Edwardsville failed to employ her as a consultant.

Stung by this treatment, Dunham turned to other sources for funding, including state and federal programs, as well as fund-raising events by private agencies. She gained the support of some local political leaders, notably state representative Wyvetter Younge. It proved to be an auspicious partnership: Younge was effective in realizing some of Dunham's and Buckminster Fuller's aspirations for East St. Louis. She succeeded in gaining funding for a children's center—the Mary Brown Center—which was part of the original proposal, and she has worked to obtain financing of Dunham programs at the state level.

In 1975, the Dunham Fund purchased from the university three adjoining houses on Tenth Street: Dunham and Pratt's residence, a middle building used as an office and later for storage, and a stone building referred to as the "corner house," in which students, instructors, and visitors have resided through the years. In 1976, the Dunham Fund bought and adapted for use as a museum the old Maurice Joyce House, occupied by Judge Joyce's family until 1975 and then occupied by the YWCA until it was purchased by Dunham. It was transformed into a museum for art, artifacts, and mementos collected by Dunham and donated by others. Later, the carriage house on the grounds was converted into a studio for the Children's Workshop. The museum building, an English regency townhouse, was built at the turn of the twentieth century and is listed in the Federal Register, as well as on the Illinois Historic Register. Visitors from around the world, as well as local people, tour the museum, which stands out in a neighborhood of dilapidated buildings. On a street of once dignified and spacious houses, it is the only building that has been preserved—all others are burned out, run-down, or torn down.

Inside the museum's spacious rooms, carved oaken doors and fireplaces set off a display of African woodcarvings, instruments, Haitian art, and Dunham memorabilia, including costumes and pictures. Dunham's museum office is lit by massed suspended paper-shaded lamps, designed by John Pratt. An enlarged picture of Dunham in Tokyo, posed before a statue of Buddha, dominates the room.

The preview opening of the museum was in 1977, and an international opening was held in 1979, attended by former company members and representatives from Senegal, Haiti, and other African and European countries. The Friends of the Museum, made up of community and university representatives, held fund-raisers, including birthday banquets for Katherine Dunham, as well as workshops and "cleanup" days, until the mid-1980s, when flagging support for the arts discouraged many members. The Friends' first president, the art historian Floyd Coleman in the art department at SIU at Edwardsville—now at Howard University—was, in the words of one of its members, "an inspiration to a lot of people [in East St. Louis]."[67]

John Pratt designed an African village on the museum grounds; the huts were designed for concessions for fairs and outdoor performances. The outdoor stage is used for Children's Workshop performances. Mor Thiam's Drum and Dance Conference, the forerunner of the current Dunham Technique Seminar, was held on the museum grounds in the 1980s; it included classes in mask-making, jewelry-making, sculpture, and other crafts, as well as dance and music. A tradition of serving African and African American food at museum events continues to the present.

When the museum opened, Dunham appointed a board to oversee museum operations, primarily made up of East St. Louis businessmen, with Buckminster Fuller as honorary chairman. The board has been reconstituted several times in a checkered career. That successive boards have proved ineffective may reflect a paradox in establishing an unconventional program. In the 1990s, the museum fell on bad times as bills piled up and utilities were turned off. Two burglaries occurred in that period, even though none had taken place prior to 1996. After considerable publicity in the local media, objects from the first robbery were returned by a conscience-stricken collector; however, the culprits were not identified.

Representative Younge was instrumental in obtaining line-item funding in the state budget, as well as Illinois Arts Council funds, for Dunham programs. These grants, as well as assistance from the local casino and the power company, enabled the Dunham center to pay off the money owed for utilities bills; the electricity was turned on, a new alarm system was installed, and the plumbing, which had frozen during the winter, was repaired. A grant from the Urban Resources Partnership, a state program to fund urban environmental enhancement, provided for the refurbishing of John Pratt's African village and the museum grounds, according to a design by a local architect.

As Southern Illinois University decreased its involvement in East St. Louis, Younge challenged the University of Illinois to play an active role in the community. As a result, the School of Architecture at the University of Illinois at Urbana-Champaign established the Neighborhood Technical Assistance Center (NTAC) in East St. Louis, with the goal of assisting in neighborhood renewal and economic development. NTAC staff members were working in the Olivette Park neighborhood in which the Katherine Dunham Museum was located when Younge persuaded them to support the Dunham Center programs through technical assistance in fund-raising and financial management.

The current museum staff includes Robert Lee; Darryl Braddix, his assistant and adult class teacher; Donna Pollion, the audio-visual coordinator; and an education coordinator/acting curator (the author). Stovall meets with local and visiting officials, on occasion conducts educational tours, and is responsible for fund-raising. At the beginning of the twenty-first century, the building and grounds were fairly well-maintained, and bills were being paid. But the fortunes of the museum and other Dunham programs remain uncertain, contingent on adequate and dependable funding.

The Children's Workshop

When PATC as Dunham envisioned it was essentially disbanded, she felt it was important to continue teaching the children of East St. Louis. In 1970, she had presented sixty-six children, ages four to twelve, at the White House Conference on Children. They performed dances, songs, and karate and played drums and guitars. For the program, she choreographed "Rainforest," which was to become a staple of the Children's Workshop. An article in the *Evening Star* in Washington, D.C., remarked on the "strong echo in Dance and Music of Miss Dunham's own tremendous intensity and vitality. . . . Everything Miss Dunham's kids did was exactly right, absolutely spontaneous." The writer continued to describe it as reflecting the "sounds of children," while what preceded it were "the sounds of adults" imposed on children.[68]

In 1981, a CBS grant enabled her to continue working with children and to transform the carriage house on the museum grounds into a dance studio. The program began officially in 1982, with children between the ages of four and twelve. The core teaching staff included Darryl Braddix and Ruby Streate. Other teachers, from the greatly reduced PATC and from Cosaan—Mor Thiam's dance company—as well as Lee Nolte, a ballet teacher currently with the St. Louis Center of Contemporary Arts, joined the staff on a rotating basis. There have been considerable staff changes through the years, and Streate is now coordinator of the workshop.

The children's education included many subjects in addition to dance. In 1982, workshop children attended the Intercultural Conference on Drum and Dance at the museum, where they were taught drum and dance rhythms from Africa and the Caribbean countries by masters from those areas. They had the opportunity to learn African cooking, leather-working, and drum-making and to view and purchase imported clothing, oils, incense, jewelry, and art objects.

An emphasis is placed on African and Caribbean cultures in workshop classes as well, and children are eager to learn about their heritage. In one of the classes, a Senegalese woman spoke to them on common misconceptions about Africa, pointing out that there are large cities, rural areas, and poor and rich people in Africa, just as in the United States. She taught them Wolof words, proverbs, songs, and games. In another class, a master drummer from Senegal stressed the necessity of learning dances, drumming, and songs—all three—to be a dancer or drummer, and he taught them rhythms. Another time, a griot demonstrated the kora—a stringed instrument—and talked about his family, how they live and function as griots. Jeanelle Stovall, who is fluent in several languages, on occasion has taught Wolof, French, and Spanish conversation.

The children learn Dunham technique, ballet, African ritual movements, and dances of Haiti and other Caribbean countries. A favorite piece, "Rainforest," employs African and Haitian themes; it includes the Malinke—vigorous movements performed at puberty ceremonies, Mahis—gestures describing the planting of crops, and the Watusi, an adrenaline-increasing movement in preparation for war or other aggressive acts. It also includes a "resting step," uncannily similar to the resting step of black church choirs. *Yonvalou,* the dance of the Haitian god Damballa, represents the motions of a serpent, his symbolic animal counterpart. It is practiced while leaning forward with a flat back at the barre and involves an arch and roll of the spine, the head following through on the motion. Away from the barre, the spinal motion is accompanied by slow, deliberate steps. It is a calming movement and also projects a feeling of buoyancy.

These and other movements, along with associated drum beats, are practiced at home and elsewhere by the children; they have become familiar motifs, shared by many young people in the local area. The young dancers gain distinction through their knowledge of their heritage and a sense of style by being able to perform the movements expertly and displaying distinctive clothing and hairstyles.

The children perform at local events and in schools and also travel to other states. They are especially popular in Columbus, Ohio, and students from Columbus have come during the summer breaks to take classes. They accompanied Dunham to Detroit for a series of workshops in schools. Her plane arrived early, Streate recalled: "They had dancers and drummers, a welcome committee for Miss Dunham and the Children's Workshop. Because we were late Miss Dunham wouldn't allow the festivities to begin . . . she let them know how important these kids were to her." There was a photographic display of Dunham and the company at Marygrove College in Detroit. "The children were very excited and they got a chance to see some of the things that they are helping to make come alive—like 'Rara Tonga'—in photographs," Streate recounted.[69]

In 1997, the children performed at a festival of traditional and ethnic arts at Issoire, France, near Bayonne. They had been planning to attend in previous years but were unable to raise enough money. To make the trip, they gave performances, sold T-shirts and sweatshirts, and, with their parents' assistance, finally accumulated the funds. They were received enthusiastically and were given the key to the city. It was a crowning achievement for the children, as well as for the parents. "A lot of them could not imagine this kind of dream becoming a reality, because they'd never dreamed anything this big. And certainly if they ever dreamed it, no one ever told them that it could come true," Streate remarked. The children were learning that through their commitment and devotion, they could fulfill lofty ambitions. Streate told them the story about Katherine Dunham's cabaret when she was a young girl: "She taught us that you're never too young to commit yourself to your own personal growth and development. . . . People probably said to her, 'You're too young, you don't know what you're doing.' But she didn't let them discourage her in what she thought she could do."[70]

Following Dunham's model, the children worked very hard to prepare for the twenty-fifth anniversary celebration for Katherine Dunham's work in East St. Louis and, looking beyond, for the European trip. "So," Streate explained, "they're working diligently, they've been working until seven every evening because they want this community to know what they are doing. . . . And that's the kind of passion that they have for the legacy that she has left for them."[71]

In the workshop, Streate has used the lesson about education she learned at PATC: learning can be fun. She has assigned reports on the body—the functions of bones, tendons, and muscles in movement—on Katherine Dunham, and on African and other cultures. The children have been motivated to learn languages and about other cultures because of their friendship with peers. "They had to present reports on China because we had a young girl who was from China, she was talking about her country and I wanted them to get an understanding of what she was talking about. . . . We had a young lady from Martinique, who spoke no English, and with the kids learning French, it was a very opportune time for them to try to get some experience with French and help her learn English," Streate reported. Parents told her that their children who previously would not read books they were assigned at school were suddenly going to the library to get books for their reports.[72]

As the children have grown and become more proficient, their instructors have concentrated more on polishing their performances and developing something like the PATC semiprofessional dance group. Reviewing a workshop performance, Jennifer Dunning of the *New York Times* wrote a glowing report: "Here were children who traveled through space with an appetite for movement that in no way blurred the lines between the ballet, modern dance, tap and traditional-style African and Caribbean dance they were performing. . . . Discipline and a respect for technique and style shone through the students' self-assured abandon. Yet they had gone beyond the classroom, becoming performers alive in their every moment on the stage."[73]

The recognition given the performers and their instructor raises the possibility that the younger and less proficient students will not receive as much attention as the star performers. Streate has extended the upper age limit of participants to sixteen, retaining some of the more experienced dancers in the program. Both Dunham and Stovall stress that the recruitment and education of younger children at a lower level of skills are of equal importance to polished performance. Although tensions between performance and broader education goals are realities, given limitations of time and resources, the union of the two is at the heart of Dunham technique and philosophy.

In this, Katherine Dunham has an ally in the superintendent of District 189 schools. The two, along with other community educators, have met to make plans for the Katherine Dunham Academy of Performing, Visual, and Cultural Arts. The superintendent attended an institute at City Center in New York in August 2000, at which dance educators considered pedagogy incorporating Dunham's methods and ideas about dance and society. In the same month, Illinois governor George Ryan announced a $57.4 million educational grant to the East St. Louis district at a meeting with Harry Belafonte and Danny Glover, who, at Dunham's instigation, were conducting a fact-finding mission in East St. Louis as a preliminary to seeking funding for cultural and economic development projects.[74] Katherine Dunham's visionary ideas on integrating dance with other fields of knowledge, as well as in all aspects of life, seem on the brink of realization in her adopted city.

11   Legacy

> Dunham Technique, while it consists of a system of
> learnable transferable qualities . . . is also dynamic . . . it
> continues to incorporate and merge methods of teaching
> style and application from earlier generations, with the
> contemporary ideas, methods, and philosophies which
> emanate from, and are taught by, Katherine Dunham.
> —Albirda Rose, *Dunham Technique: A Way of Life*

IN THE ANNUAL Dunham Technique Seminar, the atmosphere
vibrates with the force of percussion and the élan vital of energetic dancers. The two-week seminar, held since 1984 in the St. Louis–metro-east
(Illinois) region, is an intensive learning experience. It is also a celebration of Katherine Dunham's long, eventful, and influential career.

Those attending the seminar have included through the years—many
of them every year—former members of the Dunham Company, as master instructors. Drummers from Senegal, Ghana, Argentina, Barbados,
Brazil, Cuba, Haiti, New York, and the St. Louis–East St. Louis area provide complex, diverse rhythms for the dancers. Dunham technique students of various skill levels, as well as other dancers and nondancers,
come to learn from the masters. The origins of those traveling to the
seminar reflect the international tours and influence of the original Dunham Company: Australia, Peru, Paris, Spain, Germany, California, Con-
necticut, New York, Chicago, Denver, Trinidad, Haiti, Jamaica, Rome,
Senegal, Japan, Israel, and Brazil are some of the locations in and outside
the United States. They arrive in St. Louis to retrain, reenergize, and re-
store the unique qualities of Dunham technique that they have lost or
that have been diluted by practicing other dance styles during the year.

203

Many are dance instructors, and quite a few have dance schools and groups of their own.

Several generations of Dunham technique students mingle and learn from one another. All participants learn about "Miss D's" philosophy and the history of the Dunham Company and technique. The master instructors discover the differences that have developed in other regions where the technique is taught. The rapport and camaraderie that develop are crucial to the transmission of Dunham traditions.

Dunham has dreamed of holding the seminars at her residence in Port-au-Prince; however, the political situation there has persuaded her to continue housing it in various schools in the metropolitan St. Louis area, most recently, at East St. Louis Community College. Although it is very demanding and difficult for her, the seminar is too important and valuable an experience to all participants to be abandoned. In 1998, when she was eighty-nine, she said she could not be concerned about how old she is, that these last years she is just "scrabbling" to get the things done she needs to. In the summer of 2001, at ninety-two, she seemed even more driven, extending the master class beyond the allotted time and exhausting many of the dancers, who had already had classes in Cuban, African, "jazz" dance, or Dunham technique. Her desire to communicate what she has learned, to get things right, comes through clearly in these sessions, and the students respond with great respect and a concern to carry on her mission.

In the master class, Dunham—dressed in an African robe or other distinctive garb—presides with absolute authority and dignity. In recent years sitting in a wheel chair, she directs with incisive comments, expressive hand gestures, and her total body; she works closely with the drummers, in a fashion reminiscent of the *voudun* priest. As Lucille Ellis explained, "They carry the power of the drum that she needs."[1] When the dancers are slow to pick up the beat or get into formation, she threatens that the drummers will get bored or tired waiting for them and will quit.

The drummers greet her with a spirited salute when she arrives for the master class. The mutual respect between master instructors and the drummers forms the solid foundation of all seminar classes and reflects the honor and regard all drummers accord "Madame," who recognizes and appreciates their power. She learned intricate and subtle rhythms and movements from such drummers as Papa Augustin and the Cubans La Rosa Estrada and Julio Mendez. On tour in Brazil, Puerto Rica, and Cuba, and in Haiti, she visited the drummers' families.

When the Cubans entered her life, Dunham asserted, they greatly influenced her. "They have a way of externalizing their religions; the music, drums, and dance form a religion that is with them all the time," Dunham explained.[2] She was introduced to Estrada and Mendez by the Cuban anthropologist Fernando Ortiz.[3] The Cuban *rhumba* and the *nanigo*, portraying gauchos, or cowboys, became staples of the Dunham Company repertoire. Marta Vega, the director of the Caribbean Cultural Center in New York, has pointed out that Katherine Dunham was the first to take the *bata*, or Cuban double-headed drum, to New York.[4]

Dunham brought an appreciation of the origins of Latin rhythms in African religions to audiences in the Latino community in New York, as well as elsewhere. Her staging of the dances, displaying the cultural context, influenced Cubans and other Latinos to make their own artistic presentations. Recordings of Latin rhythms by Tito Puente and Chano Pozo acquainted North Americans with the vitality of the Cuban beat.[5] Pozo, who was a drummer in the Dunham Company, played with Dizzy Gillespie's band, introducing Latin rhythms into jazz. Other Cuban drummers in the company included Francesco Aquabella and Albert Laguerre, and Gilberto Valdes, "a brilliant young composer and conductor," wrote music based on Afro-Cuban themes for the company.[6]

When she visited Senegal and trained the royal dance troupe, Dunham worked closely with Senegalese drummers and musicians, bringing them to the United States to perform and teach in her program. Drummers paid homage to Dunham in a 1988 tribute performance in Chicago. Mor Thiam, the Senegalese master drummer, started the program with a crash of his *jimbe* from the back of the auditorium, then he led a parade of thirteen or more drummers down the aisle to the front where she sat, and they serenaded her for several minutes. It was a spirited introduction, and it raised the excitement level of both audience and performers to a high pitch.[7]

Marta Vega maintains that it is Dunham's relationship with the drummers that gives her technique a solid grounding in the spiritual life of those in the African diaspora. Knowledgeable drummers help control the spirits that can otherwise disrupt performances, while ensuring the authenticity of rhythmic movement. In 1979, Dunham wrote, "I would, when developing exercises which later became Dunham Technique, work closely with what drummers were available. As a school, we taught Haitian, Cuban and Brazilian drumming, with smatterings of what I had recorded or could remember from first-hand experience."[8]

The master instructors sit at her side or nearby in the master class. In recent years, there has been a serious erosion of staff. In 1993, Talley Beatty received a Scripp's Award and took time out for personal renewal.[9] Ricardo Avalos traveled from Los Angeles to take his place. Avalos, an Argentinean, was originally hired as a drummer, but he also danced with the Dunham Company and taught at PATC. He had not returned to the area for many years. Beatty came back to attend the seminar in 1994, but he died the following year. His death was keenly felt by participants, especially Dunham.

Through the years, other instructors have died or dropped out because of ill health, and others have taken their places. When Lucille Ellis, who had had a serious stroke, missed the 1995 seminar, her classes were taught by Dana McBroom Manno, a former Dunham Company dancer. Joe Sircus, a Cuban drummer, was memorialized in the 1996 seminar, and Lucille Ellis, Tommy Gomez, and Ronnie Marshall all died in 1998–99. Walter Nicks, a former dance director at the Dunham school in New York, stepped in to teach Dunham technique classes, while Sara Marshall, Ronnie Marshall's wife, picked up Ghanaian dances that he had taught.

Dunham was absent from the 1995 seminar because she was in Haiti, where she had been honored in a ceremony at the Presidential Palace. Hurricane Andrew and then ill health delayed her return. This was the first seminar she had missed, and the dancers, some of whom had come primarily to see her, were disappointed. In the spirit of the Dunham Company, others substituted in master classes, and the seminar presenters VèVè Clark and Marta Vega provided dynamic learning experiences about the sources and social and cultural contexts of Dunham technique.

In the 1995 seminar, Vanoye Aikens, serving as master of ceremonies in the final demonstration performance, referred to himself as "Miss D's" third partner and jested that perhaps she would have a fourth, since lately he was short of breath. A muscular, imposing figure, he exuded an aura of power and masculinity, yet he spoke with fastidious precision. A Copenhagen reviewer had commented in 1959, "Vanoye Aikens, the leading man, is a dancer and acrobat of unusual style, a tall, handsome negro who controls his body to perfection."[10] In 1998, when "Miss D" was attempting to reconstruct the original "Shango," it was Aikens to whom she looked for accuracy in details.

Dunham rules the demonstrators for the master class—most often Theodore ("Theo") Jamison, tall and solidly built; Keith Williams; and, on occasion, Doris Bennett-Glasper—with an iron hand. They are accomplished dancers who were among the original students in PATC. Jamison and Bennett-Glasper, along with Ruby Streate and Darryl Braddix, have been instructors at the Children's Workshop, which represents the only current dance group—except for Cleo Robinson's Denver company—that has permission to perform Dunham choreography and copy her costumes.

In the master class, Dunham educates the dancers about subjects ranging from politics and culture to love and sex, relating them to dance. She instructed the students to achieve the sinuous movements of the *yonvalou* by envisioning what it was like to be a snake, with no legs and having to project itself forward through a series of wavelike motions. She described this type of imitation through mental imaging as characteristically African. In the same class, Dunham noted that Congolese movement stresses the middle part of the body as the focus of power, medical treatment, and sexuality. She alluded to the fierceness and independence of the Congolese in Haiti and the tall, very dark, handsome men. She is aware that some people criticize her for spending too much time talking, so that the dancers are not warmed up when they perform the movements. Nevertheless, she feels that they need to know these things and that she will never get all of her views and ideas written down.

She also imparts detailed information about the dance movements, how they were developed, as well as the philosophy behind her technique. When she first returned from Haiti, she incorporated into her pieces movements taken from dances she had learned in the Caribbean. She described the first movement she used from her field research, based on the *combité* procession in which the toes grip the earth and then release in a zigzag pattern across the ground, leaving furrows. She used such isolation of body parts in choreography before she incorporated them into a technique. She pointed out the difference between a dance movement and technique: as a system of prototypes providing the basis for choreography. Dunham technique consists of paradigms utilizing different muscle groups, displayed in progressions across the floor. It is fundamentally a synthesis of African and balletic movement, with the systematic isolation of body parts characteristic of African and East Indian dance. She worked with Uday Shankar and Vera Mirova in developing isolation technique, although the basic movements and choreographic patterns were African.[11] A flexible back and relaxed knees are central to the technique; these are characteristic of the *yonvalou*, so important in Dunham's life.

The East Indian influence continues to be felt in the master classes. She emphasizes the seven *chakras*, points on the body where energies are focused, and the need to be aware of them at all times. She admonished the class, "Don't be afraid of that *chakra* [groin], that's where most of your energy comes from. Get acquainted with it."[12] The externalization of sexual energy in African and Latin movements that has energized audiences and brought about critical reaction to performances was also therapy to the girl and woman who had fought against a strict Methodist upbringing and a domineering father.

Dunham is a severe taskmaster. She characterized her role in the class as one of providing criticism, and she takes her charge seriously. A reviewer wrote in 1957, "Hard on herself, she is hard on others, but despite long hours, stormy scenes and low pay . . . the company stays with her."[13] In 1993, while students were working strenuously in ninety-five-degree temperatures and high humidity, with no air conditioning, their energy sometimes flagged. Resolutely, the eighty-four-year-old woman, weakened by a spell of pneumonia, insisted, "Never say I'm hot, never say I'm tired, just go on."[14] These were the words of a star performer who went on stage while suffering from knee pain and many bouts of illness. Marjorie Scott commented, "[She missed] one performance in Quito, Ecuador, [when] she went on a trip somewhere and the boat got stranded and she didn't get back. That was the only time in all the time I was with her that she missed a performance . . . you'd see her going on [stage] sick or sorry."[15]

Dunham has stated that "dancing hurts," although some do not acknowledge it. Tommy Gomez felt she sometimes had the dancers in the master class do deep knee bends too soon, before they were ready, but he understood that she was teaching a master class and expected them to be prepared.[16] Because the group is made up of a mix of the young and the middle-aged, professional dancers, teachers, nondancers, and former dance students attempting to renew skills, she is faced with some of the same problems of lack of preparation and occasional lack of skill and discipline she encountered in the early days.

According to a seminar student, Dunham technique has been developed through the years to minimize dance injuries, including modification of the neck and back releases in back rolls to avoid strain on those sensitive body parts.[17] Nevertheless, leg injuries, foot problems, and muscle sprains are endemic in the dance world. All of the master instructors have had physical disabilities necessitating a range of medical treatments, including foot surgery, knee and hip replacement, and leg amputation and prosthesis. Although such handicaps often accompany aging, they are no doubt exacerbated by the wear and tear on the body from dancing.

Dunham occasionally allows her assistants scope, although because of limited time, she usually concentrates on producing proficient dancers and choreographers who go on to earn their own plaudits. When Dunham was once expressing difficulty in establishing a desired sequence of movements at the barre, Jamison requested her "indulgence" to demonstrate a series he had practiced. She liked the result, and Jamison admitted that he had learned it in her class at PATC in 1975. She expostulated, "That reminds me of Ethel Waters saying, 'What? Imitate my imitators?'" when someone gave her advice on how to be more "authentic" in her performance. But she informed the class that Jamison's contribution was welcome. "We went back and found what I'd forgotten, and it works," she exclaimed.[18]

But praise in the master class is sparing: the participants clap when demonstrators—especially master teachers—illustrate a difficult movement at Dunham's request. If she is not greatly impressed—especially if the exhibitor is a student—she may admonish the others not to applaud unless the person deserves it. When Jamison and Bennett-Glasper lead the classes, they often receive sharp criticism; but when Bennett-Glasper once executed triple turns, Dunham praised her and encouraged applause. Lithe, ebony-skinned, Bennett-Glasper radiated pleasure.

Dunham encourages individuality within her basic artistic conception. At times the drummers will release energy in an aggressive tattoo or will spontaneously erupt into chanting. When there are seven or more percussionists, there is a veritable cacophony of rhythm. Lucille Ellis once commented, "It doesn't matter what country they're from, all drummers are into their own thing."[19] Jamison may burst into an African chant: "Ah Bobo. . . ." But Dunham demands seriousness and mastery of technique on the part of drummers, dancers, and observers, including master instructors, all of whom she occasionally castigates for talking or otherwise showing lack of attention during the class.

Eartha Kitt wrote in her memoir about the teasing—occasionally barbed—that Dunham engaged in during company rehearsals. In the seminar master class, she occasionally makes playful, sometimes pointed remarks about members, particularly the men. She commented when Jamison gained weight, then commended him when he took it off. She teased Beatty about his youth when he joined the original group in Chicago and then remarked, "One of my high points was when I stood on the side of the stage and saw Talley Beatty do 'Rites de Passage'—so beautiful, so pure."[20] At times she displays what seems to be a great deal of forbearance. Aikens, imposing and dignified, who teaches jazz dance at the seminar, occasionally stopped the master class to ask questions about a movement, and Dunham repeated the directions patiently to him while the class members, who quickly picked up her intent, fidgeted restlessly. Having gained her attention momentarily, he would sit down, satisfied.

Seminar classes convey an international orientation. Former company members remark that on tour, elements inspired by national folk dances and ballets were adopted into the choreography. In like manner, seminar students are constantly introduced to new dances from many traditions. In the tenth annual seminar, Ricardo Avalos, agile and animated despite a recent serious heart attack, demonstrated the *rhumba, sam-*

ba, the Brazilian *sha-sha-da*—dance of the gauchos—and a visceral *tango.* "His superb control has already brought him to a prominent place in the troupe," a reviewer commented in 1957.[21] "Don't announce that you are teaching the *tango,*" Dunham warned the seminar participants, concerned about the depth and quality of the instruction of her student teachers. She frequently warns them about teaching something before they are ready: "Keep things within yourself until you know they're pretty complete."[22] The seven *chakras,* based on East Indian cosmology, that she has incorporated into master classes during the last few years are particularly problematic for the inexperienced; if the instructor does not have absolute control over them, Dunham repeatedly stresses, the consequences for students may be serious.

Katherine Dunham has stated her criteria for teaching Dunham technique: first, one must have a sense of compassion; second, absolute honesty is critical; finally, one must study as much as possible and be a perennial student, constantly learning.[23] "I don't believe you can teach choreography," Dunham lectured in a class, "Your teacher gives you materials and you put it into your own ideas."[24]

In other seminar classes, instructors have taught African, Caribbean, and Latin American dance. In one seminar, C. K. Ganyo, a master drummer and the director of the National Ballet in Ghana, and Ronnie Marshall taught Ghanaian movement. They worked on a dance developed by two warring tribes to express their aggressions in a harmless manner: by vigorously and rhythmically striking sticks, to the front and to the rear, meeting and weaving in and out in double-line formation. It was a popular class: the students learned about African culture and worldview, which they shared with those unable to take the class. In 1994, Ganyo, who was performing a healing ceremony for a compatriot, did not attend; Ronnie Marshall took the Ghanaian class, and they performed funeral and Ashanti war dances. Joe Sircus, a Cuban drummer with the Alvin Ailey group who attended seminars regularly, collaborated with a drummer from Mexico in a class in Cuban and Brazilian rhythms. Louisnes Louisnis, a dancer and drummer from Haiti, and Avalos worked together with students on Haitian and Argentinean movement and rhythms. In the 1994 seminar performance, the Haitian dances won the greatest ovation, partly due, no doubt, to the political situation in Haiti.

Two recent Haitian immigrants performed the *yonvalou* in the 1994 master class. James Hunter, a professional dancer, was teaching in New York, and Phenel Colastin, who had came to live with and be trained and educated by Dunham at Habitation Leclerc when he was a young boy, was living and working at her home in East St. Louis. There was a sharp contrast between the two Haitians' styles of performance, although both were skilled. Colastin had learned the movements when he was a boy, and his performance was more like that of the Haitian peasants. Hunter combined sweeping arm movements, which represent Aida Ouedo, the female *loa*, with the torso movements of Damballa. Dunham pointed out that this is part of an acculturation process that begins with innovations by individuals. In this instance, Dunham technique employs the more traditional pattern. She has noted that she has observed dances performed in Senegalese villages that have adopted some of the innovations she has introduced, in an instance of cultural syncretism. She recounted an incident in London in which an African king responded to her presentation of the *yonvalou* by sending her a beaded bag, an act that was symbolic of engagement. "He did his best to make me his twelfth wife," she exclaimed.[25] The wives of a ceremonial king of Dahomey danced the *yonvalou* at the First World Festival of Negro Arts in Dakar in 1966, which demonstrated the close relationship between the Haitian and African religious ceremonies. Dunham uses this and other examples of cultural change and continuity to educate dancers in the cultural backgrounds of dance.

The seminar provides a time for former company members to reminisce and recapture some of the feelings and energy they experienced at the height of the Dunham Company's success. The family feeling, including rivalry, jealousy, and deep affection, that prevails in the seminar is an evocation of that which existed in the original company. In seminars, too, there has been a certain amount of rivalry, though muted, among the master dancers over the years. Gomez sometimes expressed impatience with Aikens, who, Gomez rather ruefully admitted, had supplanted him at one time as Dunham's favorite. Lucille Ellis, however, would never admit any lessening in the intensity of her relationship with Dunham: "Miss Dunham and I are inseparable; we're joined at the hip."[26] Both Ellis and Gomez were at times resentful that younger, aggressive seminar attendees seemed to attract more of Dunham's attention.

Gomez and Ellis taught with surrogates into their seventies, conducting rigorous classes despite Gomez's leg amputation and open heart surgery and Ellis's two hip replacement operations. One of Ellis's students said in the earlier 1990s, "[Miss Ellis] is one of the greatest repositories of the Dunham choreography that I have ever seen. She is feisty, dynamic and insistent upon excellence in the execution of the technique, and has the vanity of Erzulie!" She commented that in their seventies, Gomez and Ellis were impeccable in appearance and could still astonish their students, for which they would credit "The Man up above and Dunham Technique."[27] They, along with Aikens, were among the most faithful of

Dunham disciples. Ellis brought many of the students from her Chicago school to the seminar until she suffered a stroke in 1995.

Over the years, Ellis had a profound effect on many dancers. When Mary Vivian auditioned to attend the Julliard School in the 1960s, Martha Graham, who was on the board, told her she was the right physical type to dance and sent her to the Dunham School in New York. Excited that all the dancers were black, Vivian knew this was just where she belonged, though when she first saw Dunham, she was frightened: "I had never experienced so much personal power." She also thought Ellis, who taught the younger members at the time, was much too strict with her. But when she went to the school Dunham established in Sweden and Claude Marchant, an early company member, informed her that she had been properly taught the requisite skills for performance and teaching, she wrote a letter to Ellis, thanking her for working so hard with her and apologizing for thinking her "mean."[28] Vivian, along with Dana McBroom Manno, went to the 1994 seminar, the last one Ellis attended.

Dana McBroom Manno had started studying at the Dunham School when she was thirteen. She was with her mother, a travel agent, who was discussing travel arrangements with Dunham in the lounge of the Chelsea Hotel, where Dunham was staying and teaching classes. She recalled, "Lucille Ellis came out of nowhere with a pair of leotards, threw them at me and said there's a class starting in ten minutes, get in there to the class." When she protested that she was there with her mother, Ellis replied, "Yes, but you're going to take the class, put on these leotards." She began taking classes that day. Later her sister Marsha joined her at the Dunham School on Forty-second Street. Their family was from the island of Montserrat, and their mother, a classical pianist, also loved Caribbean music: "It was our culture." Less than a year after they began, Dunham got them the audition for the Metropolitan's dance company in *Aida.* McBroom Manno performed for five years at the Met; then she taught dance at Adelphi University for twenty-one years and subsequently joined the Dance Theatre of Harlem.[29]

At present, Dunham technique is being taught by former company members and their students, by others who studied at the Dunham School, and by former PATC company members. Lavinia Williams and Pearl Reynolds taught Dunham technique in the Alvin Ailey Company. Their places were later taken by Joan Peters, who had held a children's scholarship at the Dunham School in New York. When Syvilla Fort, who directed the dance division of the school while Dunham was on tour, left to form her own school, she took Peters and others in the children's group with her.

According to one scholar, Richard Long, Fort became "for many years one of the leading teachers in New York City."[30] He referred to Dunham, along with Pearl Primus, as "canonical" in producing dance teachers and mentioned a considerable number of dancers associated with Dunham who have international reputations as teachers. Among others, he cited Carmencita Romero, who has taught in Cuba, Italy, Japan, Spain, and Germany; Lavinia Williams, who taught in Haiti, the Bahamas, Guyana, Jamaica, Germany, and New York; Vanoye Aikens, a faculty member for many years at the Royal Swedish School of Dance; Walter Nicks, who taught in New York, Scandinavia, and France and in the 1970s had his own company in the United States; and Syvilla Fort, Claude Marchant, Tommy Gomez, Archie Savage, Ruth Beckford, Glory Van Scott, and Pearl Reynolds, all of whom have taught primarily in the United States. Lucille Ellis, Clifford Fears, Lenwood Morris, Ural Wilson, and many of those who have attended the seminar also taught in universities and community centers.

Beginning with the 1990 seminar, participants from San Francisco State University led a discussion about a certification process for teachers of Dunham technique. A number of regular seminar attendants were concerned that people were claiming to teach Dunham technique with very little training or understanding of the system or of Dunham's philosophy. There was some feeling that as the original Dunham dancers died or became less active, there was a need for the authentication of Dunham teachers and basic agreement on issues of pedagogy.

A lack of unanimity existed for this undertaking, however. Ellis felt that Dunham technique could not be codified: "Miss D does not like format, and [it won't be formalized] until she makes that decision within herself, 'OK, now I will give this to the world.'" Ellis claimed, "You can't put it on paper because it's of the spirit," and insisted that the seminar was the only legitimate means of transmitting the technique: "When people ask me about Dunham technique, I say you have to come to the seminar. Because that is what the seminar is for, so people can learn about Dunham technique." At the seminar, students are challenged to find out for themselves what Dunham technique is, she asserted: "because to me there is no distinctive explanation: I don't think there is, because I have never heard her say it and I have been with her almost sixty years."[31]

But pressures from some of the dance instructors, especially those in Dunham's "West Coast cult," as she ironically refers to them, led her to agree to the certification. In 1993, a group was selected to undergo a program beginning one week before the seminar. The program included a demonstration of knowledge about Dunham's philosophy, anthropolo-

gy, life history, and teaching methods. Twelve participants were selected for the first group.

Portrayals of some of these instructors who were authorized to educate others in Dunham technique, as well as of those who taught and
inspired them, lend insight into the qualities of instructors chosen to
carry on the tradition. The variety of their backgrounds and activities
reveals the different developments in the technique over the years, as well
as the diverse functions and applications of Dunham technique. Their
apprenticeships and relationships with company members provide significant insights into the makeup of the Dunham Company.

Alicia Pierce studied Dunham technique with Nontsizi Cayou, a
student of Ruth Beckford at the University of California at Berkeley. She
also worked with Pearl Reynolds, who taught at the seminar until her
death in 1990, and with the late Syvilla Fort. According to a former company member, Fort worked out Dunham's choreographic designs for the
dancers and was a repository of the technique. Reynolds also had a comprehensive knowledge of the movements, along with a clarity and a
meticulous approach to teaching; but, most of all, in Pierce's words, she
was "special," with a "spirit about her" that helped her form a link between the original technique—represented by the earlier Dunham Company members—and the ways in which it was developed by younger
members.[32] Seminar participants remember Pearl Reynolds with affection and respect.

Pierce, her quiet demeanor often enlivened by an impish sparkle,
grew up in New Orleans, where a Caribbean flavor permeates cultural
life; she moved to San Francisco in 1969. She teaches at San Francisco
State University and coaches teenagers at the Center for African and
African-American Arts and Culture in San Francisco. During the 1960s
and 1970s, she became politically active in the social movement that
culminated in the establishment of a black studies program at the university. She worked in recreational centers for the Berkeley Parks and
Recreation Department in the Bay Area and helped form the Wajumba
Cultural Ensemble, a group of dancers, drummers, and singers who performed in penal institutions, schools, and community centers in California and other states; the group also traveled to Jamaica and performed
at the Second World Festival of Black Arts in Nigeria in 1977.

Although Pierce had been teaching Dunham technique for several
years, she did not meet its creator until 1986, when she attended her first
Dunham Technique Seminar. She expressed her admiration for the courage of Katherine Dunham, who instilled black dancers with the knowledge that "what we were doing was legitimate," with pride and self-

esteem, and with respect for diverse cultures.[33] She led them to learn about the cultural backgrounds of dance, including their own heritage as well as those of others.

The late Ronnie Marshall, a tall and rangy dancer with a strongly expressive face and intense eyes, was the only male in the certification group. He originally studied Dunham technique with Lucille Ellis in Chicago. When he attended his first class, Ellis recognized him as the son of Delores Marshall, a well-known Chicago performer. She also knew his aunts, who taught tap, as well as popular dances like the lindy and the Charleston. Ellis was his "theater mother"; she taught him the basic technique and theatrical skills. He spent a lot of time learning about Dunham theory and intercultural communication in private conversations with Ellis, and, with her encouragement, he attended PATC in East St. Louis.[34]

When young Ronnie Marshall was dancing in the 1960s, he became active in the black power movement and grew disillusioned with dance, concluding it was irrelevant to the economic and political situation for black people. Dunham technique and philosophy gave him the medium through which he could employ his talents and skills in the service of African American culture and society. Inspired by the strong and talented male dancers he studied with during his years at PATC and by Dunham's example, Marshall traveled to Africa to learn about his cultural background. After his return, at Dunham's instigation he decided to study at the University of California at Los Angeles.

Marshall toured the United States, Europe, Korea, and Japan in a show he developed with Chester Whitmore, tracing the history of black dance. There were twelve in the company—ten dancers, a singer, and a technician—in addition to the impresario and his wife. They danced the cakewalk, lindy, blues tap, spiritual, hip-hop, rap, and break dance and added anything new that appeared in popular culture.

Marshall's family represents a lineage of black dancers. His aunt Sara often performed at the Regal Theater in Chicago, his aunt Mary at the Apollo in New York. Aunt Mary purportedly moved her school to New York so that her sister could dominate the Chicago scene. Dunham was acquainted with the two women, and John Pratt created costumes for them. Marshall hoped to develop a foundation to keep his aunts' schools and their heritage alive in Chicago and New York.

Marshall's widow, Sara, is one of Kenya's top singers; she was singing in Europe when she was brought by UNICEF to do a concert in New York. She and Marshall were introduced in 1983 by Olatunji, a Nigerian drummer with whom Marshall worked, while Marshall was staying in New York with one of his aunts. After she and Marshall married, she was the primary breadwinner, he remarked, since dance does not pay well. In 1998, when he was stricken with cancer, she taught at the seminar. He died in the fall of that year, and she has continued to teach classes.

Articulate and knowledgeable about dance, Penny Godboldo has performed the difficult barre exercise set to Tomaso Albinoni's "Adagio" at several final class demonstrations. She began studying dance at twelve years of age, late for a dancer, and she learned classical ballet in high school. She studied modern dance with Garth Fagan, originally from Jamaica, who founded the popular Bucket Dance Company, later the Garth Fagan Dance Company. She learned Dunham technique from Clifford Fears in Detroit; he had joined the Dunham Company in the early 1960s. Godboldo became acquainted with Dunham when Dunham visited Detroit in 1970 and was awarded the Katherine Dunham Day Award, and she met her again in 1971, when Dunham received the Dance Division Heritage Award of the American Association of Health, Physical Education and Recreation.[35]

Godboldo received a scholarship for the Alvin Ailey School in New York, where she worked with Lavinia Williams. Ailey had brought Williams from Haiti to develop the sense of movement his students had lost; he felt that black dancers were losing their soul. Williams's workshops at the Ailey School were intensive. She taught Haitian material and included a repertory of songs. She mixed Dunham technique with traditional Haitian material; her progressions used Haitian movement and were accompanied by song.

According to Godboldo, Williams's interpretation of Dunham technique was similar to that of Tommy Gomez and Lucille Ellis. All Dunham dancers have the same essence of technique and "look" to their bodies, but styles were influenced by the different countries in which the company toured. Godboldo was impressed by the "vast array of the diaspora" and was herself encouraged to travel and to study Cuban, Ghanaian, and Brazilian dance and culture.

Godboldo described herself as obsessed about maintaining Dunham technique; she worries about its continuance as a vital movement. Its strength lies, she believes, in the fact that Dunham never specialized, she never "mass produced" the technique to make money but has taught it as a way of life.

Jeanne Speier and Geraldine Williams, also certification students at the 1992 seminar, have developed careers centering on the therapeutic aspects of Dunham technique. Dance therapy is now an established discipline; Katherine Dunham recognized the healing possibilities of dance during her *lavé-tête*. Speier saw Dunham as the first dance therapist, having attempted to help her brother work out his problems through movement when he was hospitalized. Speier attended classes at the Performing Arts Training Center in the 1970s and studied dance therapy at St. Louis University. In the 1990s, she taught staff and patients at the Chicago Read Mental Health Center to communicate feelings and thoughts through dance. Previously she had traveled and studied, supporting herself with temporary positions. She was chosen to perform with the PATC Company at Carnegie Hall in 1979. Of German descent, she has danced with black dancers for many years. "I don't even see color when I'm here," she asserted.[36]

Speier has found that a background in Dunham technique is broadening for any dancer. She was inspired to travel to Bali, quitting her job and selling her car to raise funds. There she studied dance for nine months, learning one dance in depth, embedded in its cultural setting. Speier provides workshops in Balinese dance and occasionally performs it on stage. In 1994, she won a scholarship to return to Indonesia for twelve months and hoped to return again in 2001. Katherine Dunham has been attracted to Balinese dance since her work with Vera Mirova, and in the 1993 seminar she asked Speier to teach the movements. Speier is impressed by Dunham's low-keyed manner as she teaches. There are differences among the group, although all share the same focus and there is "unity in diversity." Something of a mystic, during the period of meditation at the end of a master class, Speier envisioned people who were not present at the seminar: in particular, Lenwood Morris and Archie Savage. She was reminded of Savage's account of visualizing his students after class, mentally preparing for the next class while driving through the field near the East St. Louis Center.

Geraldine Williams works with mentally handicapped people in Chicago, using Dunham technique to instruct those with behavior disorders on how to release tension. She teaches epileptic patients to prepare themselves for seizures so they will not tighten up when they feel one coming on. She explained that seizures may be brought on or intensified by tension, so that by relaxing the muscles they can avoid serious attacks.[37] Through Williams's work, Dunham's experience with the *voudun* is used to help ill people in Chicago.

Besides her work with mentally handicapped people, Williams teaches low-income elementary school children. Once when there was to be a performance, she arranged with gang leaders to keep the peace during the affair. The neighborhood remained quiet; not even a tire was slashed during the period of détente. She had learned this technique from Dunham during her stay in East St. Louis.

Williams studied in Chicago with Lucille Ellis, who brought her and other students to study at PATC. Dunham technique helped build her self-confidence, and she made a commitment to Ellis that she would continue with the technique.

Like many Dunham dancers, Williams supports herself with a variety of activities. She models in and choreographs shows for the Ultimate Ladies African Fabrics in Chicago. Unassuming, with a subtly humorous air, she, like many participants, often wears striking African dress and headpieces during the two weeks of the seminar, adding to the slightly exotic atmosphere.

The 1994 certification students ranged from thirty-seven to nearly fifty years in age and represented the broad spectrum of talent, experience, and knowledge characteristic of Dunham technique teachers and students. They all expressed a commitment to carry on the spirit of Dunham's life work, using their art both for self-expression and in the service of others. A second certification class was started in 2000.

Dr. Albirda Rose—dignified and Ethiopian in appearance, with close-cropped hair—is the moving force behind the certification program. She is both assertive and reflective in temperament, and in discussions she is given to authoritative statements, alternating with extended periods of silence.

Rose met and studied with Ruth Beckford as one of the "recreation brats" in the Oakland Parks and Recreation Program, of which Beckford was the director.[38] "Bird," as her friends call her, published a book, *Dunham Technique: A Way of Life*, in which she addressed three of Dunham's principles: socialization through the arts, intercultural communication, and form and function in dance.[39] She explained that the first principle, socialization through dance, was most important to her: "Miss Beckford was my first teacher, and she really built that program on that concept. Dance was just a tool . . . used as [a] means of having us become socialized within the system we would be living in."[40] It was after she had taught for awhile and encountered people of the many ethnic backgrounds in the Bay area that she became aware of the importance of the other two principles of Dunham technique.

In the recreational program, Beckford formed honor societies, for which the girls had to audition. "Hundreds of girls all across Oakland would come on a Saturday morning and audition one at a time in front of Miss Beckford. . . . All we had to do was to introduce ourselves and say what recreational center we were from, and then dance. [It] gave me the courage to go in front of people and present myself, and [say] this is who I am and this is what I have to offer," Rose asserted.

When Rose was in college, the Black Panthers and the "Black Pride" movement were in full sway, and there was a push for black studies in the university. There was also a great demand in the Bay area for African culture, especially African Caribbean dance. Trained in Dunham technique, she and her peers were in a position to take advantage of this: the universities would come to Beckford for recommendations, and she would say she had trained these dancers. Rose and the others began teaching in colleges throughout the area. When programs for children were severely cut in California under Proposition 13, she continued to teach in the public schools on a volunteer basis.

Largely through Beckford's teaching, Dunham technique is well represented throughout the Bay area. The Community of Black Dance, a group of dancers and activists in the area, monitors the local dance performances to see that the proper credit is given to artistic creators.

Rose met Dunham in 1976, when Dunham was a resident artist at Berkeley. When Rose was doing research for her book, comparing her own training with that she observed by watching hours of tape made at the Performing Arts Training Center, she was struck by the way Dunham technique had changed during the years. "When [Dunham] got [to East St. Louis], something else started happening; living here and living in Haiti, she was actually using [dance] as a means of dealing with people, of training people, and of teaching people how to live and not just to dance. I think that's the aspect of this technique that sets it aside from any other technique that I've studied as a dancer," Rose explained. At this time, she came to understand better Dunham's concept of form and function in dance.

During Dunham's residency at Stanford during May of 1989, Rose and Pierce demonstrated in the master class. They knew many of the students in the class and were irritated by some who became upset when Dunham lectured to them instead of teaching them technique for the full period. "They knew Miss Dunham as the technician, the dancer, the mover and shaker and they wanted to move and shake and jump up and down on the floor; but they could not see that what she was saying would make you jump higher, possibly, if you would understand what she was saying," Rose said.

Rose thought that certification should be accomplished through the seminar, while Dunham is still available to give her "stamp of approval." "I'd always be concerned whether or not that's really the way she wanted it," she remarked. She realized the hazards of codifying a creative expression: "I am split down the middle. One is the creative person and one is the academician. As the academician [I feel] that it needs to happen on this level, coming from this [group]. I think somebody might come along and make it so set, so clinical, that her intent will be lost." Along with former Dunham Company members, she was very dissatisfied with the Alvin Ailey Company's presentation of Dunham choreography in 1987: "It was obvious they had not studied Dunham technique, to someone who has. There was a whole quality missing, an inner spirit that projected 'L'Ag'Ya,' [and] 'Shango,' that wasn't there. . . . It was technically very good, but that was it."[41]

In teaching, Rose stresses the meaning projected by the movement and what the students themselves bring to it. "Dunham technique does that," she commented. She recounted her experience in a seminar class in which Beatty wanted the class to feel the hard percussion of the beat and project it, but she could not feel it. She thought this was perhaps because she was breast-feeding and the aggression was alien to her life at that time.

In discussing Dunham's choreography for the "Adagio," she explained that the lyrical element has always been a part of Dunham technique and was especially prominent in the pedagogy of Syvilla Fort. Beckford had not included it in her repertoire, concentrating more on the percussive and Caribbean movements; nor did she employ the progressions, which usually include balletic movements. Rose was fascinated by the graceful leg extensions of the "Adagio." "It's fabulous," she exclaimed.

Rose is one of the participants who have brought other members of their family along to the seminar. Rather late in life, she gave birth to a son, who became the center of attention when she brought him to the seminar. Dunham was entranced; she remarked that the smile of a baby, with the innocence and purity it brings with it, is the most miraculous thing in the world. She saw in a baby's beatific expression evidence of the place she or he came from, still remembered. Rose's son has returned in subsequent years, provoking exclamations over his growth and progress.

The Dunham legacy is ultimately dependent on the children, who are learning how to express themselves in the Dunham mode, and the teachers who are responsible for developing their creativity. The high point of the seminar's final demonstration-performance is the children's presentation, in which students at the Children's Workshop in East St. Louis are joined by children from St. Louis and those of older seminar participants. Glory Van Scott, small and sylphlike, with enormous, dramatic eyes, directs and teaches them.

Glory Van Scott first came to East St. Louis in 1971 to do a production with the children, and Dunham asked her if she would come back and continue to work with them. She had been a younger member of the

Dunham Company; in the Carnegie Hall Gala, she had played Dunham's role—the widowed queen in "Rites de Passage"—opposite Vanoye Aikens. She teaches and organizes productions in New York City. She loves to work with children because they have incredible energy: "They're great! And they try things that you tell them to try, you know, unabashedly."[42]

On the first day of class, she studies the children to discover temperaments and talent; she brings with her a concept of what she wants to do with them, then translates the idea into a dramatic presentation that suits the group. Then she goes back to her room and begins to write. As she creates, she discusses ideas and values with the children so that they can relate their performance to their lives. "Robots I'm not interested in, but I am interested in kids developing their awareness of the world. I want them to have fun with it, I want them to be excited about it, I want them also to know about commitments in the world and want them to make commitments," she exclaimed. Subjects of discussion range from the importance of voting (Van Scott feels strongly about this) to what's happening at school, even pranks in which they may have engaged. "So there's a real camaraderie that happens, that I share with them, and I love them, and they know it," she declares, adding, "I'm a disciplinarian, but the discipline I do is done with love [and] they understand. And they get leeway, they get breaks." She provides them with snacks: "You know, when you work with kids, some of them may not have had anything to eat . . . you cannot assume that you can walk in there and work with them. You could say, their mothers should give them something: you can't operate on that. Some of these kids, perhaps, they don't have anyone in the house at that time."

Van Scott appreciates Dunham's social involvement and intellectual breadth, saying that just to sit with her is like attending a class. She used to call her and say, "Well, Miss Dunham, I'm getting ready for Dunham 101." "There's never a moment when you spend any time with her that she doesn't leave you thinking . . . your brain is going when you walk away from her." Van Scott believes students should go on to achievements beyond what Dunham provides in terms of creativity and direction, and she feels it is a "crime" if you do not do anything further with what she offers. "She expects that: she should give you all those treasures and you should sit on your bum and do nothing?"

The theater is all-important to Van Scott: "I can't imagine life without it: it's life, it's full." Practicing theater art, which she learned from Dunham and others in the company, is a special way of life that she shares with children. She believes that Dunham has done great things for children. Dunham exemplifies Van Scott's idea of the artist: "She's a genius. . . . She's eighty-one with a vision, a better vision than people walking around twenty, twenty-one or thirty." Van Scott believes younger people will never attain her vision because Dunham looks further into the future.

Van Scott shares Dunham's view of time as nonlinear. In her "Conversations" with students and others, Dunham depicts it as a spiral: actions and events are repeated, but we continuously advance and accumulate experiences as we move through our lives. Van Scott apprehends time as represented by people she has known, who have gone away but are still in a profound sense with her, including those participants in the creative venture of the Dunham Company who continue to influence her even after their deaths.

Seminar attendants represent a large part of Dunham's kindred, extending across political, social, and cultural boundaries. Births and deaths are events affecting everyone and are recognized accordingly. In 1999, a memorial service was held for Lucille Ellis, Tommy Gomez, and Ronnie Marshall. Commencing as a Christian service, with Albirda Rose, an ordained minister, leading, it soon became unrecognizable as such, with African invocation, drumming, and dancing. C. K. Ganyo spoke movingly of Ronnie Marshall's first journey to Ghana when he took the day name of "Yao," or "Thursday," not because he was born on Thursday but because he arrived in Ghana on that day. He and Marshall had kept in touch after Ganyo came to the United States, through the seminars and while on tours.

Theo Jamison and Keith Williams recalled Tommy Gomez's softspoken manner, describing him as a "gentleman" but totally dedicated to his art.[43] Jamison recalled his last contact with Gomez when both taught classes in Port-au-Prince in 1998. Gomez was deftly maneuvering with only one leg and with IVs in his arm.

Van Scott spoke of Lucille Ellis as "our mother." She became teary when she described looking to "Miss D's left" where Ellis always sat and how the line of company members had dwindled; she could not proceed for awhile. "I told myself, 'You're a professional; you're supposed to go on, no matter what,' but I just couldn't," she admitted.[44]

Rose announced that something important was missing from the occasion: the *voudun*. Then the service mounted to a passionate celebration of the life force. It commenced with the movement that had launched Dunham's life adventure: the graceful, calming *yonvalou*, with Sara Marshall and others joining in. "Breaks" were introduced, and a seminar participant from Trinidad introduced a Shango-like movement—angular, abrupt—and embraced Marshall, as the drummers switched to a rapid pace. The dancers—with Marshall at the center—addressed impassioned gestures to Mor Thiam as he pounded his *jimbe* with great energy.

The cathartic effects of the dance could be seen in Sara Marshall's transformation after the observance. Throughout the day, she had been sad and withdrawn, but the dancing seemed to revive her. She came up to me afterward, embraced me warmly, and said, "I'm so happy to see you, I'm glad you could come." Overcome with emotion, I could only respond, "I'm glad, too." It was a wrenching but appropriate conclusion to a triumphant celebration of Katherine Dunham and her dancers.

Promises to Keep

Despite pressures exerted on Dunham to move her programs from East St. Louis and to give up her property in Haiti, she feels her lot has been cast with the two localities. She feels compelled to ensure that her aspirations for their development are realized. In spite of the despoiling of her property in Haiti, she persisted in plans to develop a botanical garden on part of her estate. The international organization of 140 Botanical Gardens, led by the British contingent, had expressed an interest in the undertaking. Her continuing goal was to "stabilize Haiti" by means of establishing something of international significance. She also received a tentative offer of sale to a church interested in establishing an educational institute, with a Dunham program as a central part. These and other developments fell through for a number of reasons, including the political situation, lack of funding, and Dunham's deep reluctance to give up the property. She became discouraged: "You know when you've gone as far as you can, and I have."[45]

But Dunham's innate optimism unfailingly asserts itself. The experience of synchrony often brings new life to her sense of mission. Twice her path has crossed that of Garry Davis, head of the World Government of World Citizens. He came to her dressing room in Paris in 1949; she had met his brother, Meyer Davis, who conducted a society orchestra in New York. Their mother was the sister of Pierre Monteux, whom Dunham had met in Los Angeles. Dunham was surprised when Davis appeared in her dressing room, since she was avoiding the press and had given orders to keep everyone out. "He was not stopped by any false barriers; he echoed my own feelings against false barriers, gained at the University of Chicago." At his invitation, she became a World Citizen and holds a world passport. She admires Davis's dynamic personality, his "wonderful energy and spirit"; he renounced his U.S. citizenship because of U.S. militarism and imperialism. "We are all citizens of earth," she explained. During her fast in 1992, Davis contacted her and he and his brother joined her fast. He asked her if she saw a relationship between world citizenship and the environment. "Both have to do with caring, care for people, care for the environment; respect for man, for all living things, not destroying. . . . Anything that makes us feel hope should be appreciated and lauded," she replied.[46]

Another "soul mate," Buckminster Fuller, also stressed the existence of one world; in his futuristic design, energy would replace currency, and he projected a worldwide grid in which energy was shared, creating conditions of wealth. His "World Game" is based on developing strategies for solving problems of poverty and unequal resources throughout the world. Dunham regards Davis and Fuller as representatives of an avant-garde, forerunners of another civilization—a theme that recurs in her public and private conversations. She includes Erich Fromm in this elect group. Deploring the human euphoria relating to violence—as Fromm depicted it, the "ecstasy of killing"—she lamented, "I've got to get away from this planet." She misses her regular and therapeutic visits to Residence Dunham in Port au Prince, but "I don't have to cling to things lost in Haiti."[47] The themes of hope, regret, and discouragement with the present, as well as millenarian beliefs in a superior civilization—based on the efforts of the enlightened—run throughout her public and private statements.

In East St. Louis, she can see concrete results, although she is often critical of the inadequate vision and commitment of some who try to carry on her work. She can point to successful careers launched, but she expects more from those she has touched. The ultimate misfortune of such dreamers and doers as Katherine Dunham is that they rarely find others who are equally committed. When she has met those who were on her wave length and on whom she could rest her hopes, they have had their own dreams, often different from her own.

The greatest disappointment to many of her colleagues and supporters is a general lack of recognition of the achievements of Katherine Dunham and other dance pioneers in African American dance and the consequent failure of career advancement for many young black dancers. In a 1998 PBS presentation, produced by the late Henry Hampton, which documents a history of African American art, Katherine Dunham's name and work were not mentioned. Alvin Ailey's name was alluded to in passing only; and most of the treatment on dance dealt with ballet, the difficulties black dancers had in trying to enter white companies, and modern dance that has little affinity with African American themes.[48] Individuals attending a scholarly conference on Dunham's legacy criticized the 1998 documentary as unrepresentative of African American art and artists.[49] That the historical role and importance of black-directed companies was overlooked in a national broadcast by a respected black producer shows that such companies as that of Denver-based Cleo Robinson, which performs Dunham choreography, as well as others who teach Dunham technique, have an unenviable task. The questions arise: Will another "Katherine Dunham" appear to take up the struggle for black dancers? Or will the responsibility fall on the shoulders of the Dunham followers in their studios and classrooms?

Dunham and her colleagues have been interested in establishing a permanent record of Dunham technique by videotaping her choreography. This has been discussed with interested parties on many occasions, but so far funds have not been obtained for this gargantuan task. Apart from those who are currently teaching Dunham technique, the Children's Workshop, and the Cleo Robinson Dance Company, the resources are sparse for those who wish to see the original choreography, and few of the Dunham Company are left. "Rites de Passage" was taped in 1980, with Glory Van Scott, Vanoye Aikens, Doris Bennett-Glasper, Norman Davis, and Emilio Lastarria dancing the leading roles; it was presented on a PBS special that year.[50] Dunham and former company members worked with the Alvin Ailey Company on *The Magic of Katherine Dunham*, which had a successful but limited tour of U.S. and European cities in 1986–9.[51] In that production, "Choros," "L'Ag'Ya" "Shango," "Flaming Youth," and "Cakewalk," among other pieces, were performed. But these performances and the university courses in Dunham technique at Southern Illinois University in East St. Louis and at other schools fall short of the standards set by Dunham. Tommy Gomez lamented the "distortions" of the technique that he had seen in his classes: "There are so many people that have taken some Dunham technique and they think that they are informed enough to teach it. . . . It takes years to grasp the technique and the philosophy behind the technique."[52]

It is perhaps the mystery and worldview of Dunham herself that are missing from the re-creations. Dunham has described her dance technique: "It is about movement, forms, love, hate, death, life, all human emotions. . . . Dunham Technique, which has been called a way of life, is about life in the Universe."[53] Her mysticism—Dunham identifies herself as a "non-theistic mystic"—is expressed through her teaching as well as in living. Adam Pinskcr, former executive director of Dance St. Louis, commented during Dunham's fast, "Fasting is an intrinsically spiritual act, and Dunham's very nature and her art have always been intensely spiritual."[54]

An aspect of Dunham's art that has been controversial throughout her career, both in the black and mainstream communities, is the expression of sexuality. Eugene Redmond values that expression: "There's a deep psychology that Miss D employs, and sexuality. [She] confirmed the goodness and the righteousness and the integrity, and even the justice, if you will, of the sensual human being; and I think that one of the hallmarks of black culture is sensuality. Miss Dunham confirmed it in some very interesting ways for me . . . beyond the saying, 'Black is Beautiful.'"[55] A society that expresses a duality of attitudes toward sexuality—puritanism, on the one hand, commercial exploitation, on the other—might well view with ambivalence an artist who treats it an integral part of religion, human relationships, and artistic expression.

In discussing the impact of the artist on a society, Dunham asserted that to make a difference, it takes not many but someone who is dedicated. Certainly she has made an impact on American dance and society, the extent of which cannot be measured. According to one assessment, "She has influenced everyone from George Balanchine to Jerome Robbins, Alvin Ailey, Bob Fosse, and Twyla Tharp. American dance, including ballet, modern dance, Hollywood and Broadway, would not be the same without her."[56] More important to Dunham is the fact that she has challenged countless students and colleagues to live and think more deeply.

Although she left Joliet, Chicago, and Illinois in the 1940s feeling resentment about privations and humiliations suffered during her youth, Katherine Dunham's achievements as a dancer and educator have since been recognized in her home state. In 1978, she was honored, along with the poet Gwendolyn Brooks, at the First Annual Governor's Awards for the Arts in Illinois. A coalition of the Chicago chapters of the American Association of University Women and the National Council of Negro Women, among other groups, presented the "Illinois and Chicago Salute to Katherine Dunham," on the occasion of her Kennedy Center Honors Award; the program noted that "Katherine Dunham is a native of Chicago, an alumna of the University of Chicago, and the Choreo-Laureate of Illinois."[57] Joliet—the "mean city," as she described it—inducted her into the Hall of Pride in 1989, nearly sixty years after she left for Chicago.

In June 1998, Southern Illinois University at Edwardsville renamed its communications building Katherine Dunham Hall. At the same time, the name of the East St. Louis Katherine Dunham Performing Arts Training Center was changed to the East St. Louis Center for Performing Arts, fulfilling a wish she had expressed since her retirement to remove her name from the title since she no longer directed the program. This was a recognition of the artistic requirement of control over productions identified with her name. Henceforth, the Children's Workshop would represent her work in East St. Louis and reap any financial and cultural benefits from her accomplishments.

Dunham's crusade to abolish racial and social boundaries is yet to be accomplished in her country of birth. She believes that Dale Wasserman and others who had expressed an interest in producing a film on her life were ultimately put off by her marriage to John Pratt, which in the United States is still not socially acceptable. Their alliance survived the vicissitudes of a mixed marriage, but Dunham commented after his death that at the Kennedy Center Award presentation, Pratt was placed in the back row where he could barely be seen.

Despite these setbacks, Dunham is far from capitulating: "activism"—physical, mental, and spiritual—still characterizes her life. Her fast in support of Haitian refugees was quite a feat for an eighty-two-year-old woman. She had been feeling depressed as a result of a sense of helplessness. The following account of a day of her activities during the twenty-seventh day of her fast reveals the revitalization of a woman with a cause:

> Katherine Dunham sat up in her hospital bed, giving interviews with the press, talking to friends, making phone calls to political leaders, to leading figures in the world of art, film and theater, receiving calls from around the nation and around the world, getting her hair braided, listening to Haitian, classical, and rock music, giving directions, receiving and advising young people who have been fasting while in jail for protesting, watching TV news reports, giving support to her god-daughter, scolding and calming her aides when they became stressed or when they did something in her name she does not approve of. She tires out those who are around her with her incessant activity. All the while, she is refusing food, ingesting only water and cranberry juice. . . . She is in her 27th day of fasting; a rally, one of many, is planned for her 30th day, with Dick Gregory, Silvester "Sunshine" Lee, Cleo Willis and others speaking. These men are fasting and have spent several days in jail for chaining themselves to the Federal Building.[58]

Eight years later, she would be celebrating her ninetieth birthday, with a "live birthday card"—which included former Dunham Company members and their students, as well as others from around the country she has known through the years—and a community celebration in East St. Louis that commemorated the experiences and accomplishments of PATC alumnae of "Tenth Street Tech."

As Dunham's friends and colleagues prepared for her ninetieth birthday celebration, she worried that the community program would not come together as she had hoped. Despite advice by others that she not be involved in the activities, it was not her wont to just let things happen. She had remained in the public eye and received numerous awards and wide recognition for herself and her artistic collaborators by dint of unceasing effort, not by passively standing by. It is a matter of personal pride that her objectives and values are realized. And she had spent a third of her life committed to her work in East St. Louis. So she asked an East St. Louis native—the daughter of a member of the first museum board— and me to organize a local celebration. We felt we could hardly refuse her.

We had only two or three months to produce an event that would do justice to her achievements in the city. We wanted to stage it on the museum grounds, which meant we would have to not only build a new outdoor stage but also complete the landscaping and rehab the African village, work that was supported by an Urban Resource Partnership grant but had barely begun. Attempting to accomplish a task of this magnitude in any period of time in East St. Louis is a near Herculean task because of the political factions and long-standing rivalries and grudges. We managed to nearly complete the landscaping and construction by the time of the ceremonies consecrating the refurbished African village—conducted jointly by Mor Thiam and Evelyn Voelker of the American Indian Center. Voelker's participation was in recognition of Dunham's long-standing desire to include American Indian cultural events in museum activities. A tractor that was spreading gravel in the muddy pathways around the village was temporarily halted for the ceremony but then resumed its endless rounds in an attempt to eradicate the mud in time for the birthday gala.

Two parallel activities vied with the celebration for time and resources. The Dunham Technique Seminar was moved from August to June to allow participants to commemorate Dunham's birthday. Robert Lee and helpers, including student volunteers from Southern Illinois University at Edwardsville, worked tirelessly to complete a stage for the final performance of the seminar. In addition, efforts were poured into completing interior repairs and redecorating the corner house for visitors. The entire process resembled the assemblage of a gigantic production, with similar pressures of time, deadline, and artistic demands.

Dunham's power to accomplish the apparently impossible and to enlist others in her efforts was confirmed, though not without a hitch. The designated day dawned clear and sunny and the museum was ready, but the weather did not cooperate. By program time, there was a torrential downpour, and the entire crowd was redirected to the local community college, where the seminar was being held. Fortunately, the stage there was finished. Dunham arrived, resplendent in pink from the top of her head to her toes—a costume provided by the local Nation of Islam group. After she was interviewed at length by a French television correspondent, delaying the proceedings even further, Anne Walker, a highly articulate emcee— PATC graduate, now an advertising executive—opened the program.

Among others who appeared that night, Eugene Redmond—the program chairman—read his poetic biography of Katherine Dunham to drums and dancing by members of the Children's Workshop, and Sunshine Lee presented his spirited and talented group of singers, drummers, and dancers. Sunshine's life had been changed by Dunham; he was one of the young East St. Louis men who was "raising hell" during the sixties. At the time of the assassination of Martin Luther King Jr., he was ready to destroy and ravage and to "shoot anyone." Darryl Braddix brought him to meet Dunham, and after that he became a changed person. Today, he drives a van with his name and logo on the side, and his group is known and in demand for performances throughout the region.

Other highlights of the night included Representative Wyvetter Younge's announcement of a grant from the Illinois Arts Council and the presentation of the "Smith" award by Smithsonian representatives. Dunham was tired even before the program began—it was an exhausting week for her, since the Dunham Technique Seminar was being held at the same time. But she stayed for nearly all of the program and announced before she left that she had enjoyed the show and that—unusual for her—she had no criticisms to make. She announced at the next seminar master class, "I'm happy . . . they can say, 'Lord, she's on her way,'"[59] and that she felt more optimistic about the future for African American dancers. Those of us who had worked to bring the party off felt we had received our reward.

Throughout the lean times and even after finances improved, Dunham's personal comfort and welfare have weighed heavily on her friends. Residing in the second story of an old house with structural defects— including a leaky roof and a lack of wheelchair access—she was physically isolated except when transported by a van to the airport or to a local event. Because of staff shortages, Stovall and others often have little time to spend with her. The world news—she is an inveterate CNN viewer —frequently depresses her, as does her weakened condition and the many deaths in the Dunham extended family.

Besides these worries, Dunham is often compelled to wrestle with staff problems. For a time, there was a question about the immigration status of her Haitian nurse and concern that she would have to return to Haiti. She is physically dependent on the nurse, but despite care, she suffered frequent bouts of bronchitis that caused her to be hospitalized. Her inability to take accustomed breaks in Haiti—especially in winter months—as well as her concerns about the country and her property there often leave Dunham dispirited.

Concerned about the long-term fate of the Dunham legacy, Marta Vega, the founder of the Caribbean Cultural Center in New York, the art historian VèVè Clark, and the dance historian Richard Long initiated a series of meetings in an attempt to set the Dunham Centers for Arts and Humanities on course. Operating with a skeleton staff, the activities of the centers could not be expected to long outlast Dunham's lifetime. The immediate goal was to attract funding from private foundations and to set up an endowment. To create confidence in the management of any future funds, the trio pointed out, the centers needed organizational changes. Dunham's personal welfare and artistic agenda—including completing her memoirs and teaching master classes—needed to be separated from the operations of Dunham programs.

In the fall of 1999, the Caribbean Cultural Center sponsored an intensive series of workshops to identify sources of Dunham materials. It was attended by representatives of the New York Public Library, Smithsonian Institution, Library of Congress, Lincoln Center, Missouri Historical Society, and Southern Illinois University at Carbondale, by filmmakers who have access to Dunham films, and by staff members of the Dunham centers. The assignment was to discover what materials are available and existing plans for developing the resources, as well as ways of making them more widely accessible. The long-planned documentation of Dunham technique with living Dunham Company members had never been realized because of a lack of support. The announced aim was at least to make available what film footage existed from company performances, as well as photographs, music, reviews, designs, stage directions and notes, and other documentation. Foundation support to maintain Dunham's legacy was sought and obtained, to be administered through the Library of Congress; however, since Dunham refused to sign away her rights to all her choreography, writings, and other materials, the award remained in limbo.

The infusion of state monies in the late 1990s brought about an improvement in Dunham's personal and programmatic fortunes and provided a new roof and other repairs for her home. Friends in New York, including Julie and Harry Belafonte, persuaded her to enter a clinic that has a record of success in strengthening nonambulatory patients. Since the fall of 1999, she has spent most of her time in New York, seeing old friends and catching up on events there, returning to East St. Louis for her birthday celebrations and the Dunham Technique Seminar in June. Enjoying a needed break, she continued to brood over the problems in her two adopted homes. Thwarted by conditions in Haiti, she focused on East St. Louis. Harry Belafonte, who was identifying communities that could benefit through reinvestment, reported that she phoned him saying, "'East St. Louis is where you must go. . . . You must look and pay heed.'" "She knew there was a richness here," he affirmed.[60]

Harry Belafonte, whose mentor was Paul Robeson, has worked through his position with the United Nations to connect people in the African diaspora to their homeland. He heads a private-public coalition to fund cultural and economic development in African American communities. He said that he listened to Dunham's advice to involve East St. Louis in his plans because he respects her wisdom and insight: "When Katherine Dunham called we responded because she is our elder."[61] At a city hall meeting in 2000, Mayor Debra Powell addressed plans to make East St. Louis a cultural "mecca" for African Americans, where they can learn about their cultural traditions. Seemingly, Dunham's and Fuller's visions of East St. Louis, also articulated by Representative Younge, were on the brink of fulfillment.

Dunham's longevity, allowing her to see the realization of many of her dreams—despite illness, handicaps, and financial and political adversities—is largely a result of her remarkable talent for living. Whether in her room or in a clinic or hospital, in East St. Louis or elsewhere, Dunham surrounds herself with amenities and memorabilia.[62] On her capacious bed in East St. Louis, she kept near at hand a phone, address book, letters, reading and writing materials, a tray with her crystal collection, and specially prepared foods. Her medicines and favorite candies were positioned on a bedside table. The walls and shelves display a collection of some of her awards, represented by plaques and objets d'art. Wherever she resides, her bed is covered with colorful spreads, and she receives her frequent guests graciously, dressed in comfortable, distinctive styles and with strategically applied makeup. For several years, a beautician whom she met through friends, styled her hair becomingly in the multiple small braids favored by the young. Lately, however, she has worn a short hairstyle.

Dunham loves to cook and eat fine food, and she regrets the loss of taste that comes with age and illness. She invariably offers food and drink to visitors. Although she is unable to cook, she consults at great length with those who prepare meals for her—usually one of two or three friends who work for her for love more than money—about menus and recipes.

What new forms and transformations Katherine Dunham's mission assumes are yet to unfold. Harry Belafonte remarked that several times he had assumed she had retired from active life, only to find that she was involved in a new undertaking.[63] Those who have been close to her through the years have not been under such illusion. Still restless and active in her nineties, she sees the work as never completed, just as no account of her life can be complete. Though not able to walk unassisted since her fast, she has frequently traveled to cities in the United States to accept awards, lecture, and teach classes.[64] Despite her many achievements, she asserts that her goals have yet to be realized. She has avowed, "I was put here by some force; this child is supposed to grow up into a woman who has courage and wisdom to do certain things."[65] As she has reiterated in many contexts, she has composed her own epitaph: "She tried." And, it might be added, few have tried harder or achieved more.

APPENDIX A
Timeline

1909	Katherine Mary Dunham is born in Chicago on June 22
1928	Enters University of Chicago
1930	Forms first dance group
1933	Appears with Chicago Opera in *La Guiablesse*
1935	Awarded a Rosenwald Foundation grant; begins fieldwork in West Indies
1937	Performs at YMHA in New York City
1938	Federal theater performance of "L'Ag'Ya"
1940	Performs at Windsor Theater in New York; performs and choreographs for *Cabin in the Sky*; forms the Katherine Dunham Dance Company
1940–41	First U.S. tour with *Cabin in the Sky*
1941	Marries John Pratt
1941–47	Second tour, United States and Canada, *Tropical Revue, Carib Song*
1945	Katherine Dunham School of Dance opens in New York
1947–49	Tours Mexico, Europe
1949	Brother, Albert Jr., dies
1950	Tours South America; purchases Habitation Leclerc
1951–3	Tours Europe, North Africa
1951	Adopts four-year-old Marie-Christine
1956–57	Tours South Pacific and Far East
1957	Disbands company; writes *A Touch of Innocence*
1959–60	Third European tour
1962	*Bamboche* opens after recruitment in Morocco
1963	Choreographs *Aida*
1964–65	Artist-in-residence at Southern Illinois University at Carbondale; choreographs *Faust.*
1966	Trains, choreographs for Ballet National de Senegal; represents United States at the First World Festival of Negro Arts in Dakar
1967	Receives EOC funding for Performing Arts Training Center; is jailed in East St. Louis

1970	Takes children to Washington, D.C., for White House Conference on Children
1979	International opening of the Katherine Dunham Museum
1980	CBS grant for Children's Workshop
1982	Retires from Southern Illinois University
1983	Receives Kennedy Center Honors Award
1986	John Pratt dies
1991–92	Fasts for Haitian refugees
1999	Ninetieth birthday celebration in June

APPENDIX B
Selected Performances
and Choreography

Theater

Chicago Opera, guest star, 1933–36
Chicago World's Fair, 1934
Run Li'l Chil'lun, Goodman Theatre, Chicago, 1938
Caribbean Rhapsody, London, Paris, European tour, 1938–49; South America, 1950–51; Europe and North Africa, 1952–53; United States and Mexico, 1953; Germany and European tour, 1954; South America, 1954–55; Mexico, 1955; Broadway, 1955–56; Australia and New Zealand, 1956–57; Far East, 1958; Europe, Near East, Argentina, 1959–60
Pins and Needles, New York, 1939
Tropics and *Le Jazz Hot*, New York, 1939
Cabin in the Sky, New York and tour, 1939–42
Tropical Revue, New York and tour, 1943–44
Carib Song, New York, 1945
Bal Nègre, New York and tour, 1946; Mexico, Canada 1947
Windy City, Great Northern Theater, Chicago, 1947
Bamboche, U.S. tour, 1962; New York, 1963

Films

Carnival of Rhythm, Warner Brothers, 1939
Star Spangled Rhythm, Paramount, 1942
Pardon My Sarong, Universal, 1942
Stormy Weather, Twentieth Century–Fox, 1943
Casbah, Universal, 1948
Botta e riposta, Ponti–de Laurentiis, Italy, 1950
Native Son, Argentina, 1951 (film company unknown)
Mambo, Paramount, 1954
Liebes Sender, Germany, 1954 (film company unknown)
Musica en la noche, Allianza Cinematografica, Mexico, 1955
Green Mansions, Metro-Goldwyn Mayer, 1958
The Bible, Twentieth Century–Fox, Rome, 1964

Opera

Aida, Metropolitan, New York, 1964
Faust, Southern Illinois University, Carbondale, 1965
Treemonisha, Atlanta, 1972; Wolftrap Farm Park for the Performing Arts,
    Vienna, Virginia, 1972

Theater Direction

Tropical Pinafore, Chicago, 1939
Pins and Needles, New York, 1939
I Hear America Singing, New York, 1939
Deux Anges, Paris, 1965
Ciao, Rudi, Rome, 1965
San Remo Festival, New York, 1966
Ballet National de Senegal, 1966–67
A Dream Deferred, East St. Louis, 1968
Ode to Taylor Jones, East St. Louis, 1968
Some Rags and Such, Wolftrap, 1975

Television

NBC telecast, 1939
BBC, London, 1952
National Television, Paris, 1952–53
Spectacular, Buenos Aires, 1955
CBC, Toronto, 1956
Australian television, Sydney, 1957
"Karaibishe Rhythmen," WDR Fernschen, Cologne, Germany, 1960
Performance of PATC company at Wolftrap Park, PBS, 1976
McNeil-Lehrer Report, PBS, 1978
"Dance in America, Divine Drumbeats: Katherine Dunham and Her Peo-
    ple," WNET-TV, New York, 1980
"Eye on St. Louis," KMOX-TV, 1981

Night Clubs and Hotels

College Inn and Sherman Hotel, Chicago, 1939
Chez Paree, Chicago, n.d.
Mark Hopkins, Fairmont, and Las Fiesta, San Francisco, n.d.
Ranch Vegas and Sahara, Las Vegas, 1947, 1959
Mapes Hotel, Reno, n.d.
Lake Towhee and Palm Springs, n.d.

Ciro's, Hollywood, 1947–48, 1952, 1955
Little Trocadero, Hollywood, n.d.
Versailles, Mexico City, n.d.
Sporting d'Ete and Sea Club, Monte Carlo, n.d.
Casinos in Nice, Cannes, Juan les Pins, Menton, Biarritz, Archachon, La
    Boule, Annecy, n.d.
La Martinique, New York, n.d.
Chalfonte, Atlantic City, n.d.
Latin Quarter and Eden Roc, Miami, n.d.
Benibashi, Tokyo, 1957
Mar del Palata, Argentina, n.d.

APPENDIX C
Major Honors and Awards

Honorary Degrees

Doctor of Humane Letters, MacMurray College, Jacksonville, Ill., May 21, 1972
Doctor of Literature, Atlanta University, Atlanta, Ga., May 16, 1977
Doctor of Fine Arts, Westfield State College, Westfield, Mass., May 26, 1979
Doctor of Fine Arts, Brown University, Providence, R.I., June 4, 1979
Doctor of Fine Arts, Dartmouth College, Hanover, N.H., June 10, 1979
Doctor of Fine Arts, Washington University, St. Louis, Mo., May 22, 1981
Doctor of Fine Arts, Southern Illinois University at Edwardsville, June 10, 1983
Doctor of Laws, Lincoln University, Lincoln, Pa., May 6, 1984
Doctor of Fine Arts, Howard University, Washington, D.C., May 12, 1984
Doctor of Humane Letters, University of South Carolina, Columbia, May 18, 1985
Doctor of Fine Arts, Tufts University, Medford, Mass., May 17, 1987
Doctor of Fine Arts, Buffalo State College, Buffalo, N.Y., October 13, 1987
Doctor of Humane Letters, Spelman College, Atlanta, Ga., April 11, 1990
Doctor of Humane Letters, Chicago State University, Chicago, Ill., June 5, 1993
Doctor of Fine Arts, University of Southern California, Los Angeles, May 12, 1995

Major Awards

Note: The selections indicate the range of activities for which Katherine Dunham has received recognition.

Chevalier, Haitian Legion of Honor and Merit, 1952
Grand Officer, Haitian Legion of Honor and Merit, 1968
Professional Achievement Award, University of Chicago Alumni Association, 1968
President's Council on Youth Opportunity Honoree, Washington, D.C., 1968

Dance Magazine Award, 1969

Eight Lively Arts Award, 1969

Certificate of Merit, International Who's Who in Poetry, 1970–71

Dance Division Heritage Award, American Association for Health, Physical Education and Recreation, 1971

National Center of Afro-American Artists Award, Elma Lewis School of Fine Arts, Boston, 1972

Black Filmmakers Hall of Fame, 1974

Entertainment Hall of Fame Foundation, 1974

International Women's Year Award, United Nations Association, St. Louis Chapter, 1975

Dance Pioneer Award, Alvin Ailey American Dance Theatre, 1978

Black Heritage Commemorative Stamp, United States Postal Service, 1978

Albert Schweitzer Music Award, 1979

National Dance Week Award, Dance Concert Society, April 1980

Kennedy Center Honors Award, Washington, D.C., 1983

"Grand Cross," Legion d'Honneur et Merite, Embassy of Haiti, 1983

National Council on the Aging, Inc., Service Award, April 5, 1984

Samuel H. Scripps American Dance Festival Award, 1986

Oral Self-Portrait, the National Portrait Gallery, Smithsonian Institution, April 1986

Distinguished Service Award, American Anthropological Association, 1986

Medal of Artistic Merit in Dance, International Council on Dance, UNESCO, 1986

Southern Cross, Award of Honor and Merit, Government of Brazil, 1986

Founders of Dance in America Honoree, Mr. and Mrs. Cornelius Vanderbilt Whitney Hall of Fame, National Museum of Dance, Saratoga Springs, N.Y., 1987

Candice "Trailblazer" Award, National Coalition of 100 Black Women, 1987

Ebony Magazine American Achievement Award, Fine Arts, Los Angeles, November 1987

President's Award, National Council for Culture and Art, Inc., New York, September 1988

Officier de L'ordre des Arts et des Lettres, Le Ministre de la Culture et la Communication, Haiti, 1988

Officer, Legion d'Honneur, Order of Arts and Letters, Government of France, March 29, 1988

The Caribbean Award, Trinidad and Tobago, 1990

National Medal of the Arts, 1992

Full Citizenship of Haiti, 1993

Smith Award, Smithsonian Institution, 1999

Tribute to a Black American Award, National Conference of Black Mayors, Inc., 1999

APPENDIX D
Lectures and Publications

Lectures and Master Classes

University of Chicago, 1937
Yale University, 1939
Bellas Artes, Mexico, 1947
Royal Anthropological Society, London, 1948
Royal Anthropological Society, Paris, 1949
Teatro Experimental do Negro, Rio de Janeiro, Brazil, 1950; Auckland University, New Zealand, 1957; University of Salzburg, Salzburg, Austria, 1965
Southern Illinois University, 1964–82
First World Festival of Negro Arts, Dakar, Senegal, 1966
Case Western Reserve University, Cleveland, 1973
International Institute of Ethnomusicology and Folklore, Caracas, Venezuela, 1974
Artist-in-Residence/Lecturer, Afro-American Studies, University of California at Berkeley, 1976
"Conversations with Katherine Dunham," Dunham Technique Seminar, 1984–2001
Buffalo State College, 1987
Artist-in-Residence/Lecturer, Stanford University, 1989
Missouri Historical Society, 1990–96
Artist-in-Residence/Lecturer, University of Hawaii, 1994

Selected Publications

BOOKS

Journey to Accompong. New York: Henry Holt, 1946; reprint, Westport, Conn.: Negro Universities Press, 1971.
Las danzas de Haiti. Acta Anthropologica (Mexico City), 2, no. 4 (1947). Also published as *Les Danses de Haiti* (Paris: Fasquel, 1957) and as *Dances of Haiti* (Los Angeles: Center for Afro-American Studies, University of California at Los Angeles, 1983).

A Touch of Innocence. New York: Harcourt Brace, 1959, 1969; reprint;
   Chicago: University of Chicago, 1994.
Island Possessed. New York: Doubleday, 1969; reprint, Chicago: University of Chicago, 1994.
Kasamance: A Fantasy. New York: Third Press, 1974.

ARTICLES

"La Boule Blanche" (under the pseudonym Kaye Dunn). *Esquire,* September 1939.
"L'Ag'ya of Martinique" (under the psyeudonym Kaye Dunn). *Esquire,* November 1939.
"Thesis Turned Broadway." *California Arts and Architecture,* August
   1941.
"Interrelation of Form and Function in Primitive Dance." *Educational
   Dance,* October 1941.
"The American Negro Dance and Its West Indian Affiliations." In *The Negro Caravan,* edited by Sterling A. Brown, Arthur P. Davis, and Ulysses
   Lee. New York: Dryden, 1941.
"Goombay." *Mademoiselle,* November 1945.
"Notes on the Dance." In *Seven Arts,* edited by Fernando Puma. New
   York: Doubleday, 1954.

SHORT STORIES

"Afternoon into Night." *Bandwagon* (London), 13 (June 1952). (Reprinted
   in Langston Hughes, *Best Stories by Negro Writers* [Boston: Little,
   1967].)
"Audrey." *Phylon* 15 (June 1954): 147–53.
"Crime of Pablo Martinez." *Ellery Queen's Magazine,* 1964.

APPENDIX E

Resources on Katherine Dunham

Barnet, Dr. Miguel. Fundación Fernando Ortiz, Havana, Cuba
   Photos, films, programs
Caribbean Cultural Center. New York City, New York
   Photo exhibit
Dance Collection. New York Public Library, New York City, New York
   Films, videos, photos, books
Dunham, Katherine. Collection. Missouri Historical Society, St. Louis, Missouri
   Letters, photographs, documents, with emphasis on Performing Arts Training Center
Dunham, Katherine. Dance Company. Films of company shows are in private collections, including those of Katherine Dunham; Madison D. Lacy of Free to Dance, American Dance Festival, 1697 Broadway, Room 203, New York City; Patrick Bensard, Cinematheque de la Dance, 4 Rue de Longchamp, Paris, France; Terry Carter of the Council for Positive Images, PMB 332, 244 Madison Avenue, New York City; the last also holds sixteen hours of original, broadcast-quality footage on the Dunham technique, recorded during the Dunham seminars of 1992.
Dunham, Katherine. Museum. East St. Louis, Illinois
   Photos, costumes, reviews, proposals; Dunham Technique Seminar videos.
Dunham, Katherine. Papers. Special Collections. Morris Library, Southern Illinois University, Carbondale, Illinois
   Letters, photographs, documents—1919–68
Herskovits, Melville. Papers. Northwestern University, Evanston, Illinois
   Correspondence with Katherine Dunham and Zora Hurston
Montiel, Dr. Luz Maria. Afroamerica Mexico Colonia Hipodromo-Condesa, Mexico
   Mexico materials.
Nascimenta, Abdias Do. Rio de Janeiro State Secretary for Human Rights and Citizenship, Rio de Janeiro, Brazil
   Clippings, lecture by Katherine Dunham, photos

New York Public Library for the Performing Arts at Lincoln Center. New
  York City, New York
    CD-ROM, Dance on Disc; photos, books
Osumare, Dr. Halifu. Dance Department, University of Hawaii, Honolulu
  Photos and videos of Stanford University and University of Hawaii resi-
  dencies; photos, clippings, posters, programs
Schomburg Center for Research in Black Culture. New York Public Li-
  brary, New York City, New York
    Books, clippings, photos

NOTES

Introduction

1. See Joyce Aschenbrenner, *Lifelines: Black Families in Chicago* (New York: Holt, Rinehart, Winston, 1975; reprint, Prospect Heights, Ill.: Waveland, 1983).

2. See, for example, Sue Barry, "Woman of the Week: Modern Dance Owes a Lot to Lovely Katherine Dunham" (1941), in *Kaiso! Katherine Dunham, an Anthology of Writing*, ed. VèVè A. Clark and Margaret B. Wilkerson (Berkeley: University of California Institute for the Study of Social Change, 1978), 82–84.

3. Joyce Aschenbrenner, *Katherine Dunham: Reflections on the Social and Political Contexts of Afro-American Dance* (New York: Congress on Research in Dance, 1980).

4. Dunham prefers the term *dance anthropology* to the *anthropology of dance* because it weds the two more integrally, attributing to the study of dance the central role she believes necessary in understanding societies.

5. Katherine Dunham, *A Touch of Innocence* (1959; reprint, Chicago: University of Chicago Press, 1994); Katherine Dunham, *Island Possessed* (1969; reprint, Chicago: University of Chicago Press, 1994).

6. When I asked Dunham why she had written *A Touch of Innocence* in the third person and claimed it was not an autobiography, she replied, "I didn't touch that book until after my mother died . . . it was too close to me, I was too tender to be objective" (Katherine Dunham, conversation with author, February 27, 1993, East St. Louis residence).

7. Elizabeth Janeway, Review of *A Touch of Innocence, New York Times Book Review*, November 8, 1959, sec. 7:54.

8. Langston Hughes, Book Reviews, *New York Herald Tribune*, October 25, 1959. Fanny Butcher described *A Touch of Innocence* as having "the fascination of fiction, the exciting impact of fact" and attributed to its author the "sureness, incisiveness of a seasoned novelist" (*Chicago Tribune*, October 25, 1959). A reviewer in Portland, Maine, spoke of her "smooth, clear flow of language" and deemed her "skillful at painting word pictures" (Harold L. Cain, "Two on the Aisle," *Evening Express*, February 11, 1960).

9. Grace P. Comons, "The Hard Way," *Hartford Courant*, November 21, 1959, Katherine Dunham Museum, East St. Louis, Illinois.

10. See Erika Bourguignon, Review of *Island Possessed, American Anthropologist* 72 (December 1970): 1132–33.

11. Barbara G. Myerhoff, *Remembered Lives: The Work of Ritual, Storytelling, and Growing Older* (Ann Arbor: University of Michigan Press, 1992).

Chapter 1: More Than a Touch of Innocence

1. Quoted by Dunham, conversation with author, February 27, 1993.

2. Dunham, *A Touch of Innocence*, 15.

3. Ibid., 124

4. See Colin Wilson, *The Mind Parasites*, 2d ed. (Berkeley, Calif.: Wingbow, 1990). Dunham recommended this book.

5. Quoted in Dunham, *A Touch of Innocence*, 218.

6. Dunham, conversation with author, February 27, 1993. Throughout her life, Dunham has carried a negative view of the places that formed her: "I wanted something different. I loathed Joliet, the Midwest, Chicago" ("Conversations with Katherine Dunham," August 3, 1992, Dunham Technique Seminar, University City High School, University City, Mo. [all Dunham Technique Seminar "Conversations with Katherine Dunham" and "Master class" videotapes are at the Katherine Dunham Museum in East St. Louis. There are no videotapes for the 1997 seminar or for the "Conversations with Katherine Dunham" that were held at the Missouri Historical Society. Notes for some of the latter are with the author]); "Joliet was a mean town, even then" (Katherine Dunham, interview by author, February 8, 1999, East St. Louis residence).

7. Clarissa Pinkola Estés, *Women Who Run with the Wolves: Myths and Stories of the Wild Woman Archetype* (New York: Ballantine Books, 1992), 172. The Dunham siblings held that they were from Jupiter; such fantastic claims are not uncommon among highly creative people, even as adults. For example, a contemporary popular artist whose music is unconventional claims to be from Saturn, and the late Sun Ra, who throughout his life was in the avant-garde of jazz, contended he was from "outer space."

8. "Conversations with Katherine Dunham," August 3, 1992. In 2001, while spending most of the year in New York City, she distinguished between New York as a base and East St. Louis as "home." Steven Spearie, "Dunham's Dancers," *Heartland Magazine* of the *State Journal-Register* (Springfield, Ill.), July 13, 2001, 6A.

9. Janeway, Review of *A Touch of Innocence*, sec.7:54.

10. Dunham, *A Touch of Innocence*, 98.

11. Ibid., 98–99.

12. "Conversations with Katherine Dunham," August 10, 1992, Dunham Technique Seminar, Missouri Historical Society, St. Louis.

13. Dunham, *A Touch of Innocence*, 54.

14. Ibid., 58–59.

15. Ibid., 130.

16. Ibid., 187.

17. Katherine Dunham, conversation with author, August 1990, East St. Louis residence.

18. Dunham, *A Touch of Innocence*, 191.

19. Ibid.

20. Ibid., 104.

21. "Conversations with Katherine Dunham," August 10, 1992.

22. St. Clair Drake and Horace Cayton, *Black Metropolis: A Study of Negro Life in a Northern City* (New York: Harcourt, Brace, 1945); Alan H. Spear, *Black Chi-*

cago: *The Making of a Negro Ghetto, 1890–1920* (Chicago: University of Chicago Press, 1967).

23. Dunham, *A Touch of Innocence*, 178.

24. Ibid., 179 (emphasis added).

25. Ibid.

26. Katherine Dunham, interview by Frederic L. Orme, "The Negro in the Dance as Katherine Dunham Sees Him," *American Dancer* (March 1938), in *Kaiso!* ed. Clark and Wilkerson, 60.

27. Dunham, *A Touch of Innocence*, 156.

28. Ibid., 156–57.

29. Ibid., n.p.

30. Dunham, conversation with author, February 27, 1993, East St. Louis residence.

31. Robert Plant Armstrong, in *The Affecting Presence: An Essay in Humanistic Anthropology* (Urbana: University of Illinois Press, 1971), defines all art expressions in terms of "objective correlatives," because connections between art and feeling are intrinsic rather than symbolic or metaphorical.

32. Dunham, *A Touch of Innocence*, 285. A resolution of family conflict was demonstrated as early as 1933, when Dunham's parents came to Chicago for her performance of *La Guiablesse* and reportedly stated they "never had enjoyed anything so much before." Quoted in Terry Harnan, *African Rhythm, American Dance: A Biography of Katherine Dunham* (New York: Alfred A. Knopf, 1974), 53.

33. Ibid., 312.

Chapter 2: At the University of Chicago

1. Katherine Dunham, "Minefields," unpublished memoir, a work in progress, 3.

2. Drake and Cayton, *Black Metropolis*, 22.

3. Studs Terkel, *Talking to Myself: A Memoir of My Times* (New York: Random House, 1973).

4. Ibid., 125. The Haymarket Riot in 1886 was a union action that, according to Drake and Cayton, "became America's first left-wing *cause célèbre*" (*Black Metropolis*, 21).

5. Richard Wright, Introduction to *Black Metropolis*, by Drake and Cayton, xvii.

6. Arna Bontemps, "Famous WPA Authors," *Negro Digest* 7 (June 1950): 47.

7. Robert Bone, "Richard Wright and the Chicago Renaissance," *Callaloo* 9, no. 3 (1986): 446–68.

8. Ibid. See Richard Wright, *Twelve Million Black Voices* (Manchester, England: Ayer Publishing, 1969).

9. Drake and Cayton, *Black Metropolis*, 379–80.

10. Dunham, "Minefields," 21.

11. Katherine Dunham, conversation with author, May 1992, East St. Louis residence. Elsewhere Dunham refers to the theater as "The Little Theatre Group of Harper Avenue," in V. Clark, M. Hodson, C. Neiman, and F. Bailey, "Excerpt from *The Legend of Maya Deren*" (interview in *Film Culture Magazine*, 1978), in *Kaiso!* ed. Clark and Wilkerson, 37.

12. Dunham, quoted in Clark et al., "Excerpt from *The Legend of Maya Deren*," 36.

13. Dunham, "Minefields," 48.

14. Dunham was criticized in the *Chicago Defender* for using *Negro* instead of *colored* for her dance group. Katherine Dunham, conversation with author, June 1992, East St. Louis residence.

15. Alain Locke, *The New Negro: An Interpretation* (New York: Albert and Charles Boni, 1925), 10, 11.

16. Clark et al., "Excerpt from *The Legend of Maya Deren*," 36.

17. W. C. Handy, *Father of the Blues: An Autobiography*, ed. Arna Bontemps (1941; reprint, New York: Collier Books, 1970), 227.

18. Katherine Dunham, conversation with author, August 1992, East St. Louis residence.

19. Bone, "Richard Wright and the Chicago Renaissance," 463.

20. Ruth Page, *Page by Page* (New York: Dance Horizons, 1978), 126.

21. Etta Moten Barnett, telephone conversation with author, June 1, 1993.

22. Lucille Ellis, conversation with author, June 1993, Dunham's East St. Louis residence. Moten celebrated her hundredth birthday on November 11, 2001, and Harry Belafonte "led well-wishers in singing 'Happy Birthday'" (Jeff Daniels, "People in the News," *St. Louis Post-Dispatch*, November 11, 2001).

23. According to Dunham, "We did not like each other" (Katherine Dunham, conversation with author, July 1993, East St. Louis residence).

24. Terkel, *Talking to Myself*, 119.

25. Katherine Dunham, conversation with author, June 22, 1993, East St. Louis residence.

26. Terkel, *Talking to Myself*, 121.

27. Richard Wright, *American Hunger* (New York: Harper and Row, 1977).

28. Dunham, "Minefields," 33.

29. Because of her acquaintanceship with Randolph, she would reproach her dancers when, on tour, they did not tip porters.

30. Charles H. Nichols, ed., *Arna Bontemps–Langston Hughes Letters, 1925–1967* (New York: Dodd, Mead, 1980), 12.

31. Later, on her world tours, she at first refused to perform in Franco's Spain; however, she decided that she should not punish the Spanish people for the sins of their government: "You can't hold an entire country responsible for what a few does" ("Conversations with Katherine Dunham," August 7, 1992, University City High School).

32. Dunham, "Minefields," 53.

33. Dunham, quoted in Clark et al., "Excerpt from *The Legend of Maya Deren*," 38.

34. Page, *Page by Page*, 126.

35. John Martin, *John Martin's Book of the Dance* (New York: Tudor Publishing, 1963), 1978–79.

36. Dunham, "Minefields," 3.

37. "Conversations with Katherine Dunham," August 10, 1992, Dunham Technique Seminar, University City High School.

38. Katherine Dunham, "Dunham Technique: Prospectus" (1978), in *Kaiso!* ed. Clark and Wilkerson, 210.

39. In *Black Bourgeoisie* (Glencoe, Ill.: Free Press, 1957), the Chicago sociologist E. Franklin Frazier depicts black middle-class characteristics strikingly similar to those Dunham attributed to the parents of her Chicago students. He has been strongly criticized for his generalizations.

40. Dunham, "Minefields," 39.

41. John Bennett, address, January 31, 1991, Washington University, St. Louis.

42. Edward Shils, "Robert Maynard Hutchins," in *Remembering the University of Chicago: Teachers, Scientists and Scholars,* ed. Edward Shils (Chicago: University of Chicago, 1991), 185–96.

43. William H. McNeill, *Hutchins' University: A Memoir of the University of Chicago, 1929–1950* (Chicago: University of Chicago Press, 1991), vii.

44. Dunham, quoted in Clark et al., "Excerpt from *The Legend of Maya Deren,*" 36.

45. Quoted in Harry S. Ashmore, *Unseasonable Truths: The Life of Robert Maynard Hutchins* (Boston: Little, Brown, 1989), 97.

46. Ibid., 194. These methods were still practiced in the anthropology department at Chicago in 1970.

47. Marianne Eismann, "Dunham," *University of Chicago Magazine,* Summer 1985, 14–19, 32.

48. Dunham, quoted in Clark et al., "Excerpt from *The Legend of Maya Deren,*" 36.

49. Bennett address.

50. Quoted in Regna Darnell, *Edward Sapir: Linguist, Anthropologist, Humanist* (Berkeley: University of California Press, 1990), 224.

51. Quoted in ibid., 226. The term *primitive* was commonly used by anthropologists at the time but has been since abandoned in favor of more accurate terminology.

52. Watkins wrote his dissertation on a Ugandan Bantu language with Sapir as his adviser.

53. Dunham joined Fred Eggan, Ruth Bunzel, Leslie White, and Robert Redfield in finding Sapir "far out of their depth." Darnell, *Edward Sapir,* 233–34.

54. Ruth Benedict, *Patterns of Culture* (New York: Houghton Mifflin, 1934).

55. Richard Handler, "The Dainty and the Hungry Man: Edward Sapir," in *Observers Observed: Essays on Ethnographic Fieldwork,* ed. George W. Stocking Jr. (Madison: University of Wisconsin Press), 210.

56. Edward Sapir, "Culture, Genuine and Spurious," in *Selected Writings of Edward Sapir in Language, Culture and Personality,* ed. D. Mandelbaum (Berkeley: University of California Press, 1949), 94–119.

57. Melville J. Herskovits, "Freudian Mechanisms in Primitive Negro Psychology," in *The New World Negro: Selected Papers in Afro-American Studies,* ed. Frances S. Herskovits (Bloomington: Indiana University Press, 1966), 135–45.

58. Dunham, "Minefields," 39.

59. Katherine Dunham, "A Lecture-Demonstration of the Anthropological Approach to the Dance and the Practical Application of This Approach to the Theater" (October 1942), in *Kaiso!* ed. Clark and Wilkerson, 200.

60. Quoted in Dorathi Bock Pierre, "A Talk with Katherine Dunham," *Educational Dance* (August–September 1941), Dance Scrapbook, Dance Collection, New York Public Library, New York City.

61. Katherine Dunham, conversation with author, July 1990, East St. Louis residence.

62. I took this course from Katherine Dunham in 1978–79 and taught it in 1983.

63. Bennett address.

64. Robert Redfield and Milton Singer, "The Cultural Role of Cities," *Economic Development and Cultural Change*, vol. 3 (Chicago: Research Center in Economic Development and Cultural Change, University of Chicago, 1954), 53–73.

65. Milton Singer, "Robert Redfield," in *Remembering the University of Chicago*, ed. Shils, 414.

66. Ashmore, *Unseasonable Truth*, 67.

67. Dunham, "Minefields," 14.

68. Dunham, quoted in Clark et al., "Excerpt from *The Legend of Maya Deren*," 38.

69. Katherine Dunham, conversation with author, June 1986, East St. Louis residence.

70. Ibid., May 1993.

71. Ibid., July 1985.

72. Dunham, "Minefields," 12

73. Franz Boas, *Race, Language and Culture* (New York: Macmillan, 1940).

74. W. E. B. Du Bois, *Dusk of Dawn: An Essay toward an Autobiography of a Race Concept* (New York: Harcourt, Brace and World, 1940), 66, 322.

75. Bone, "Richard Wright and the Chicago Renaissance," 455.

76. Darnell, *Edward Sapir*, 217.

77. W. Lloyd Warner, Buford H. Junker, and Walter A. Adams, *Color and Human Nature: Negro Personality Development in a Northern City* (Westport, Conn.: Negro Universities Press, 1941), 292.

78. Katherine Dunham, "The State of Cults among the Deprived" (paper presented at the Royal Anthropological Institute, London, 1937, in Dunham's possession).

79. Wright, Introduction to *Black Metropolis*, by Drake and Cayton, xvii, xix.

80. Ibid., xvii.

81. Studs Terkel, telephone interview by author, August 31, 1993.

82. George W. Stocking, *Anthropology at Chicago: Tradition, Discipline, Department: An Exhibition Marking the Fiftieth Anniversary of the Department of Anthropology* (Chicago: Joseph Regenstein Library, University of Chicago, 1979), 21. In a personal conversation at her residence in June 1993, Dunham recalled that he was "very English" in manner.

83. Darnell, *Edward Sapir*, 236, 250.

84. Fred Eggan, "A. R. Radcliffe-Brown," in *Remembering the University of Chicago*, ed. Shils, 401–12.

85. Quoted in Stocking, *Anthropology at Chicago*, 23.

86. Dunham, "A Lecture-Demonstration of the Anthropological Approach to the Dance and the Practical Application of This Approach to the Theater," 200.

87. Ibid., 201.

88. Ibid., 203.

89. Katherine Dunham, "Interrelation of Form and Function in Primitive Dance," *Educational Dance*, October 1941, 2–4.

90. Stocking, *Anthropology at Chicago*, 21.

91. Quoted in Pierre, "A Talk with Katherine Dunham."

92. Katherine Dunham, "Notes on the Dance," in *Seven Arts*, ed. Fernando Puma (New York: Doubleday, 1954), n.p.

93. Robert Redfield, *The Folk Culture of Yucatán* (Chicago: University of Chicago Press, 1941), 132.

94. Clifford Geertz, *The Interpretation of Cultures: Selected Essays* (New York: Basic Books, 1973).

95. See Fred Eggan, "Social Anthropology and the Method of Controlled Comparison," *American Anthropologist* 56 (August 1954): 743–63.

96. Victor Turner, Clifford Geertz, David Schneider, and Louis Dumont, for example.

97. Dunham, *Island Possessed*, 66.

98. For more on this, see, for example, Lynne Fauley Emery, *Black Dance in the United States from 1619 to Today*, rev. ed. (Princeton, N.J.: Princeton Book, 1988); and Richard A. Long, *The Black Tradition in American Dance* (New York: Rizzoli, 1989).

99. Page, *Page by Page*, 136, 126.

100. Dunham, "Minefields," 7.

101. Dunham, *Island Possessed*, 69.

102. Bone, "Richard Wright and the Chicago Renaissance," 453.

103. McNeill, *Hutchins' University*, 137.

104. Ibid.

105. W. E. B. Du Bois, *The Souls of Black Folk* (New York: Washington Square, 1970).

106. Warner, Junker, and Adams, *Color and Human Nature*, 295.

107. Dunham, conversation with author, August 1992.

108. "Conversations with Katherine Dunham," August 3, 1992. Approaching her ninetieth birthday, Dunham remarked, "My life has been influenced so much by Erich Fromm and Dr. Jacobson. They've gone and I feel left hanging out here" (Dunham interview, February 8, 1999).

109. Dunham, conversation with author, August 1992.

Chapter 3: Fieldwork at the Cutting Edge

1. George W. Stocking Jr., "The Ethnographer's Magic: Fieldwork in British Anthropology from Tylor to Malinowski," in *Observers Observed*, ed. Stocking, 70–120.

2. Katherine Dunham to Melville Herskovits, March 9, 1932, folder 12, box 7, Papers of Melville J. Herskovits, University Library, Northwestern University, Evanston, Illinois (hereafter Herskovits Papers).

3. Herskovits to Dunham, March 23, 1932, folder 23, box 7, ibid.

4. Patrick J. Gillpin, "Charles S. Johnson: Entrepreneur of the Harlem Renaissance," in *The Harlem Renaissance Remembered; Essays Edited with a Memoir*, ed. Arna Bontemps (New York: Dodd, Mead, 1972), 215–46. *Opportunity: A Journal of Negro Life* was a publication of the National Urban League. Johnson became president of Fisk University in 1947.

5. Bone, "Richard Wright and the Chicago Renaissance."

6. The Rosenwald grant, awarded on February 13, 1935, provided the follow-

ing: $2,400—one year; $500—tuition and living expenses at Northwestern ($200 for February, $100 monthly for March, April, and May). Rosenwald grant, folder 2, box 1, Katherine Mary Dunham Papers, 1919–68, Morris Library, Southern Illinois University at Carbondale (hereafter Dunham Papers).

7. In a conversation with the author in July 1998, she stated that she had trouble in the tropics with the wax cylinders, which tended to melt in the heat.

8. Edwin Embree to Melville J. Herskovits, February 15, 1935, folder 12, box 7, Herskovits Papers.

9. Dunham, *Island Possessed*, 65.

10. Stocking, *Anthropology at Chicago*, 21.

11. Oscar Lewis, *Life in a Mexican Village: Tepoztlán Restudied* (Urbana: University of Illinois Press, 1951).

12. See George W. Stocking, "The Ethnographic Sensibilities of the 1920s and the Dualism of the Anthropological Tradition," in *Romantic Motives: Essays of Anthropological Sensibility*, ed. George W. Stocking (Madison: University of Wisconsin, 1989), 208–79.

13. Recounted in Bennett address.

14. Redfield's position anticipated current views about "contextualizing" ethnography with autobiographical and biographical particulars concerning ethnographers. See, for example, Clifford Geertz, *Works and Lives* (Stanford, Calif.: Stanford University Press, 1988); and James Clifford and George E. Marcus, eds., *Writing Culture: The Poetics and Politics of Ethnography* (Berkeley: University of California Press, 1986).
Further, current theoretical views of ethnography represent the text as a dialogue between the fieldworker and the people encountered in the field and as requiring specification of the ethnographer's relationships with those people. See Helen Callaway, "Ethnography and Experience: Gender Implications in Fieldwork and Texts," in *Anthropology and Autobiography*, ed. Judith Okely and Helen Callaway (London: Routledge, 1992), 1–28; and Kirsten Hastrup, "Writing Ethnography, State of the Art," in *Anthropology and Autobiography*, ed. Okely and Callaway, 116–33.

15. Quoted in Philip K. Bock, *Modern Cultural Anthropology: An Introduction* (New York: Alfred A. Knopf, 1979), 279.

16. Robert Redfield, *Aspects of Primitive Art* (New York: Museum of Primitive Art, 1959), 39.

17. Kant based intersubjectivism on the innate structure of the human mind rather than on social agreements, that is, culture.

18. For a discussion of fieldworkers' motivations, see Stocking, *Romantic Motives*.

19. Norman E. Whitten Jr. and John F. Szwed, *Afro-American Anthropology: Contemporary Perspectives* (New York: Macmillan, 1970), 28.

20. Quoted in Orme, "The Negro in the Dance as Katherine Dunham Sees Him," 60.

21. Ibid. In a letter to Herskovits dated November 15, 1935, Dunham referred to Boas's suggestion that she study whether rhythm was inherent or acquired; she noted that a woman in a film she sent from Trinidad "was dancing while seven months pregnant," from 8:00 A.M. to 1:30 P.M., supporting her own view that rhythm was learned, even starting in the womb (folder 12, box 7, Herskovits Papers).

22. For a discussion of Malinowski's personal dilemma, see Geertz, *Works and Lives*, 73–101.

23. For a further treatment of this subject, see Aschenbrenner, *Katherine Dunham*, 53–58.

24. Dunham, *Island Possessed*, 144.

25. Conversation with author, March 1991, Port-au-Prince.

26. Conversation with author, August 1993, East St. Louis residence.

27. Franz Boas to Zora Neale Hurston, May 3, 1927, Franz Boas Papers, American Philosophical Society Library, Philadelphia.

28. Franz Boas, Preface to *Mules and Men*, by Zora Neale Hurston (1935; reprint, New York: Harper and Row, 1970). See also Gwendolyn Mikell on Hurston's fieldwork in "Feminism and Black Culture in the Ethnography of Zora Neale Hurston," in *African-American Pioneers in Anthropology*, ed. Ira E. Harrison and Faye V. Harrison (Urbana: University of Illinois Press, 1999), 51–69.

29. Margaret Mead, who collaborated with Jane Belo in a study of Balinese dance, suggested that Dunham observe the use of dance in enculturating children.

30. Eismann, "Dunham," 18.

31. James Clifford, "Power and Dialogue in Ethnography: Marcel Griaule's Initiation," in *Observers Observed*, ed. Stocking, 121–56.

32. Barbara Speisman, "Voodoo as Symbol in *Jonah's Gourd Vine*," in *Zora in Florida*, ed. Steve Glassman and Kathryn Lee Seidel (Orlando, Fla: University of Central Florida Press, 1991), 86–93.

33. Zora Hurston, "Dance Songs and Tales from the Bahamas," *Journal of American Folklore* 43 (July–1930): 294–312; Zora Hurston, "Hoodoo in America," *Journal of American Folklore* 44 (October–December 1931): 317–415.

34. Hurston, "Hoodoo in America," 317.

35. Zora Neale Hurston, *Tell My Horse* (New York: J. B. Lippincott, 1938), 114.

36. Ibid., 153.

37. Ibid., 179.

38. In a letter dated April 22, 1936, Herskovits attempted to dissuade Hurston from spending much time in Haiti, recommending that she instead concentrate on the Bahamas (folder 20, box 9, Herskovits Papers).

39. Hurston to Herskovits, January 6, 1935, folder 32, box 9, ibid.

40. Ibid.

41. Herskovits to Hurston, September 28, 1936, ibid.

42. Hurston to Herskovits, April 6, 1937, ibid.

43. Hurston, *Mules and Men*.

44. Dunham, "Minefields," 47.

45. Zora Neale Hurston, "Thirty Days among Maroons," *New York Herald Tribune Weekly Book Review*, January 23, 1947, 8.

46. Hurston, *Tell My Horse*, 35. Actually, Dunham spent a month in Accompong.

47. Zora Neale Hurston to Melville Herskovits, July 30, 1936, folder 32, box 9, Herskovits Papers.

48. Zora Neale Hurston, *Their Eyes Were Watching God* (New York: J. B. Lippincott, 1937). See also Zora Neale Hurston, *Dust Tracks on a Road* (New York: J. B. Lippincott, 1942).

49. Ralph Linton, Introduction to *Journey to Accompong*, by Katherine Dunham (New York: Holt, Rinehart, 1946), viii.

50. Claude Lévi-Strauss, Foreword to the French Edition, trans. Jeanelle Stovall, in *Dances of Haiti,* by Katherine Dunham (Los Angeles: Center for Afro-American Studies, University of California at Los Angeles, [1957]), xv–xvii.

51. Claude Lévi-Strauss, *Tristes Tropiques: An Anthropological Study of Primitive Societies in Brazil* (New York: Atheneum, 1964), 63–64.

52. Geertz, *Works and Lives,* 10.

53. Phyllis McDonoge, "Katherine the Great—An Interview with Katherine Dunham, Sydney, Australia, ca 1957," folder 1, box 1, Dunham Papers.

Chapter 4: Katherine Dunham's Possessed Island

1. Dunham, *Island Possessed,* 66.

2. Alan Lomax to Katherine Dunham, July 16, 1937, folder 5, box 1, Dunham Papers.

3. Katherine Dunham, conversation with author, January 29, 1991, Port-au-Prince.

4. Katherine Dunham to Melville Herskovits, June 3, 1935, folder 12, box 7, Herskovits Papers.

5. Dunham, *Journey to Accompong,* 1, 2.

6. Ibid., 6.

7. Ibid.

8. Ibid.

9. Dunham to Herskovits, August 25, 1935, folder 12, box 7, Herskovits Papers.

10. Dunham, *Island Possessed,* 209.

11. Robert Redfield to Katherine Dunham, September 13, [1936?], folder 4, box 1, Dunham Papers.

12. *Obeah* is the system of African-based religious beliefs and practices in Jamaica that corresponds to the Haitian *voudun.*

13. Dunham, *Journey to Accompong,* 71.

14. Herskovits to Dunham, October 24, 1935, folder 12, box 7, Herskovits Papers.

15. Dunham to Herskovits, November 15, 1935, ibid.

16. Linton, Introduction to *Journey to Accompong,* by Dunham, viii.

17. Dunham to Herskovits, August 26, 1935, folder 12, box 7, Herskovits Papers.

18. Herskovits to Dunham, October 25, 1935, ibid.

19. Ibid.

20. Dunham to Herskovits, November 15, 1935.

21. Quoted in McDonoge, "Katherine the Great—An Interview with Katherine Dunham."

22. Dunham to Herskovits, October 27, 1935, folder 12, box 7, Herskovits Papers.

23. Ibid.

24. Ibid., November 15, 1935.

25. Dunham, *Island Possessed,* 3.

26. Quoted in ibid., 159.

27. Ibid., 13.

28. An exception she noted was Mrs. Price-Mars, wife of the intellectual who was trying to improve the status of all women in Haiti. Ibid., 23.

29. Ibid., 74.

30. "Conversations with Katherine Dunham," August 10, 1988, Dunham Technique Seminar, Nerynx Hall High School, Webster University, Webster Groves, Mo.

31. Herskovits to Dunham, December 19, 1935, folder 12, box 7, Herskovits Papers.

32. "Conversations with Katherine Dunham," August 5, 1992, Missouri Historical Society.

33. Dunham, *Island Possessed*, chaps. 4–7.

34. Ibid., 59.

35. There are many alternative spellings for the African and creole terms; the spellings here are those used in her *Island Possessed*, although there are differences in other Dunham writings. *Rada* is the creole term for the African tribal group Arada.

36. "Conversations with Katherine Dunham," August 10, 1988.

37. Dunham, *Island Possessed*, 98.

38. Ibid., 111–12; Dunham to Herskovits, January 13, 1936, folder 12, box 7, Herskovits Papers.

39. Dunham, *Island Possessed*, 105–6.

40. Ibid., 106.

41. Ibid., 109.

42. Ibid., 122.

43. Ibid., 93.

44. Ibid., 128.

45. Ibid.

46. Ibid., 69.

47. Ibid., 107.

48. Ibid., 92.

49. Ibid., 91, 131, 134. The levels of the *voudun* include *lavé-tête*, or washing of the head; *kanzo*, trial by fire; *prise-de-l'asson*, sanctioning use of the rattle; *prise-de-la-cloche*, involving the bell used in ceremonies; and the *prise-des-yeux*, the highest degree, granting clairvoyance.

50. Ibid., 130–31.

51. Ibid., 124.

52. Ibid., 110.

53. Ibid., 75.

54. Ibid., 106.

55. Ibid., 79.

56. Ibid., 132.

57. Ibid., 113.

58. Ibid., 128.

59. Dunham, *Dances of Haiti*, 31.

60. Dunham, *Island Possessed*, 68.

61. Ibid., 132.

62. A. Métraux, "Katherine Dunham, an Appreciation," Program notes to *Bamboche* (1962), in *Kaiso!* ed. Clark and Wilkerson, 184.

63. Dunham, *Island Possessed*, 109.

64. "Conversations with Katherine Dunham," August 10, 1988.

65. Dunham, *Island Possessed*, 118.

66. Ibid., 211.

67. Ibid., 182.

68. "Conversations with Katherine Dunham," August 12, 1994, Central City Visual and Performing Arts High School, St. Louis.

69. Friedrich Nietzsche, *Thus Spake Zarathustra*, trans. Thomas Common (Mineola, N.Y.: Dover, 1999), 24, cited in Dunham, *Island Possessed*, 117.

70. Dunham, *Island Possessed*, 136.

71. Hastrup, "Writing Ethnography."

Chapter 5: Anthropology and Dance

1. For previous and subsequent anthropological research on dance, see Gertrude Prokosch Kurath, *Half a Century of Dance Research* (Flagstaff, Ariz.: Cross Cultural Dance Resources, 1986). Joann Kealiinohomoku critically views boundaries between "art dance" and "ethnic dance" in "An Anthropologist Looks at Ballet as a Form of Ethnic Dance," *Impulse: The Annual of Contemporary Dance* (San Francisco: Impulse Publications, 1969–70), 24–33.

2. Dunham, *Dances of Haiti*, xiv, xv, 11.

3. "Conversations with Katherine Dunham," August 11, 1993, Dunham Technique Seminar, Missouri Historical Society. It would be instructive to discover whether the Petro gods returned with renewed force in the political upheaval in Haiti in the 1990s.

4. James Clifford, Introduction to *Writing Culture*, ed. Clifford and Marcus, 13.

5. Dunham, *Island Possessed*, 93.

6. George Devereux, *From Anxiety to Method in the Behavioral Sciences* (The Hague: Mouton, 1967), 197–274.

7. Callaway, "Ethnography and Experience."

8. See, for example, Elinor Bowen, *Return to Laughter* (London: Victor Gollancz, 1954); Charlotte J. Frisbie, "Fieldwork as a 'Single Parent': To Be or Not to Be," in *Collected Papers in Honor of Florence Hawley Ellis*, ed. Theodore J. Frisbie (Norman, Okla.: Published for the Archaeological Society of New Mexico by Hooper Publishing, 1975), 98–119; Hurston, *Mules and Men*; and Hortense Powdermaker, *Return to Laughter* (London: Secker and Warburg, 1967). See also Callaway, "Ethnography and Experience."

9. Clifford, Introduction to *Writing Culture*, ed. Clifford and Marcus, 11.

10. Judith Okely, "Anthropology and Autobiography: Participatory Experience and Embodied Knowledge," in *Anthropology and Autobiography*, ed. Okely and Calloway, 1–28.

11. "Conversations with Katherine Dunham," August 12, 1994. It should be remembered that Jane Belo and Margaret Mead studied Balinese dance and its role in child development.

12. Dunham also studied Polynesian dance in this respect while she was in residence at the University of Hawaii.

13. "Conversations with Katherine Dunham," August 15, 1994, Dunham Technique Seminar, Central City Visual and Performing Arts High School. Robert Farris Thompson in *African Art in Motion* (Berkeley: University of California

Press, 1974) speaks of the "orchestral use" of the body, in which parts of the body are played as instruments, each with a different rhythm.

14. Richard Schechner, "Magnitudes of Performance," in *By Means of Performance: Intercultural Studies of Theatre and Ritual*, ed. Richard Schechner and Willa Appel (Cambridge: Cambridge University Press, 1990), 19–49.

15. Gregory Schrempp, "Aristotle's Other Self: On the Boundless Subject of Anthropological Discourse," in *Romantic Motives*, ed. Stocking, 10–43.

16. Katherine Dunham pointed out that "women aren't supposed to touch drums until after menopause. . . . I just started playing drums [and] they said, 'Go ahead'" ("Conversations with Katherine Dunham," August 10, 1988).

17. Quoted in Pierre, "A Talk with Katherine Dunham."

18. Millicent Hodson, "How She Began Her Beguine: Dunham's Dance Literacy" (1978), in *Kaiso!* ed. Clark and Wilkerson, 198.

19. Colin Turnbull, "Liminality: A Synthesis of Subjective and Objective Experience," in *By Means of Performance*, ed. Schechner and Appel, 80.

20. Schechner, "Magnitudes of Performance," 19–49.

21. See Ivan Strenski, *Malinowski and the Work of Myth* (Princeton, N.J.: Princeton University Press, 1992).

22. Mètraux, "Katherine Dunham, an Appreciation," 184.

23. Geoffrey Gorer to Katherine Dunham, January 20, 1941; George Murdock to Katherine Dunham, January 20, 1941; and Donald Horton, January 22, 1941, all in folder 10, box 1, Dunham Papers.

Chapter 6: Ethics and Politics

1. Claude Lévi-Strauss, "Anthropology: Its Achievements and Future," *Current Anthropology* 7, no. 2 (1966): 126

2. For an explanation of "thick description," see Clifford Geertz, "Thick Description: Toward an Interpretative Theory of Culture," in his *Interpretation of Cultures*, 3–30.

3. Bourguignon, Review of *Island Possessed*, 1132–33.

4. Joyce Aschenbrenner, "Anthropology as a Lifeway: Katherine Dunham" (1978) in *Kaiso!* ed. Clark and Wilkerson, 186–91.

5. The Haitian anthropologist and statesman Antenor Firmin, in his treatise *De l'egalité des races humaines* (Paris: Librairie Cotillon, 1885), made this point persuasively in answer to Comte Joseph Arthur de Gobineau's *Essai sur l'inegalité des races humaines* (Paris: Belford, 1853–55). Unfortunately, Gobineau's racist views dominated thought until recently, and Firmin's book was only recently translated into English (*The Equality of the Human Races*, trans. Asselin Charles [New York: Garland Press, 2000]) and his work recognized by anthropologists (see Carolyn Fluehr-Lobban, "Antenor Firmin: Haitian Pioneer of Anthropology," *American Anthropologist* 102 [September 2000]: 449–66).

6. Dunham, *Island Possessed*, 228.

7. In responding to a current controversy in the discipline concerning alleged ethical transgressions of a noted anthropologist (see Patrick Tierney, *Darkness in El Dorado* [New York: W. W. Norton, 2000]), Dunham instanced her close supervision by Herskovits (telephone conversation with author, New York, September 18, 2000). Unfortunately, all advisers are not as scrupulous as Herskovits.

8. Dunham, *Island Possessed*, 228.

9. "African American Dance in Research and Applied Theory: Katherine Dunham and Pearl Primus," Joyce Aschenbrenner and Yvonne Daniel organizers; presenters: Yvonne Daniel, Vèvè Clark, Katrina Hazzard, Joyce Aschenbrenner, and Eugene B. Redmond; discussant: Anya Peterson Royce. Annual meeting of the American Anthropological Association, Chicago, Illinois, November 1991.

10. Dunham, *Island Possessed*, 42.

11. Despite his opposition to *voudun*, during Estimé's presidency he founded Le Theatre de Verdure, the national theater, "in the attempt to make known to the foreign visitors the vast richness of Haitian folklore and Voudoo dancing," as well as to provide playwrights the opportunity to produce their plays at a modest expense. Lavinia Williams Yarborough, *Haiti Dances* (Frankfurt-am-Main, Germany: Bronners Druckerei, n.d.), 6.

12. Dunham, *Island Possessed*, 45.

13. Ibid., 172–78.

14. Ibid., 178.

15. In *Island Possessed*, published in 1969 during Duvalier's regime, Dunham candidly described Duvalier's tyrannical rule and personal characteristics.

16. Ibid., 178.

17. Katherine Dunham, conversation with author, February 22, 1992, East St. Louis residence.

18. Ibid.

19. Ibid.

20. Katherine Dunham, conversation with author, February 27, 1992, East St. Louis residence. The final title was *Katherine Dunham: A Simple Act of Faith*, according to Silverman in a telephone conversation with the author, February 23, 1999.

21. Dunham, conversation with author, February 27, 1992.

22. Ibid.

23. Katherine Dunham, interview, April 12, 1992, KWMU–St. Louis, National Public Radio.

24. John Donnelly, "Dancer Fasting to Support Refugees: Katherine Dunham's Protest Centers on People, Not Politics," *Portland Oregonian*, February 19, 1992. Clipping sent by a relative.

25. Dunham, conversation with author, February 22, 1992.

26. Ibid.

27. "All Things Considered," March 4, 1994, National Public Radio.

28. Quoted in Dunham, *Island Possessed*, 236. Also recalled later, at her residence in August 1992.

29. Dunham, conversation with author, February 27, 1992.

30. Ibid.

Chapter 7: Creating the Company

1. Melville Herskovits to Katherine Dunham, May 8, 1937, folder 5, box 1, Dunham Papers.

2. Melville Herskovits to Edwin Embree, May 27, 1936, folder 12, box 9, Herskovits Papers.

3. Dunham, quoted in Clark et al., "Excerpt from *The Legend of Maya Deren*," 36.

4. Jack Harris to Katherine Dunham, May 9, 1937, folder 5, box 1, Dunham Papers.

5. Dunham to Herskovits, May 5, 1937, folder 12, box 7, Herskovits Papers.

6. Herskovits to Dunham, May 8, 1937, folder 5, box 1, Dunham Papers.

7. Katherine Dunham, conversation with author, November 25, 1993, East St. Louis residence.

8. Talley Beatty, interview by author, August 13, 1991, Dunham Technique Seminar, Center of Contemporary Arts, St. Louis.

9. Ibid.

10. Ibid.

11. Beatty interview, August 13, 1991.

12. Ibid.

13. Edward Barry, "Miss Dunham Is Sensation in Haitian Dances," *Chicago Tribune* (June 4, 1937), in *Kaiso!* ed. Clark and Wilkerson, 58.

14. Talley Beatty, interview by author, August 14, 1992, Soldan High School, St. Louis.

15. Robert Hemenway, *Zora Neale Hurston: A Literary Biography* (Urbana: University of Illinois Press, 1977).

16. Emery, *Black Dance in the United States from 1619 to Today*, 250.

17. Archie Savage studied with both Winfield and Dafora.

18. "Conversations with Katherine Dunham," August 14, 1992, Soldan High School, St. Louis.

19. Beatty interview, August 14, 1992.

20. Hodson, "How She Began Her Beguine," 197, 198.

21. Agnes de Mille, *Dance to the Piper* (Boston: Little, Brown, 1951), 197.

22. Ibid., 196.

23. Beatty interview, August 13, 1991.

24. Ibid.

25. Quoted in Orme, "The Negro in the Dance as Katherine Dunham Sees Him," 61–62.

26. For more on these projects, see Hallie Flanagan, *Arena: The History of the Federal Theatre* (New York: Benjamin Blom, 1940); Lorraine A. Brown, "Introduction: The Federal Theatre Project and Research Collection," in *The Federal Theatre Project, a Catalog-Calendar of Productions,* comp. Staff of the Fenwick Library, George Mason University (Westport, Conn.: Greenwood, 1986); and Ira A. Levine, *Left-Wing Dramatic Theory in the American Theatre* (Ann Arbor, Mich.: UMI Research Press, 1985).

27. E. Quita Craig, *Black Drama of the Federal Theatre Era* (Amherst: University of Massachusetts Press, 1980).

28. Warner, Junker, and Adams, *Color and Human Nature;* Ina Corrine Brown, *The Story of the American Negro* (New York: Friendship, 1936).

29. Richard Wright and Jack Conroy, "Native Sons, the Theatre," "The Negro in Illinois" Project, box 052, Illinois Writers Project, Vivian T. Harsh Collection, Carter G. Woodson Branch, Chicago Public Library.

30. Bontemps, "Famous WPA Authors," 46–47.

31. Arna Bontemps and Jack Conroy, *Anyplace but Here* (1945; reprint, New York: Hill and Wang, 1966), v.

32. Katherine Dunham, conversation with author, November 9, 1993, East St. Louis residence.

33. Arna Bontemps, Preface to *Anyplace but Here,* v.

34. Katherine Dunham, conversation with author, March 21, 1992, East St. Louis residence.

35. Quoted in Bontemps and Conroy, *Anyplace but Here,* 232.

36. Dunham, "The State of Cults among the Deprived," 1.

37. Dunham, "Minefields," 53.

38. Beatty interview, August 13, 1991.

39. Barry, "Miss Dunham Is Sensation in Haitian Dances," 58.

40. Flanagan, *Arena,* 141–42.

41. Dunham, conversation with author, November 25, 1993.

42. Eugene Stinson, "Music Views, Some Dancing," *Chicago Daily News,* February 3, 1938.

43. Dunham, "Minefields," 25.

44. Terkel interview.

45. Bone, "Richard Wright and the Chicago Renaissance."

46. Dunham, "Minefields," 13, 14.

47. John Pratt, interview by author, September 6, 1983, East St. Louis residence.

48. Eartha Kitt, *Thursday's Child* (New York: Duell, Sloan and Pearce, 1956), 83.

49. Bernard Berenson, February 26, 1950, in his *Sunset and Twilight* (New York: Harcourt, Brace and World, 1963), 162.

50. In *African Art in Motion,* Robert Farris Thompson demonstrates the unity of the arts in African performance, which is paralleled in the aesthetic totality of Dunham Company performances.

51. Cecil Smith, "Federal Dance Project Gives First Program," *Chicago Tribune,* January 28, 1938, Katherine Dunham Museum.

52. Robert Pollak, "All-Negro Folk Ballet Steals Federal Show," *Chicago Daily News,* January 28, 1938, ibid.

53. June Provines, "She's Got Haitian Rhythm," *Chicago Tribune,* February 26, 1938, ibid.

54. Consuelo Young-Megahy, "Preface," *Chicago Defender,* March 12, 1938, ibid.

55. Quoted in Orme, "The Negro in the Dance as Katherine Dunham Sees Him," 60.

56. Some of the information on the *Ballet Fedré* was obtained from the National Archives Special Collection on the Federal Theatre Project, on loan to George Mason University.

57. Flanagan, *Arena,* 23.

58. It should be noted, however, that Arna Bontemps wrote to Langston Hughes in 1941 that "Katherine Dunham gave two most successful programs with her dancers—Haitian dances, carnival stuff, etc. Excellent houses at 75 cents a head" (in *Arna Bontemps–Langston Hughes Letters,* ed. Nichols, 67).

59. Craig, *Black Drama of the Federal Theatre Era,* 154–71.

60. Flanagan, *Arena,* 145, 146.

61. Katherine Dunham to Arthur Mitchell, July 8, 1938, folder 7, box 1, Dunham Papers.

62. Levine, *Left-Wing Dramatic Theory in the American Theatre,* 144.

63. Quoted in ibid.

64. Dunham, conversation with author, November 9, 1993.

65. Beatty interview, August 13, 1991.

66. Lucille Ellis, interview by author, August 13, 1991, Dunham Technique Seminar, Center of Contemporary Arts.

67. Ibid.

68. Craig, *Black Drama of the Federal Theatre Era,* 199.

69. Aschenbrenner, *Katherine Dunham,* 41–47, 71–79; Harold Cruse, *The Crisis of the Negro Intellectual* (New York: William and Morrow, 1967).

70. Craig, *Black Drama of the Federal Theatre Era,* 97–112.

71. John Martin, *New York Times,* February 25, 1940, sec.9:2.

72. See chapter 5, endnote 1.

73. Beatty interview, August 13, 1991.

74. Ellis interview.

75. Dunham, "Minefields," 27.

76. "Conversations with Katherine Dunham," August 3, 1992, University City High School.

77. Bernard Taper, *Balanchine: A Biography* (New York: Times Books, 1984), 195.

78. Quoted in ibid.

79. Marshall Stearns and Jean Stearns, *Jazz Dance: The Story of American Vernacular Dance* (London: Macmillan, 1968), 309.

80. Tommy Gomez, interview by author, August 11, 1991, Dunham Technique Seminar, Center of Contemporary Arts.

81. Sol Hurok, in collaboration with Ruth Goode, *Impresario* (New York: Random House, 1946), 286 (emphasis added).

82. Don McDonagh, *George Balanchine* (New York: Twayne, 1983), 89. When Dunham choreographed *Aida* late in her career, some critics criticized the dance sequences as "too authentic" for opera patrons.

83. Ibid.

84. Al Smart to Katherine Dunham, January 16, 1941, folder 1, box 2, Dunham Papers.

85. She completed her research paper, which Chicago required for a bachelor's degree, and it was later published; however, she did not complete the requirements for a master's degree.

86. Adeline Linton to Katherine Dunham, March 11, 1940, folder 9, box 1, Dunham Papers.

87. Franziska Boas to Katherine Dunham, October 1, 1941, in *The Legend of Maya Deren: A Documentary Biography and Collected Works,* by VèVè A. Clark, Millicent Hodson, and Catrine Neiman (New York: Anthology Film Archives/ Film Culture, 1984), 469.

88. Katherine Dunham, conversation with author, August 2, 1998, East St. Louis residence.

89. Gomez interview.

90. Ibid.

91. "Conversations with Katherine Dunham," August 13, 1993, Soldan High School, St. Louis.

92. Roy Thomas, "Focal Rites: New Dance Dominions" (1978), in *Kaiso!* ed. Clark and Wilkerson, 113.

93. Long, *The Black Tradition in American Dance*, 68.

94. "Conversations with Katherine Dunham," August 13, 1993.

95. Thomas, "Focal Rites: New Dance Dominions," 116.

96. Ruth Beckford, *Katherine Dunham: A Biography* (New York: Marcel Dekker, 1979), 54.

97. Ellis interview.

98. Langston Hughes to Arna Bontemps, July 4, 1941, in *Arna Bontemps–Langston Hughes Letters*, ed. Nichols, 84.

99. Bontemps to Hughes, October 3, 1941, in ibid., 91.

100. Beckford, *Katherine Dunham*, 2.

101. Hurok, *Impresario*, 284–85.

102. Ibid., 287.

103. Dunham, conversation with author, November 9, 1993.

104. David Jampel, Review in *Mainichi* (Tokyo), September 30, 1957, folder 3, box 26, Dunham Papers.

105. Kitt, *Thursday's Child*, 84.

106. Richard Kollmar, "Katherine Dunham: Trend toward Feminine Leadership in Choreography," Biographical Sketch—Who's Who in the East—unpublished manuscript, n.d., folder 1, box 1, Dunham Papers.

107. "Conversations with Katherine Dunham," August 3, 1992, University City High School; Gloria Thornburg, interview by author, August 18, 1993, East St. Louis.

108. Quoted in "Katherine Dunham Is Weary of Hotel Trek," *PM* (September 5, 1943), in *Kaiso!* ed. Clark and Wilkerson, 86.

109. Katherine Dunham to Campbell Casad, April 5, 1941, folder 1, box 2, Dunham Papers.

110. Letters between Eleanora (Maya) Deren and Campbell Casad, April 1941, ibid.

111. Gomez interview.

112. Beatty interview, August 14, 1992.

113. Thornburg interview.

114. Ellis interview.

115. "Katherine Dunham Is Weary of Hotel Trek," 86.

116. "Miss Dunham's Comment to the Louisville Audience at Memorial Auditorium, October, 1944," in *Kaiso!* ed. Clark and Wilkerson, 88.

117. Katherine Dunham, interview by author, November 1994, East St. Louis residence.

118. Ellis interview.

119. Katherine Dunham, conversation with author, August 16, 1996, East St. Louis residence.

120. Ellis interview.

121. Beatty interview, August 14, 1992.

122. Ellis interview.

123. Ibid.

124. "Conversations with Katherine Dunham," August 12, 1994.

125. Katherine Dunham, writing as Kaye Dunn, "La Boule Blanche," *Esquire Magazine* (September 1939), in *Kaiso!* ed. Clark and Wilkerson, 52–53.

126. Ibid.

127. Beatty interview, August 13, 1991.

128. Quoted in Peter Waddington, "Katherine Dunham Raises Primitive Dance Art to New Heights of Sophistication," *Opera and Concert* (June 1948), in *Kaiso!* ed. Clark and Wilkerson, 109.

129. Ellis interview.

130. Kitt, *Thursday's Child*, 125.

131. Gomez interview.

Chapter 8: Taking It Abroad

1. Kitt, *Thursday's Child*, 132.

2. *London Observer* (September 12, 1948), in *Kaiso!* ed. Clark and Wilkerson, 105.

3. Richard Buckle, *Katherine Dunham, Her Dancers, Singers, Musicians* (London: Ballet Publications, n.d.), ix, x.

4. Gomez interview.

5. Ibid.

6. Ibid.

7. Ibid.

8. Marjorie Scott, interview by author, June 10, 1993, East St. Louis, Illinois.

9. Gomez interview.

10. Ibid.

11. Roger Caillois, program notes, n.d., Paris, Katherine Dunham Museum. Translated by Reno Cassanelli.

12. When "MC," as she is known, became an adult, she lived abroad, with periodic sojourns in the United States. She taught Dunham technique for awhile in Rome; she currently lives there and writes screenplays.

13. Gomez interview.

14. Ibid.

15. Scott interview.

16. Gomez interview. In *Katherine Dunham*, Beckford quotes Dunham in reference to Kitt's departure: "It was a very awkward time in Paris when Eartha Kitt left. I was extremely upset because I thought she could have at least completed our season. . . . She had really become a featured part of the company, so it was very difficult for us to have her leave with practically no notice. . . . But now, reflecting on it, I realize it was her time to go. . . . [I]n observing me [she] knew what being a star was like. She was also aware of her own talent as a dancer [and also] her mime talent . . . and much of her vocal talent had been put before the public" (115).

17. L. R., "The Fifth Catherine," program note, n.d., Milan, Italy. Translated by Reno Cassanelli.

18. Scott interview.

19. Vanoye Aikens, comments at closing ceremonies, Dunham Technique Seminar, August 16, 1995, Parks College, Cahokia, Illinois.

20. Scott interview.

21. Madeline Preston, interview by author, January 7, 1994, East St. Louis.

22. Scott interview

23. Ibid.

24. Ibid.

25. Dunham, *Island Possessed,* 174.

26. VèVè Clark, "Performing the Memory of Difference in Afro-Caribbean Dance: Katherine Dunham's Choreography, 1938–1987" (paper presented at the annual meeting of the American Anthropological Association, Chicago, Illinois, December 1991).

27. Notes in Katherine Dunham Museum, East St. Louis, Illinois.

28. Correspondence with author, February 1996. Zannoni has coproduced a number of films with Franco Zeffirelli, including *Tea with Mussolini,* which opened in the United States in 1999.

29. "Program of 'Southland'" (January 1951), in *Kaiso!* ed. Clark and Wilkerson, 117–20.

30. Constance Valis Hill, "Katherine Dunham's *Southland:* Protest in the Face of Repression," *Dance Research Journal* 26 (Fall 1994): 1–10.

31. "Program of 'Southland,'" 118.

32. Beckford, *Katherine Dunham,* 59–60.

33. Hill, "Katherine Dunham's *Southland,*" 8.

34. Dunham quoted in ibid., 6.

35. Ellis interview.

36. Scott interview.

37. Telegram to Dr. Max Jacobson, December 22, 1959; Dunham to Jacobson, December 29, 1959, both in folder 16, box 12, Dunham Papers.

38. Scott interview.

39. Ibid.

40. Berenson, *Sunset and Twilight,* 166.

41. Hill, "Katherine Dunham's *Southland,*" 5, 6.

42. Dunham, conversation with author, November 25, 1993.

43. Preston interview.

44. Ibid.

45. Ibid.

46. Ibid.

47. David Wisely, "Dance Show Is Done on a Necklace," *Auckland Star,* April 10, 1957, 7.

48. Scott interview.

49. Josephine Beckwith, interview by author, June 29, 1995, Alton, Illinois.

50. Scott interview (quote); Harnan, *African Rhythm, American Dance,* 159.

51. Dunham, conversation with author, February 27, 1993.

52. Katherine Dunham, interview by author, August 1978, East St. Louis residence.

53. Preston interview.

54. Dunham quoted in Beckford, *Katherine Dunham,* 107.

55. William Gaston to Katherine Dunham, November 4, 1959, folder 1, box 26, Dunham Papers.

56. Nikki Mariano to Dan Wickenden, Harcourt, Brace and Co., December 7, 1959, folder 2, box 26, ibid.

57. Sig B, "Success for the Dunham Ballet," *Dagens Nyheder* (Copenhagen), June 15, 1959.

58. "DK a Success—All the Same," *Aktuelt* (Copenhagen), June 15, 1959.

59. "From Interviews with Katherine Dunham, May 24, 25, 1977," in *The Legend of Maya Deren*, by Clark, Hodson, and Neiman, 430. In a 2001 master class, she chided a student for overacting in a "street walk" improvisation and not sufficiently reserving energy and feelings.

60. Doris Hering, Review, *Dance Magazine* 30 (January 1956): 8.

61. "The Sitter Out: A Caribbean Rhapsody," *Dancing Times* (London), July 1948, 526.

62. Magdeleine Cluzel, *Glimpses of the Theatre and Dance* (New York: Waldon, 1953), 68.

63. O. W., "Success for Dunham Ball," *Land OG Folk* (Copenhagen), June 15, 1959.

64. "Ballet on Bare Toes," *Ekstrabladet* (Copenhagen), June 15, 1959.

65. Allan Fridencia, *Information* (Copenhagen), June 15, 1959.

66. Katherine Dunham to M. Felix Marouani in Paris, November 11, 1959, folder 1, box 26, Dunham Papers.

67. Dunham to Lee Moselle, November 14, 1959, ibid.

68. Dunham to Edith Lutyens (Bel Geddes), November 19, 1959, ibid.

69. Bel Geddes to Dunham, November 29, 1959, ibid.; Lee Moselle to Dunham, December 18, 1959, folder 2, box 26, ibid.

70. Dunham to Bel Geddes, March 3, 1960, folder 7, box 26, ibid.

71. Dunham to Moselle, April 11, 1960, folder 2, box 27, ibid.

72. Dunham to Bel Geddes, March 3, 1960.

73. Dunham to Preston, June 21, 1960, folder 5, box 27, ibid.

74. Harnan, *African Rhythm, American Dance*, 186.

75. Bel Geddes to Dunham, April 3, 1960, folder 2, box 26, Dunham Papers.

76. Dunham to Moselle, April 11, 1960.

77. *New York Times*, December 3, 1961, sec. XX:27.

78. Dunham to Ricardo Avalos, January 30, 1961, folder 4, box 26, Dunham Papers.

79. Allen Hughes, "Dance: Revue by Katherine Dunham," *New York Times*, October 23, 1962, 43.

80. Dunham, conversation with author, February 27, 1993.

81. "Aida at the Met," Metropolitan Opera House Program (December 14, 1963), in *Kaiso!* ed. Clark and Wilkerson, 125.

82. Quoted in Hodson, "How She Began Her Beguine," 198.

83. Dana McBroom Manno, interview by author, August 18, 1995, St. Louis.

84. Ibid.

85. Ibid.

Chapter 9: Katherine Dunham and Her Dancers

1. Ellis interview.

2. "Conversations with Katherine Dunham," August 15, 1994.

3. "A Burdensome Responsibility," interview with John Pratt, May 23, 1977, in *The Legend of Maya Deren*, by Clark, Hodson, and Neiman, 466.

4. Kitt, *Thursday's Child*, 96.

5. Gomez interview.

6. Ellis interview.

7. "Conversations with Katherine Dunham," August 9, 1993, Soldan High School.

8. Ellis interview.

9. Gomez interview.

10. Theresa Woosley to Katherine Dunham, February 9, 1941, folder 1, box 2, Dunham Papers.

11. Katherine Dunham, conversation with author, August 1991, East St. Louis residence.

12. Katherine Dunham, Master Class, Dunham Technique Seminar, August 5, 1992, University City High School.

13. Wisely, "Dance Show Is Done on a Necklace," 7.

14. Kitt, *Thursday's Child*, 89.

15. Thornburg interview.

16. This and some of the other details about dancers' careers in this chapter are from Long, *The Black Tradition in American Dance.*

17. "Conversations with Katherine Dunham," August 11, 1993.

18. Thornburg interview.

19. "Conversations with Katherine Dunham," August 11, 1993.

20. Penny Godboldo, interview by author, August 11, 1993, University High School, St. Louis.

21. Clark, Hodson, and Neiman, *The Legend of Maya Deren*, 467.

22. "Conversations with Katherine Dunham," August 12, 1994, commenting on Maya Deren's book *The Divine Horseman.*

23. Archie Savage, telephone conversation with author, November 5, 1993, Los Angeles.

24. Beatty interview, August 13, 1991.

25. Mary Hunter to Katherine Dunham, n.d. (circa 1941), folder 1, box 2, Dunham Papers.

26. Beatty interview, August 13, 1991.

27. Katherine Dunham, conversation with author, July 1998, East St. Louis residence.

28. Katherine Dunham to Campbell Casad, April 5, 1941, folder 1, box 2, Dunham Papers.

29. Ellis interview.

30. Denishawn was a dance group founded by Ruth St. Denis and Ted Shawn, which pioneered in modern dance, especially, "ethnic dance," and in which Martha Graham performed at the beginning of her career.

31. Thornburg interview.

32. Kitt, *Thursday's Child*, 85.

33. Ibid., 84.

34. Ibid.

35. Ibid., 88.

36. Kitt remarked at the 1994 homage to Katherine Dunham sponsored by the Caribbean Cultural Center: "Miss Dunham saw something in me she put to use and I sure was glad she did. Under her auspices I learned about the world and became curious about the rest which I knew nothing about."

37. Godboldo interview.

38. Wisely, "Dance Show Is Done on a Necklace," 7.

39. Thornburg interview.

40. Beatty interview, August 13, 1991.

41. Ellis interview.

42. Thornburg interview.

43. Scott interview.

44. Ellis interview.

45. Scott interview.

46. Thornburg interview.

47. Dorothy Bird, quoted in Agnes de Mille, *Martha: The Life and Work of Martha Graham* (1956; reprint, New York: Random House, 1991), 149.

48. Katherine Dunham, Master Class, August 20, 1993, Dunham Technique Seminar, Center of Contemporary Arts.

49. Beatty interview, August 14, 1992.

50. Dunham, conversation with author, November 25, 1993.

Chapter 10: Arts and the Community

1. Gwen Mazer, "The Katherine Dunham Legend," *Living Together*, a magazine supplement to the *Chicago Sun Times*, November 1976.

2. Eugene Redmond, interview by author, January 30, 1995, Katherine Dunham Museum, East St. Louis.

3. Katherine Dunham, *Kasamance: A Fantasy* (New York: Third Press, 1974)

4. Quoted in Bill Smith, "Katherine Dunham Was Born to Dancing and Social Activism," *St. Louis Globe Democrat*, September 11–12, 1982, 1E.

5. "Conversations with Katherine Dunham," August 18, 1993, Dunham Technique Seminar, Missouri Historical Society.

6. For a full account of this, see Elliott Rudwick, *Race Riot at East St. Louis, July 2, 1917* (1964; reprint, Urbana: University of Illinois Press, 1982).

7. The fair, which takes place during the July 4 celebrations, was established in the early part of the twentieth century by local businessmen. The name was later changed to Saint Louis Fair because of unfortunate overtones of a veiled, robed prophet (Ku Klux Klan).

8. Katherine Dunham, "Performing Arts Training Center as a Focal Point for a New and Unique College or School," in *Kaiso!* ed. Clark and Wilkerson, 259.

9. John Brooks, interview by author, August 14, 1996, East St. Louis.

10. Ibid.

11. Ibid.

12. "The Devil and East St. Louis: The Worst Hell Hole in America," *Muhammad Speaks*, September 15, 1967, Katherine Dunham Museum.

13. Eugene Redmond, interview by author, January 20, 1995, East St. Louis.

14. Ibid.

15. Ibid.

16. The Hudlins are a large and prominent East St. Louis family whose members include a former dean and a philosophy professor.

17. Redmond interview, January 30, 1995.

18. Ibid.

19. Dunham, "Performing Arts Training Center as a Focal Point for a New and Unique College or School," 262.

20. Ibid.

21. Redmond interview, January 30, 1995.

22. Ibid.

23. Ibid.

24. Ibid.

25. Ibid.

26. Ibid.

27. William Strickland obtained FBI documents showing that a counterintelligence program based in St. Louis had prepared a newspaper, called the *Blackboard*, that "is written as an intelligent Black college student might write it," which purports to praise "relatively ineffective leaders . . . while launching a tongue-in-cheek attack on Katherine Dunham, Charles Koen and other militants." The letter to the FBI director, dated April 7, 1969, stated further, "It is felt that the anonymous distribution of copies of this newspaper will have a very disruptive effect on the Black militants in the area and discredit some of the more popular ones."

28. Redmond interview, January 30, 1995.

29. Ibid.

30. Ibid.

31. Ibid.

32. Alina Rivero, "Deadly, Dazzling Capoeira, Brazilian Art Combines Dance, Self-Defense," *Pictures*, supplement of *St. Louis Post-Dispatch*, June 24, 1979, 16–19.

33. Katherine Dunham, "Reflections on Survival" (commencement address, May 21, 1972, MacMurray College, Jacksonville, Illinois).

34. "Conversations with Katherine Dunham," August 15, 1994.

35. Redmond interview, January 30, 1995.

36. Ibid.

37. Ibid.

38. Leman Davis, interview by author, March 19, 1997, East St. Louis Salvation Army Youth Center.

39. Ronnie Marshall, interview by author, August 19, 1993, University City High School.

40. Ruby Streate, interview by author, January 10, 1996, East St. Louis.

41. Ibid.

42. Ibid.

43. Ibid.

44. Ibid.

45. Brooks interview.

46. Streate interview.

47. Marshall interview.

48. Redmond interview, January 30, 1995.

49. Brooks interview.

50. Streate interview.

51. A humorous dance-skit involving Andean women with their distinctive hunched-over stance, carrying loads up the mountainside on their backs

52. Streate interview.

53. Ibid.

54. Ibid.

55. Henrietta Knight, interview by author, July 2, 1992, East St. Louis.

56. Brooks interview.

57. Ibid.

58. Redmond interview, January 30, 1995.

59. Ibid.

60. Ibid.

61. Beckford, *Katherine Dunham*, 79–89.

62. Redmond interview, January 30, 1995.

63. Ibid. Consulting and advisory editors for the revue include Maya Angelou, Amiri Baraka, Gwendolyn Brooks, Katherine Dunham, and Quincy Troupe.

64. Redmond interview, January 20, 1995.

65. Vanoye Aikens, Ricardo Avalos, Marie-Christine Dunham Pratt, Lucille Ellis, La Rosa Estrada, Pearl Reynolds, Glory Van Scott, Julio Mendez, and Camille Yarbrough were the former company members who performed; PATC instructors and students Norman Davis, Emilio Lastarria, Ronnie Marshall, Doris Bennett, Michael Green, Jeanne Speier, Ed Brown, Ruby Streate, Eusebio Da Silva, Andrea Smythe, Keith Williams, and Lesa Huston also performed, while Talley Beatty, Julie Robinson Belafonte, Laverne French, Tommy Gomez, Marcia McBroom, Charles Moore, Walter Nicks, Carmencita Romero, Archie Savage, Lavinia Williams, and Gloria Thornburg hosted the event. Eartha Kitt was narrating Aaron Copeland's "A Lincoln Portrait" for a PBS observance of Martin Luther King Day and sent a testimonial to be read.

66. Dunham had known Lila Teer, Barbara Ann's mother, in Chicago in 1935. Dunham remarked that the young men of the Nation of Islam came to assist Lila Teer when burglars broke into her house in East St. Louis in the 1990s.

67. Ruth Taylor, a member of the Friends and the community services coordinator for PATC, speaking in East St. Louis in June 1999.

68. *Evening Star* (Washington, D.C.), December 16, 1970, Katherine Dunham Museum.

69. Streate interview.

70. Ibid.

71. Ibid.

72. Ibid.

73. Jennifer Dunning, "The Simple Secret of Teaching Dance," *New York Times*, September 15, 1991, Katherine Dunham Museum.

74. Jackie Joyner-Kersey, who has established a children's center in East St. Louis, was also present at the meeting.

Chapter 11: Legacy

1. Ellis interview.

2. "Conversations with Katherine Dunham," August 12, 1994.

3. Ortiz not only does research on African-Cuban history and culture but also is a lawyer and political activist who has served in various public offices.

4. In a presentation at the Katherine Dunham Technique Seminar, August 1995, Parks College, Cahokia, Illinois. The Caribbean Cultural Center in New York

collaborated with the New York City Department of Cultural Affairs in mounting two exhibitions, *The Worldview of Katherine Dunham* and *Katherine Dunham in Cuba, 1947: Documentary Photographs by Carmen Schiavone,* on the occasion of her eighty-fifth birthday.

5. Tito Puente and Max Roach, among others, honored Dunham at the 1994 celebration sponsored by the Caribbean Cultural Center.

6. "Program for *Bal Nègre*" (1946), in *Kaiso,* ed. Clark and Wilkerson, 98–100.

7. Tommy Gomez described this in an afternoon seminar on August 14, 1990, Dunham Technique Seminar, Center of Contemporary Arts.

8. Katherine Dunham, "Open Letter to Black Theaters," *Black Scholar* 8 (July–August 1979): 5.

9. This was the Samuel H. Scripps American Dance Festival Award. Dunham received it in 1986.

10. *Ekstrabladet,* June 15, 1959, 7, folder 1, box 1, Dunham Papers.

11. Numerous mentions in personal conversations and "Conversations with Katherine Dunham," Dunham Technique Seminar, 1975–2000.

12. Katherine Dunham, Master Class, August 8, 1994, Dunham Technique Seminar, Central City Visual and Performing Arts High School.

13. Wisely, "Dance Show Is Done on a Necklace," 7.

14. Katherine Dunham, Master Class, August 11, 1993, Soldan High School.

15. Scott interview.

16. Gomez interview.

17. Godboldo interview.

18. Katherine Dunham, Master Class, August 18, 1993, Dunham Technique Seminar, Soldan High School.

19. Ellis interview.

20. Katherine Dunham, Master Class, August 10, 1992, Dunham Technique Seminar, University City High School.

21. Wisely, "Dance Show Is Done on a Necklace," 7.

22. Dunham, Master Class, August 18, 1993.

23. "Conversations with Katherine Dunham," August 10, 1992, University City High School.

24. Katherine Dunham, Master Class, August 13, 1993, Soldan High School.

25. "Conversations with Katherine Dunham," August 14, 1992.

26. Lucille Ellis, Master Class, August 20, 1993, Soldan High School.

27. Penny Godboldo, "Katherine Dunham Technique Certification Examination," August 1993, Dunham Certification Board, Dr. Albirda Rose, Director, San Francisco State University.

28. Mary Vivian, interview by author, August 15, 1994, Central City Visual and Performing Arts High School.

29. McBroom Manno interview.

30. Long, *The Black Tradition in American Dance,* 158.

31. Ellis interview.

32. Alicia Pierce, interview by author, August 13, 1993, Dunham Technique Seminar, University City High School.

33. Ibid.

34. The information in this and the following paragraphs is from the Marshall interview.

35. Penny Godboldo, interview by author, August 16, 1992, Dunham Technique Seminar, University City High School. The following paragraphs are based on this interview.

36. Jeanne Speier, interview by author, August 9, 1992, Dunham Technique Seminar, University City High School.

37. Geraldine Williams, interview by author, August 11, 1992, Dunham Technique Seminar, University City High School.

38. Albirda Rose, interview by author, August 14, 1990, Dunham Technique Seminar, Center of Contemporary Arts.

39. Albirda Rose, *Dunham Technique: A Way of Life* (Dubuque, Iowa: Kendall/ Hunt, 1990).

40. This and subsequent Rose quotes are from the Rose interview.

41. Ibid. Many dance critics did not agree with Rose's view of the Ailey performance. Anna Kisselgoff wrote in the *New York Times* on December 13, 1987, "The Magic of Katherine Dunham is exactly that," and she employed such adjectives as "fantastically staged," "sassy, colorful and vibrant." She continued, "For the first time I can understand why Broadway audiences were thrilled by Dunham's *New Tropical Revue* or why Londoners in the austere period just after World War II adored her show."

42. This and the following quotes are from an interview with Glory Van Scott, August 20, 1990, Dunham Technique Seminar, Center of Contemporary Arts.

43. Theo Jamison and Keith Williams speaking at memorial service, East St. Louis Community College.

44. Van Scott, ibid.

45. Katherine Dunham, conversation with author, February 13, 1997, East St. Louis residence.

46. Ibid.

47. Ibid.

48. "I'll Make Me a World," broadcast, February 1–3, 1998, KETC Television, St. Louis. In contrast, "Free to Dance," a PBS documentary devoted exclusively to African American dance (June 26, 2001, on KETC), provided extensive coverage of Dunham's career and influence.

49. "Conceptualizing the Legacy of Katherine Dunham," September 9–12, 1999, St. Louis. Sponsored by the Caribbean Cultural Institute, New York.

50. "Dance in America, Divine Drumbeats: Katherine Dunham and Her People," narrated by James Earl Jones. The St. Louis premiere was on March 31, 1980, in the KETC studio.

51. At an Ailey performance at the Civic Opera House in Chicago, both Ailey and Judith Jamison, who is the present director of the company, acknowledged their debt to Dunham's influence, and Ailey said that parts of his 1958 *Blues Suite* were "rip-offs" of Dunham's work. In his review of *The Magic of Katherine Dunham*, Richard Christiansen remarked, "Ailey's dances explore a rich 'black tradition'" (*Weekend Chicago* of the *Chicago Tribune*, May 3, 1986, sec. 1:13.

52. Quoted in Jennifer MacAdam, "More Than Dance: Dunham Works toward 'Whole Artists,'" *St. Louis Post-Dispatch*, August 25, 1991, 4H.

53. Quoted in Rose, *Dunham Technique,* vii.

54. Adam Pinsker, "Katherine Dunham's Fast," broadcast, March 3, 1992, KWMU-FM.

55. Redmond interview, January 30, 1995.

56. Pinsker, "Katherine Dunham's Fast."

57. Program notes for the "Illinois and Chicago Salute to Katherine Dunham," November 28, 1983.

58. Joyce Aschenbrenner, Notes, February 27, 1992.

59. Note the chorus in *Porgy and Bess*, "Lord, we're on our way . . . to the heavenly land."

60. Harry Belafonte, public address, August 29, 2000, City Hall, East St. Louis.

61. Ibid.

62. While she was in New York in 2000, for example, Dunham asked her assistant to send her many of her personal items, leading her assistant to wonder if there was enough space in her room to accommodate them.

63. Harry Belafonte, address, August 30, 2000, Crown Hotel, East St. Louis.

64. At a meeting in June 2001 in St. Louis, she surprised those present by walking into the room, using a walker.

65. "Conversations with Katherine Dunham," August 15, 1994.

INDEX

JOYCE ASCHENBRENNER is a professor emerita in the anthropology department at Southern Illinois University at Edwardsville. She is the author of *Lifelines: Black Families in Chicago* (1975), *Katherine Dunham: Reflections on the Social and Political Contexts of Afro-American Dance* (1980), and numerous essays on Katherine Dunham; the editor of *Family Institutions in Adaptation to Change,* a special edition of the *International Journal of Sociology of the Family* (1988); and the coeditor of *The Processes of Urbanism: A Multidisciplinary Approach* (1978). She has served as treasurer of the Friends of the Katherine Dunham Museum and is currently acting curator and education coordinator of the museum.

The University of Illinois Press
is a founding member of the
Association of American University Presses.

Composed in 9.5/12.5 Trump Mediaeval
with Trump Mediaeval display
by Jim Proefrock
at the University of Illinois Press
Manufactured by Edwards Brothers, Inc.

University of Illinois Press
1325 South Oak Street
Champaign, IL 61820-6903
www.press.uillinois.edu